AN INTRODUCTION TO COMMUNITY EXPERIMENTATION

THEORY, METHODS, AND PRACTICE

AN INTRODUCTION TO COMMUNITY EXPERIMENTATION

THEORY, METHODS, AND PRACTICE

George W. Fairweather, Ph.D.
William S. Davidson, Ph.D.

Department of Psychology
Michigan State University

McGRAW-HILL BOOK COMPANY

New York   St. Louis   San Francisco   Auckland   Bogotá
Hamburg   Johannesburg   London   Madrid   Mexico   Montreal   New Delhi
Panama   Paris   São Paulo   Singapore   Sydney   Tokyo   Toronto

This book was set in Times Roman by University Graphics, Inc. (ECU).
The editor was David V. Serbun; the cover was designed by Janice Noto;
the production supervisor was Leroy A. Young.
Project supervision was done by The Total Book.
The drawings were done by Fine Line Illustrations, Inc.
R. R. Donnelley & Sons Company was printer and binder.

AN INTRODUCTION TO COMMUNITY EXPERIMENTATION

Theory, Methods, and Practice

1 2 3 4 5 6 7 8 9 0   DOCDOC   8 9 8 7 6 5

ISBN 0-07-019904-3

Library of Congress Cataloging in Publication Data

Fairweather, George William, date
    An introduction to commmunity experimentation.

    Bibliography: p.
    Includes index.
    1. Social sciences—Research—Methodology.
2. Community psychology—Research—Methodology.
I. Davidson, William S. (William Sumner), date
II. Title.
H61.F27   1986   300′.72   85-10985
ISBN 0-07-019904-3

CONTENTS

PREFACE

This book attempts to provide a scientific experience that is both action oriented and intellectually stimulating to those students who are interested in using science to improve the quality of life of the citizens in our society. Endless hours of research work in field settings with many colleagues and graduate students have led the authors to conclude that a sound field experimental philosophy and methodology for interested young scientists can be created. This book is offered as the first step in that experience.

Modeled after those sciences that have a field counterpart to their classroom work, a field research workbook accompanies this textbook so that community research experiences can be gained by the students along with classroom learning. It is our belief that the integration of classroom and field research experiences will become as central to the social sciences of the future as both currently are to agriculture. For this reason, it is as important to create a place where community science can be practiced in solving human problems as it is to understand and create scientific theory and methodology about problem solutions. It is toward both of these goals that this book is written.

This book is divided into thirteen chapters. The first chapter presents the student with a broad perspective about social change and survival. Chapter 2 provides the student with the pivotal parameters that should be considered in solving human problems. Chapter 3 attempts to describe and define the processes used to create problem solving social change. Chapter 4 introduces the student to eight methodological areas that are central to community experimentation; in Chapter 4 the student learns to define a human problem in a scientific sense. In Chapter 5 the process moves to planning an innovation solution from this definition. Once the innovation has been planned it is necessary to evaluate its benefits by using an experimental design (Chapter 6) which incorporates measuring its attributes and processes (Chapter 7) as well as implementing and administering the innovative model in a community setting (Chapter 8). Chapter 9 presents a general overview of comparative and associative methods for model evaluation and Chapter 10 provides the student with some grasp of the concepts inherent in making inferences from the large body of data collected over an extended period of time in a field experiment. Chapter 11 introduces the student to the relatively new area of scientific inquiry called dissemination or knowledge utilization.

It is the purpose of the last two chapters to give the student some view of the roles that might be available to them should they be interested in pursuing a career in community experimentation. Chapter 12 is organized around several contemporary social statuses showing how community experimentalists can become involved in a wide variety of research roles. Chapter 13 presents the students with some of the author's predictions about the future of community experimentation.

We wish to acknowledge the help of our graduate students and colleagues many of whom have contributed theoretical ideas that are expressed in this book. We are especially indebted to Lawrence Severy, Brian Yates, and James Kelly for their helpful comments. Many of them have been incorporated in this volume. To those former students whose researches are mentioned throughout this book we also express our gratitude. They include: Charles H. Tucker, Nancy J. Leedom, Amanda A. Beck, Denis O. Gray, Richard J. Coelho, Robert Harris, Jeffrey Taylor, and Martin Kushler. We are also indebted to Mitchell Fleischer, Esther Fergus, David Roitman, and Brian Mavis for their helpful comments.

The authors also express their gratitude to Julie Conrad whose typing and constructive comments have made this book more readable. We are indebted to her for tolerating the numerous changes and repeated restructuring of the book with a much needed sense of humor which probably kept her personality intact. We are also grateful to Mary Scott and Susan Pavick for their help in preparing this book for publication.

It is our hope that a new generation of socially conscious scientists will become involved in human problem solving. It is our further hope that this book will provide a background for those people who might be interested in improving human problem solving techniques or in making a career in this new field.

George W. Fairweather
William S. Davidson

CHAPTER 1

THE CENTRALITY OF SOCIAL CHANGE IN SOLVING HUMAN PROBLEMS

THE RESPONSIBILITY FOR SOCIAL CHANGE

The social change processes of societies may in some ways be similar to the biological adaptive processes of human beings. When living creatures cannot adapt to conditions in their environment they disappear and are replaced by other organisms able to adapt to the conditions that exist on the planet at that time (Leakey and Lewin, 1977). So it is with societies. Social processes are part of cultural adaptive processes and it is through their constancy that social practices are passed on from generation to generation—we don't really have to keep inventing fire or the wheel. On the other hand, there needs to be a certain amount of flexibility in the cultural system so that changes can occur in a rational and systematic fashion when they are needed for maximum adaptation.

Many changes have occurred in our society over the years. In some years— for example, the 1960s—rapid changes have occurred. These changes were an attempt by the members of society to adapt to new social conditions. Thus, for humans to live in a supportive environment it is necessary to preserve those practices of the past which are helpful in coping with contemporary problems but at the same time to discard those aspects that are detrimental to the quality of contemporary life or that appear to be leading to societal disaster (Fairweather, 1972).

Whatever the changing conditions of the society and however constant practices may remain, it is invariably true that societies will change or they will disappear. History records many revolutions that have occurred because individuals were unhappy with their society and the leaders of the society failed to respond to changes that were perceived to be necessary by the members themselves. Since the governing bodies of democratic societies are charged with the responsibility of maintaining an adequate quality of life, it is their decisions that affect the lives of current and future generations.

Adequate decisions in contemporary societies often demand changing ways of doing things, and therefore, cultural processes of continuity are frequently juxtaposed against processes of change. Any society that does not have a desirable ratio of continuing practices to innovative new ones will inevitably lose its quest for human adaptation. As a society, it will eventually disappear from the earth. Applying this thesis to contemporary societies means that the pressing human problems that exist now and those that will emerge must be solved if the society is to continue. How such a social change mechanism can be created and used by the society to promote essential social adaptation is the central issue of this book.

THE ROLE OF CULTURAL HISTORY

To modify slightly a quotation from Shakespeare, the entire world is a stage and all of us but actors. While this is only a partial truth, the essential message for those interested in human problems is that each of us inhabits the earth for a short period of time and during that time we are responsible for the culture that is left for those who follow. While we in America are blessed with many of the cultural values and achievements that have been left to us by our predecessors—we all walk on the mountains of cultural successes and wallow in the depths of cultural failures—we are faced with many unfinished problems that our predecessors either did not perceive as central survival issues or were unable to solve.

Regardless of which one of these alternatives is true, most of the problems currently facing us have resulted from a failure on the part of our social decision makers to make the necessary adaptive alterations when situations changed. Even though we have been living with some very serious human problems for several generations, many of them remain unsolved.

The advantages of our cultural heritage, of course, are numerous. The democratic system in which we live permits you to read the preceding paragraph without censorship; you are free to pursue an education; and the arts and sciences are available to you as in no other society. As we recognize the beneficial values and practices we inherit from our culture, we hope this book will present you with some ideas and potential actions that will in our judgment improve those benefits and create an adequate quality of life for the twenty-first century and beyond. Even though some of the chapters in this book will take a critical view of our society (recognizing its limitations and poor aspects is necessary for its improvement), the book's intent is to provide each student with knowledge which, in the final analysis, will improve the quality of life over the next several decades. But before this can be accomplished and positive recommendations for the future presented, it is necessary to understand that serious threats to the quality of life on this planet currently exist, and that they emanate from our cultural heritage.

Ignoring the Environment

Foremost among these threats is the supposition that humans are superior to their environment and that all living matter is subject to human rule. Historically, when the natural environment was perceived as interfering with the land demands of the occupants for farming and later manufacturing and other activities, the land was cleared of trees, and rivers and streams often became dumping grounds for toxic materials. As this happened, the land that became polluted was quickly abandoned for a better location. This perception of the environment as infinite and as a "thing to be conquered" has contributed to the environmental crises we are plagued with today (Moncrief, 1970). It also led to the idea that the entire world was a continuous frontier and that persons could move on when they desired. It was believed that humans were superior to other forms of life and could control their environment in such a way that the ruling persons could produce from it whatever they wished. Needless to say, this was a perceptual error with grave consequences because it denied the preeminence of biological nature and, perhaps worst of all, diverted attention from the need to create the ecological balance essential for the long-run survival of animals and plants on this spaceship earth. The consequences of these cultural practices are summed up by the ecologist Barry Commoner (1963) in the following manner:

> As a biologist, I have reached this conclusion: we have come to a turning point in the human habitation of the earth. The environment is a complex, subtly balanced system, and it is this integrated whole which receives the impact of all the separate insults inflicted by pollutants. Never before in the history of this planet has its thin life-supporting surface been subjected to such diverse, novel, and potent agents. I believe that the cumulative effects of these pollutants, their interactions and amplification, can be fatal to the complex fabric of the biosphere. And, because [people are,] after all, a dependent part of this system, I believe that continued pollution of the earth, if unchecked, will eventually destroy the fitness of this planet as a place for human life. . . . (p. 122).

There are several ways we may pollute the environment. One is by polluting the air (Grobecker et al., 1975; National Academy of Sciences, 1976; Barney, 1980; Turk and Turk, 1984). Industrialists, city council members, scientists, members of Congress, and ordinary citizens have long known that technological developments, particularly industrial gaseous emissions and those from the automobile and the airplane, have greatly contributed to air pollution.

Air pollution usually refers to particles that are added to the air that normally would not be there. Such substances mainly come from automobile and airplane exhausts and from industrial manufacturing processes. The pollutants given off as exhaust emissions from automobiles are carbon monoxide, nitrous oxides, hydrocarbons, sulfur derivatives, and benzopyrene. All these pollutants constitute a grave threat to human existence. It is well known, for example, that in heavily air-polluted regions such as Los Angeles, the rate of emphysema and lung cancer are much higher than in areas where heavy pollution does not exist (Costle, 1979; EPA, 1979). In addition, there is continuous and increasing damage to crops from air pollutants. Various plants and trees are daily showing the results of excessive air contamination (Postel, 1984).

But automobiles are not the only polluters that diminish the life-supporting qualities of our air. Certain industries pour pollutants into the air, as any person who has been in a heavily industrialized area can attest. In some cities, residents live in a thick smog created or worsened by industrial processes. And there are threats of new transportation developments that might make the situation worse. Some scientists have recommended a slowdown in the development of supersonic transportation (SST) until research can confirm what its actual effects upon the earth's atmosphere will be (Shurcliff, 1970). They have expressed concern about the effects a fleet of SST planes would have upon the pollution of the stratosphere. Some of the opinions expressed have stated that exhaust particles might remain in the atmosphere for several years; that water vapor in the atmosphere might be increased by 10 percent on a global basis, and up to 60 percent over the densely traveled northern hemisphere; and that exhaust particles might cause the temperature of the stratosphere to rise as much as 6 or 7 degrees. An air pollution researcher from Boulder, Colorado, is reported to have said, "When you change something on a global scale, you had better watch out." There has also been concern expressed about proceeding with massive efforts that might change the global nature of the atmosphere without adequately evaluating beforehand what the effects might be.

Thus, the effects of atmospheric pollutants are all about us. In recent years wide attention has been given by scientists to a threat to the ozone layer surrounding the earth that might be caused by the use of aerosol spray containers. Current debate among scientists questions whether the use of these containers is a primary source of ozone layer reduction, which if it occurred, would increase each person's exposure to radiation and would in all probability increase the risk of contracting cancer. While this debate is not currently resolved it is important to note that threats to the ozone layer could become critical in the next 30 to 50 years.

But unclean air and the possible threat to the ozone layer are not the only environmental pollution problems facing people today. The supply of clean water is dwindling (Goldberg, 1976; U.S. Water Resources Council, 1978; Turk and Turk, 1984). As more people occupy the surface of the earth their demands for water increase in proportion to their numbers. In fact, the increase is greater annually because industrialized societies develop more complex technological devices each year that require more water. Thus, the manufacture and use of new industrial products creates a greater demand for water. Gradually, the rivers and streams, the continental shelf surrounding the country, and even the large oceans themselves have become polluted through abuse of the natural water system (Eckholm, 1982; Pringle, 1982; Ashworth, 1982). This is particularly true in and around industrialized nations like America. Many large lakes are considered to be at least partially "dead." Lake Erie is one of the world's prime examples of a beautiful body of fresh water that has been severely polluted because of people's disregard for their environment. Linton (1970) quoted a government report showing that 271 industries discharged industrial wastes into Lake Erie in 1965, and 360 in 1968. This yields a growth rate of eighty-nine new industrial sources of pollution in a 3-year period at a time when the devastating effects of dumping industrial wastes into the lake were already known. And even though recent information suggests that pollution in Lake Erie may be abating somewhat, the lake is still far from the clean body of fresh water that it could be.

Because of the process of *eutrophication,* the waters of many other inland lakes contain less and less oxygen as a result of excessive plant growth believed to be caused by phosphates and other chemicals in detergents, agricultural fertilizers, and the like. Pesticides and toxic industrial wastes cause still other problems. These pollutants are often dumped into lakes or buried in the soil by local industries and municipalities on the lakeshores. Toxins seep in lakes and underground wells as drainage from toxic dumps and are carried to the oceans by already contaminated rivers and streams. In addition, the recently identified pollutant of acid rain affects the soil, rivers, and lakes at great distances from the pollution source. It is well known to almost everyone that formerly beautiful rivers such as the Hudson and the Tiber have become polluted.

Only recently have the public and scientists alike taken steps to avoid the health hazard produced by mercury pollution. In the spring of 1970, both the Canadian and American governments banned fishing in Lake St. Clair on the United States–Canadian border because fish from the lake were found to contain 7 parts per million of mercury. (The Canadian government had previously determined that fish containing more than 5 parts per million of mercury were unsafe for human consumption, which is the amount considered safe in drinking water by the World Health Organization.) In 1984, the Michigan Department of Natural Resources warned its residents not to eat certain fish from the Great Lakes because they might contain harmful toxins. Information about the effects of mercury contamination as a threat to human life has accumulated in several industrialized nations (Hammond, 1971). In Japan, for example, mercury-contaminated fish eaten by the residents of two fishing villages caused extensive central nervous system damage to many residents. Historically, Sweden also has had experiences with contamination associated with runoff from mercury-treated materials used in farming. Levels of mercury in the waters of Sweden showed a steady increase until the use of such mercury-treated agricultural materials was stopped. Then a drop in the level of mercury ensued.

The manner in which toxic water is disposed of is also a growing environmental problem. The effects on humans of poisonous materials entering the ecological system from toxic chemical dump sites can be seen in the Love Canal incident (Levine, 1982; Turk and Turk, 1984, pp. 186–187). Chemical wastes in steel drums were buried there only to surface later in the very land where a school was built. Persons living in this geographic area suffered serious illnesses—epilepsy, birth defects, etc. While there is some disagreement about the causative effects of the chemicals, the potential for damage to health was apparent. Turk and Turk (1984, p. 187) point out that government experts believe another environmental threat to health exists in overexposure to high-energy radiation. The failure of the Three Mile Island nuclear plant and its attendant "pollution" fears show very clearly the stress associated with known and feared environmental contamination. Chemical and radiation poisons pose a serious threat to health in this technological age (Sowby, 1984). Even though recent legislation mandating chemical cleanup will aid in this process, the problem remains one requiring a long-term solution.

Preserving the life-sustaining qualities of the environment requires major changes in the manner our air, water, and land resources are handled to prevent the ultimate pollution of clean air, water, and the land itself.

There is also growing concern about another source of environmental pollution, commonly called noise pollution (Turk and Turk, 1984), which results from the ever-increasing noise made by new technological advances, particularly in urban environments. High noise levels produced by jackhammers, excessive automobile traffic, and airplanes (epitomized by the SST) appear to be destructive to hearing and also may have emotional side effects. For those living near major airports the noise from jet aircraft poses a particularly difficult problem. The noise from powerful jet engines often continues unabated throughout the day and night. Conversation can only be carried on with great difficulty while one person tries to hear the other over the roar of jet engines. Normal interpersonal relationships are interrupted. A reduction in noise pollution would require rather drastic changes in creating and implementing techniques for noise control.

It seems quite clear from this brief review that excessive pollutants are being poured into our environment. Clean air and water, and noise abatement are necessary for an adequate quality of life. The threat to life is real (Logue et al., 1981). What is important to recognize here is that environmental degradation is occurring and that it must be regulated in such a way that the planet's quality of life is maintained or improved.

Overpopulating the Planet

The threat of a polluted natural environment to human life is made more severe by overpopulation. Although people have been warned about population growth since the time of Malthus, few have been aware of its serious implications until recently (Borgstrom, 1969; U.N. Department of Economic and Social Affairs, 1973; Brown, 1976; and Turk and Turk, 1984). However, it should be very clear to everyone by now that excessive population growth is an important survival problem that must be resolved. While most leading students of population growth assure us that there is a reduction in the fertility (birth) rate now occurring, the most optimistic current forecasts are that the world's population will double before stabilizing. This stability will only occur if fertility rates continue to decline on a worldwide basis. The only way, short of a nuclear holocaust, through which population stabilization can occur, is by achieving a zero population growth. This occurs when births equal deaths.

There are particular reasons why a drop in fertility rates is so difficult to achieve. Population control is a very challenging problem, perhaps the greatest in all human existence, because it depends upon the mastery of some features of our daily life which we have had the most difficulty in adjusting to in the past. The act of procreation stems from a biological drive in humans about which myths and attendant fears have existed since people first began to think about it. The sexual act itself is surrounded by taboos and fantasies in all societies, and few have developed norms and values that place sexual behavior in its proper perspective. Because of its central place in human behavior, sexual activity has become the focal point around which many forms of cultural mysticism are organized.

Some societies equate family size with a man's virility or a woman's femininity. Others place an emphasis on family size because a parent's children become their only source of sustenance when they become old and unable to work. In an affluent society such as America a large family is considered a person's right, particularly if one can afford it. Such justifications for determining family size are basically irrational and prevent the awareness that each person occupies space and uses resources, such as air, water, and fuel, that belong to everyone. Thus the challenge in the area of population control is very complex. It will involve solving problems as awesome as conflicts between religion and biology. Because of the central role most cultures place on sexual behavior, population control is one of the most difficult challenges to survival. And even beyond the irrational aspects of sexual behavior and family size, many other human problems are so interrelated with population growth that any effective solution requires that change must be promoted along many different avenues.

Population growth also creates or exacerbates other environmental problems (Severy, 1979; Zito, 1979). This is clearly presented in a committee report stressing the relationship between population growth and energy needs. The Committee on Resources and Man (1969) several years ago arrived at the following conclusion about the relationship of population and the use of resources:

> Looking into the future on the same time scale, and assuming that a catastrophic event such as the near annihilation of the industrialized world by thermonuclear warfare can somehow be avoided, the physical realities . . . dictate that the curve of human population must follow one of three possible courses: (1) it could continue to rise for a brief period and then gradually level off to some stable magnitude capable of being sustained by the world's energy and material resources for a long period of time; (2) it could overshoot any possible stable level and then drop back and eventually stabilize at some level compatible with the world's resources; or (3) finally, as a result of resource exhaustion and a general cultural decline, the curve could be forced back to a population corresponding to the lowest energy-consumption level of a primitive existence. The one type of behavior for this curve that is not possible is that of continued and unlimited growth (pp. 227–228).

This statement is just as true today as it was in 1969.

It is difficult to conceive of societies having a reasonably adequate quality of life if their current social practices lead to continuous increases in population. While current estimates of a reduction in population growth are encouraging, the need for change in this area seems inevitable, and change of a particular kind: Fertility rates must occur through educated choices (Miller, 1983).

Exploitation of People

The survival issues mentioned thus far have stemmed from the central problems of population growth and pollution of the natural environment. However, there is another crisis which may be even more significant in determining our future quality of life. It results from exploitation of people and involves interpersonal and social relationships. Since in everyday living people interact with other persons and things, their interactions with each other and the natural environment cannot be separated; however, for purposes of describing the problems we face it seems important to present interpersonal and social problems as separate issues.

In most societies interpersonal and social problems are perpetuated by a caste or class system that the culture of the society has developed, usually over centuries (Warner, 1960; Tumin, 1967; Burkhart, 1981). The class social structure within a society is typically related to the power one person has over another. Those in higher social positions very often use their power to perpetuate their own dominance over others. Such social arrangements are reflected in all societies. This is a particularly important element in today's complex social problems because education and communication have led people to believe that inferior social positions are not necessary in contemporary societies. Accordingly, socially marginal persons who are accorded lowly social positions with abridged rights and duties are not content with their roles, particularly in a democratic society. Nonetheless, discrimination based on age, race, sex, social class, and caste continues.

The inability and unwillingness of people to treat persons of different ages, sexes, social classes, and colors justly raises a major survival issue. The critical issue here is whether people can live cooperatively with each other so that mature interpersonal relationships based on love and justice can exist as a necessary background for creating a livable environment. The problem of social inequality is particularly well illustrated in stigmatizing factors that are often used to discriminate against a recognizable group of individuals (Stephan and Stephan, 1983; McClosky and Brill, 1983).

For this reason, inequality is a central issue in race relations. Although race is a major issue in America, it is a problem for most societies because observable racial differences exist throughout the world. People's discrimination against others because of their skin color has been a feature of societies since the beginning of written history. It is particularly critical in the United States. In over 200 years of history, racial minorities have been forced by society to live in subordinate roles. Racism is a fact of life in America, as clearly attested to in the report of the President's Commission on Civil Disorders (National

Advisory Commission on Civil Disorders, 1968; Cottingham, 1982; Banton, 1983). People's inability or unwillingness to treat other persons of different social classes and colors equally raises a major survival issue.

A solution to race relations might provide a solution to a much broader series of problems than those of discrimination against others based upon color. A solution to that problem could set in motion forces that might have implications for the entire spectrum of class relationships among people on this planet. For example, it might suggest a solution to the militant nationalism which is considered essential today by many developing nations. A disappearance of racism could improve relationships among countries where residents have different skin colors. The possibility for such changes can be seen in American history following wars. Wars have always been based upon jealousies and fears which are often irrational and in which persons from other countries have been perceived as foes and hated enemies. But later the same countries and people can be perceived as allies and friends. The position of West Germany and Japan in relationship to the United States is an obvious example of such changes in perception. These former enemies are now perceived as friends and helpers—not as potential destroyers (Barnett, 1984).

Another pervasive problem is discrimination against individuals on the basis of sex (Richardson, 1981; Breines and Gordon, 1983; Bleier, 1984). This has become a crucial civil rights issue in recent years in industrialized societies, particularly the United States. With the emergence of the feminist movement it has become clear to the members of many societies that actual equality of opportunity for women does not exist today even though it is essential to social equality, at least as perceived in American society. Sexual equality will also require drastic changes in the social organization of American society. It should be obvious to everyone by this time that major social change will be necessary if social equality for all persons is to be achieved.

Other Major Human Problems

In addition to discrimination there are other human and social problems facing the nations of the world today. One is mental health (President's Commission on Mental Health, 1978). Estimates over the last several decades consistently conclude that one out of ten people is mentally ill. The ravages of such illness can be seen all about us. Many criminals are psychotic persons. The personal, social, and economic costs of untreated mental illness are catastrophic. And current methods for treating mental illness are not sufficiently helpful to prevent a continuing accumulation of chronic mentally ill people (Fairweather, 1980). This problem is of national importance and demands immediate remedial action.

The excessive use of drugs is a major international problem (McGlothin, 1975; National Commission on Marijuana and Drug Use, 1973; Harris, 1983). The number of young persons who are experimenting with drugs could have disastrous consequences for people in any society. Excessive drug use will not go away, particularly when people can get hooked on drugs and thus become drug-dependent. With the constant use of drugs, small subcultures have arisen where taking drugs is normative for group members. This type of activity is very pronounced in America because of the acceptance of drug use by many persons and the economic incentives inherent in a continuing supply. It has thus become normative for some persons to use drugs. The end result of excessive drug use is well known to physicians and mental health workers who are often faced with the blatantly psychotic individual who is a drug user. This is a problem that requires the most serious attention.

Another exceedingly important social and interpersonal problem is alcoholism (Secretary of HEW, 1974; DeLuca, J., 1982). Excessive alcoholic indulgence is a problem for all age groups in many societies. The social and personal losses are enormous. In this country, overindulgence is often the cause of auto accidents and the physical harm to the individual is so great it is inestimable. The ability to function in work situations, to be a responsive marital partner, and a responsible parent is clearly diminished by alcoholism. It remains as one of the foremost interpersonal and social problems of our time.

The problems of mental illness, drug abuse, and alcoholism cannot be divorced from the problem of crime (Monahan, 1981). In the United States, for example, there has been an increasing crime rate for years and few, if any, adequate rehabilitative programs are now available (Goldstein et al., 1981). The imprisonment of persons convicted of criminal behavior for long periods of time in isolated places where they become well-schooled in antisocial practices is a most degrading and ineffective social practice (Martinson, 1974). That we need a completely new approach to the reintegration of such individuals into the community is obvious to people who have been involved in working daily with such persons. Adequate programs, particularly those training individuals for meaningful roles in the community, have not yet emerged. Entirely new programs need to be developed with new social positions for these persons as a primary focus.

The rapid and increasing cost of health care in this society is another major human problem. Health care is now one of the largest industries in the United States: "... national health expenditures are projected to reach approximately 756 billion in 1990 and consume roughly 12 percent of GNP" (Freeland and Schendler, 1983). The cost of getting medical care of adequate quality is fast moving beyond the reach of many citizens, particularly the poor in the American society. Nevertheless, innovative approaches to the delivery of health care have rarely been tried. And with the growing health problems created by an aging population and the increased incidence of drug addiction and alcoholism, the need for new and innovative medical programs which would be superior to any of those in America today is a social necessity. Thus, if there is to be adequate medical care for all the citizens within our society, there will need to be a series of new techniques developed for delivering health care. This is a major problem in the nation today.

In addition to issues of available health care, the need for new social roles for our aging citizens is a continuing issue (Gray, 1980). America is becoming an older society because of improved diets, new medical techniques, and changing fertility patterns. Large numbers of persons now find themselves retired without a meaningful role in society and with no place to go. These older citizens frequently have no more than a pittance to live on. Participative social positions for them have not been provided by society nor has there been any real attempt to do so. And even worse, many of them find their houses being torn down by urban renewal projects or find their taxes skyrocketing so that they are often left without access to adequate new housing to replace that which has been taken from them. The problem of growing old in a society organized mainly around the activities of young people needs to be faced by America squarely. If a meaningful life for the increasing number of older citizens is to be provided, new, more challenging, and meaningful social positions will have to be created for such persons.

Age differential may also be viewed as a problem associated with childhood. In recent years, the area of child abuse and neglect has surfaced as a major human problem. A specific problem receiving a good deal of publicity recently has been that of the sexual abuse of children (Starr, 1982). While there may be no specific change or increase in the amount and type of child abuse, generally speaking it has become a more well-known and discussed problem now than it has at any time in the past. The long-term consequences of the abuse of children can be viewed as childhood trauma. The effects of such traumas have been thoroughly documented by personality psychologists and it seems clear from such literature that when abusive practices do occur the individual affected may become emotionally disabled for a long period of time. This important problem needs to be resolved at the earliest moment.

A problem involving role change concerns the degree to which traditional roles will disappear as a result of biotechnology and other aspects of high technological industry. To take one simple example, it is often suggested that robotics will displace a considerable number of American blue-collar workers in the next several years. What is at issue here is how will dissemination of these technological changes affect people and what can be done about it? These issues are currently being addressed by a number of leaders in the new field of technological dissemination. Tornatzky et al. (1983, 1984) perceive the stress of job loss, the retraining of workers, and their job placement as a problem of growing importance in the next several years.

The physically handicapped are another group for whom an adequate social role is often limited by prejudiced attitudes concerning their ability to function as fully responsible citizens in a democratic society (Rubin, 1982). Handicapped persons are often not employed even though they have the educational and background qualifications for a particular job. They are frequently stigmatized by other individuals because of their physical characteristics rather than being perceived as qualified citizens. It is quite evident that if the quality of life for handicapped individuals is to be improved in the future, new attitudes about their abilities to function in our society will be needed, and new roles will need to be opened to them.

But why have these human problems reached such crisis proportions in a democratic society? It appears that there are certain social decision characteristics stemming from these human problems in the American culture that tend to create an impasse in problem-solving behavior. To assess our inability to solve readily the aforementioned contemporary human problems, we will briefly examine American social decision processes and their implementation in order to discover how and why the social and environmental problems just mentioned have reached such proportions.

IMPEDIMENTS TO ADEQUATE SOCIAL DECISIONS

Crisis as an Antecedent Condition to Problem Solving

What has developed in American society and, indeed, in most societies throughout the world, is that human problems are only addressed when they reach crisis proportions. Rather than being approached by long-range planning with continuous attempts at problem solution until the problem is solved, it appears that most often crises such as those just mentioned emerge even though the society has had long periods of warning. Malthus (Omran, 1960) began writing about overpopulation in 1789. Despite these warnings, and even when scientific evidence was available that social change was necessary, society did not change, it appears, until overpopulation was perceived as a crisis.

In American society, very often decisions are made *after* a crisis has occurred. In many such cases it is then too late to take anything but hurried and poorly thought-through general action. This occurs simply because an identified crisis of any magnitude cannot be tolerated for a prolonged period of time in a democratic society. But permitting crises to occur as antecedents to problem solution prevents long-range planning—an approach that is more and more demanded because of the size and complexity of the problems currently emerging. For example, the overpopulation of the earth cannot continue unchecked if there is not to be worldwide famine, an atomic holocaust, infanticide, or some other unacceptable consequence. Likewise, environmental degradation due to infiltration of toxic substances into our water supply will, if unchecked, create a crisis of inestimable proportions in the future. Once the crisis has occurred there may be no way to reverse the process; that is, it may be very difficult and perhaps impossible to obtain clean water once most natural water has become toxic.

Crisis situations of a different kind also exist in many of our social areas. Mental health and other health problems do not go away nor are they solved simply by ignoring them. Problems created by discrimination against others will also continue unless action is taken. The important point to grasp here is that continuing to base social decisions and actions upon crisis decisions will, in the final analysis, result in either an uninhabitable planet or a planet so devastated that its inhabitation will not be valued by the residents. It is for these reasons that environmental planning and action based upon sound scientific procedures must be implemented.

The Unbridled Search for Economic and Political Power

In all societies certain individuals attempt to place themselves in positions of authority and gain social control over others and to maintain this position once it is achieved. This results in what is commonly called *social stratification* in the field of sociology (Tumin, 1967; Burkhart, 1981). There is *no* known society in which social stratification does not exist, so that in this regard American society is no different than any other society. In our society, persons who rise to the top of the social stratification ladder usually have economic and political power over the lives of other individuals (Mills, 1956; Rose, 1967; Banach, 1977; Page, 1983). In a competitive society such as America persons who have such social advantages usually attempt to maintain them.

To understand more clearly how economic and political power can contribute to control of the decision process and hence restrict appropriate decisions needed for constructive change, we can examine a case study of how special interest groups can affect long-range planning and decisions in the environmental area as reported by Eipper (1970). The example involved the proposed use of a large lake for the development of a nuclear power source. Eipper discussed the proposed creation of a nuclear energy plant and the decision processes in the following way:

> The special interest groups promoting such developments may be industries that wish to use the water or other resources in a way that will yield them maximum profit, or they may be persons whose welfare or sympathies are more indirectly tied to an industry's success. The latter category includes groups of citizenry primarily concerned with immediate industrial benefits to the local economy, and persons in state or federal agencies who are much concerned with promoting the development of industrial technology. (Unfortunately, many of these agencies are assigned the dual role of promoting *and* regulating an industry.) Technological interest groups often make irrational assertions (based on questionable assumptions) to support programs that will exploit public natural resources. These assertions—or implications—include the following:
>
> > The program—as proposed—*has* to be enacted *now*.
> > The program will be enacted in any event. You can't stop progress.
> > The program is needed to fill the demand that will be created by the program.
> > No one opposes the program. It will benefit the majority and harm no one.
> > Data used to estimate effects of the program are the only valid pertinent data available.
> > Since there is no proof that the development will damage the environment, we can safely assume it will not.
> > All effects of the program have been considered.

The program, as presented, represents the sum total of the development contemplated for this particular resource.

All applicable alternatives have been considered.

Not only should such assumptions be questioned when they appear in discussion of pollution issues, but other questions should be asked, such as the following:

Who participated in formulating the assumptions and conclusions about this program's desirability?

What lasting social benefits—and costs—will this program produce?

Who will derive these benefits?

What environmental problems will, or may, be created?

What alternatives exist? Has the relative desirability of not enacting the program been evaluated (p. 15)?

The Lack of Relationship between Words and Deeds

Another deficiency in the American democratic process is the dependence upon verbal debate as the tactic for change. It is an irony of history because our revolutionary ancestors knew of the low relationship between verbal behavior and performance from their own experiences. Their verbal outcries against the tyranny of the British commonwealth when America was young were not heard and as a result the colonists eventually resorted to revolution because of the unwillingness of the British to heed their verbal outcries. Thus, the colonists' own experiences showed that corrective action did not necessarily follow verbal complaints.

These early colonial experiences are now supported by scientific evidence (Fairweather, 1960, 1964, 1969, 1980; Mischel, 1968; Wicker, 1969) which shows a lack of relationship between verbal behavior and performance. Usually the correlations are small. For this reason, persons who speak out against injustice may not take action to correct the injustice. Thus, verbal debate that occurs in state and national legislatures may not lead to constructive action.

The Filter-Down Process

Another political process that prevents adequate social programming might be called the *filter-down process.* It assumes once a law is passed and money is appropriated by Congress for a particular problem—say drug addiction—that the responsible government agency, in this case the Department of Health and Human Services, will furnish information to the states that will result in increased funds for programs to help solve the problem of drug addiction. The underlying assumption here is that the various levels of government—federal, state, county, local, drug administrators, persons seeking drug treatment, professional service persons, and so on—will adopt programs to prevent drug abuse. Nothing, of course, could be further from the truth. What usually happens is that programs are selected for a variety of economic and political reasons that may have little to do with a solution to the drug problem (Kiesler,

1980). Belief in the efficacy of the filter-down system as a means of moving from verbal agreement to effective programming deters effective problem-solving action.

Unverified Solutions

Analogous to the lack of relationship between verbal behavior and performance is the notion that heavily funding programs and giving them snappy titles will alleviate the problem. The job corps, one of the "great society's" programs, did not eliminate poverty or do away with unemployment as its proponents believed it would. To get a perspective about how such programs get started and perpetuated one need only examine the history of federal programs for family planning. Fairweather and Tornatzky (1977) have discussed this in the following manner:

> A governmental agency establishes a program designed to implement a particular social policy. Once, having established the program there is some question by the Congress or the administrators about whether or not it has accomplished the purpose for which it was established. The program is then *evaluated* by researchers who usually collect *selected* kinds of information. This information often supports the notion that the program is accomplishing its goal. Because of these reassurances, more money is appropriated to the program and more evaluations positive to the program are forthcoming. Thus, a vicious circle is created in which a particular governmental policy is supported by "*scientific*" evidence which results in the creation of a bigger and bigger bureaucratic organization with more and more funds at its disposal. *The basic question about whether the governmental program is better or worse than other programs the government might have adopted to solve the problem is never raised* (p. 8).

Thus it appears that social decision processes are often not directly aimed at problem solution. This occurs because decision processes are confounded by (1) crisis emergence, (2) the search for political and economic power, (3) the lack of relationship between words and deeds, (4) the filter-down process of implementing legislative decisions, and (5) the adoption of unverified solutions.

Given the serious nature of contemporary human problems, it seems clear that a new and more accurate problem-solving mechanism must be developed in American society if a meaningful quality of life is to be maintained. The next chapter describes what seems to be the basic parameters of such a decision process.

CHAPTER 2

PARAMETERS OF BENEFICIAL CHANGE

The need for a problem-solving process that will continuously monitor society and bring about needed changes when imbalances occur should be apparent from the first chapter. Imbalances occur and changes are needed when traditional mechanisms for handling the problem are no longer appropriate—that is, they do not bring about desired social ends. The most pervasive problem of societies—the social position of its members—can serve as an example (Tumin, 1967; Burkhart, 1981; Sowell, 1983). Since all societies are organized into some sort of social class or caste system, there are certain persons in all societies who usually have more political power and economic resources than others. Persons in the middle and lower social positions must be willing to work their way up the ladder to improve their social position within the society. But in some societies this is not possible because ascension to higher positions cannot occur, such as in the caste systems where social position is assigned at birth and is often based upon some parental characteristic or some other unchangeable aspect of a person's birth. Under such conditions those in lower social positions may revolt against their helplessness in the society to change their living situation. When this occurs, the society either creates new, more meaningful roles for such individuals through which they can ascend the social status ladder, or else the society must establish continuous domination over such individuals through police activity, isolation through institutionalization, or some other mechanism or physical control developed by that particular society to regulate social deviance. In the final analysis, therefore, the groundwork for either a revolution or a police state is being created when a society does not meet the needs of its constituents.

In American society, it has been typical that when such uprisings occur, usually based on gross social inequities, the society itself attempts to change and to implement new programs that will provide the socially deprived with more important social positions and easier access to economic and political power. Although these changes are slow, if successful they can result in the emergence of new power groups developed to represent disenfranchised persons. Union organizations, civil rights groups, the feminist movement, are all examples of this phenomenon which has occurred in American society. These emergent organizations and their constituents represent new power groups that eventually have to be taken into account by elected officials in a democratic society.

THE PARAMETERS

There are, as mentioned in Chapter 1, many human problems that not only involve America but all people on this planet, such as overpopulation, environmental pollution, and so on. Thus, whether a social crisis arises through social inequities or from severe environmental degradation, the ultimate consequence is social imbalance. When imbalances occur in American society, either as a result of social disparity, population overgrowth, environmental degradation, or any other factor, change is usually brought about hastily in the face of a *crisis* and very often such change does not solve the problem for which it was an intended solution. Such solutions, emerging as they do out of crisis situations, often lack validity, i.e., they do not alleviate the problem. Furthermore, it is not uncommon for such quickly adopted programs to do as much harm as good. For this reason, the central feature of any problem-solving process is that its ultimate aim must be to improve the quality of life through a scientific approach to human problems.

The Scientific Dimension

Not all scientists agree that scientists should attempt to solve human problems. This is often called "applied" science and is sometimes differentiated from "basic" or "pure" science. But by whatever name it is called, it must be understood that the research behavior of scientists is established by scientists themselves since scientific activity is what scientists make it. The techniques of science—its theory and methods—have been defined through the history of science. Because scientists can redefine their role in light of new developments, an ongoing debate has developed in this age of strong chemicals and nuclear power, about the appropriate use of science in human problem solution. Some scientists contend that becoming involved in solving human problems dilutes science and keeps science from being completely objective. But there are other underlying reasons for science remaining aloof from human problems which other scientists believe are equally important—if not more so—than the contention of some scientists that science was never intended to solve human problems. Some scientists, beginning in the 1960s, began to become personally involved in this debate, Schenck (1963) being one of the first. Schenck saw the division between pure and applied science as a myth which permits scientists to avoid responsibility for their actions. He states that the theory and application of science actually go hand in hand and that new theories can come just as often from data generated by research as they do from someone thinking about the problem. In discussing the relationship he believes actually exists between theory and application and its effect on social responsibility, Schenck (1963) had the following to say:

> There is no evidence of a sequential process of discovery proceeding from abstract to applied science and proving that the latter cannot happen without the former. The actual situation is far more complex; it would seem most closely to resemble a kind of dialogue between the abstract and the concrete in which neither is always first.
>
> As a single but important example, there is a law of nature called the Second Law of Thermodynamics which may well be the most fundamental and far-reaching law yet formulated by (human beings). In its applied science sense it limits the utilization of all energy sources.... In its deeper and more philosophical implications, it involves the direction of time itself and the evolution of the universe. The Second Law was first formulated by a French engineer, Sadi Carnot, a strong thinker who certainly qualifies as a pure scientist of his time. His "Reflections on the Motive Power of Heat" were the result of quite practical questions from James Watt and his derby-hatted engineering contemporaries who wished only to get more work out of a given engine. What, Carnot pondered, were the limits on such work production? His answers led to a very profound, actually very beautiful, penetration of the natural order. Yet I know of no scientific historian who alleges that Carnot's formulations could have occurred without prior work by the completely nontheoretical engineers of his day. The pure and applied worlds strike mutual sparks and neither is of pre-.dominant importance.
>
> Now why does this particular myth form a core of the scientist's belief structure? Because it is the primary myth that relieves science of responsibility (p. 142).

Just as Schenck believed that the use of "value-free" norms in scientific inquiry resulted in avoiding responsibility so did the sociologist Gouldner in Gouldner et al. (1962). While Gouldner believed that one positive aspect of a value-free label was that scientists could investigate values, he also perceived the possibility of a negative side. About this matter Gouldner (1962) said:

> ... Social science can never be fully accepted in a society, or by a part of it, without paying its way; this means it must manifest both its relevance and concern for the contemporary human predicament. Unless the value-relevances of sociological inquiry are made plainly evident, unless there are at least some bridges between it and larger human hopes and purposes, it must inevitably be scorned by laymen as pretentious word-mongering. But the manner in which some sociologists conceive the value-free doctrine disposes them to ignore current human problems and to huddle together like old men seeking mutual warmth. "This is not our job," they say, "and if it were we would not know enough to do it. Go away, come back when we're grown up," say these old men. The issue, however, is not whether we know enough; the real questions are whether we have the courage to say and use what we do know and whether anyone knows more (p. 205).

Rene Dubos (1970) believes that the traditional scientific role as defined as being concerned about only the pursuit of knowledge is not supported by the scientist's own role behavior:

> Much lip service is still being paid to the notion that science is primarily concerned with pure knowledge and has little if anything to do with the practical affairs of human life. But in fact most of the scientific knowledge is now concerned with practical problems. It seems to me unwise and ambiguous for scientists to affirm on the one hand that they are primarily searchers for truth and to claim on the other hand that everything they do is ultimately of practical importance. This ambiguity creates in the general public the feeling that scientists engage in double talk to provide a rationalization for what they really want to do, under the pretext that their findings will eventually be of social use. What is often called the anti-scientific movement is probably little more than an expression of the fact that the public is losing confidence in the ill-conceived and usually exaggerated claims of the scientific community (pp. X–XI).

It is the contention of the authors that science is one of the best and foremost problem-solving tools available to societies today. Our position is probably most adequately summed up by another statement from Dubos (1970), who had this to say about the value of science when used properly from a societal perspective:

> In the final analysis the greatest social contribution of science may well be to help people shape their own destinies by giving them knowledge of the cosmos and of their own nature. Through science we can learn about the world around us, how we emerged from it, what we can do with impunity, and the best way to reach our goals. We can even learn to formulate new goals compatible with our fundamental nature and with the constraints imposed on us by the natural forces of which we are the expression. When humans truly enter the age of science they will abandon their crude and destructive attempts to conquer nature. They will instead learn to insert themselves into the environment in such a manner that their ways of life and technologies make them once more at harmony with nature (p. XVII).

But even when scientists want to create solutions to human problems it does not automatically follow that the programs proposed by those interested in benefiting society will create valid and helpful solutions. A great deal of recent evidence indicates the fallacy of such assumptions. The "great society" programs, for example, started by President Johnson in the 1960s, were intended to eliminate unemployment with particular emphasis upon raising the social position of minorities. That we still have unemployment and social inequalities is patently obvious. The reason many of the "great society" programs did not succeed was not because they were not well-intentioned—they were typically designed and implemented with the best of intentions. However, the individuals who had the ideas about how improved social positions could be achieved and unemployment eliminated did not know the difference between a good idea and scientific evidence supporting the validity of that idea. Thus, they seemed to believe that the passage of a law would alleviate the problem. To hope for a result, to speak about a result, is quite a different process than behaviorally achieving a result.

The problems and challenges inherent in fielding large-scale social reforms are numerous. It should be quite obvious that at any step in the process, for any number of reasons, the entire program can either become disorganized, be terminated, or even, if allowed to continue, may not "work." It is for this reason that a *scientific* evaluation of any new program is essential. Such evaluations are the only way that the outcomes of new programs can be known. But this need itself raises issues for the concerned citizen. One of the authors (Fairweather, 1972) addressed the public misconception of the human problem-solving potential of science in the following manner:

Unfortunately, other roadblocks appear in a scientific approach to human problem solution. Among them is the commonly held idea that experimentation is bad. It seems immediately to conjure up ideas of another Nazi Buchenwald or Auschwitz. Experimentation with human beings has thus been judged as being bad. Persons whose children participate in new school programs, for example, are often reported to say that "my child is not going to be a guinea pig for any experimenter." And very often, persons who have been subjected to medical procedures regard themselves as paying the price for someone else's curiosity without any voice in the matter. The fact is, however, that human beings have always been the subjects of experimentation because they have been alive when certain events have taken place that have changed their environment. What their position would have been had the events not happened will never be known. For example, the development of atomic fission happened and no person, other than a few scientists and politicians, had a voice in its discovery and its use. Thus no one asked the public whether or not they wanted the atomic and hydrogen bombs. The bombs were manufactured and the people of the world were therefore participating in one of the most potentially dangerous experiments of all times. Who decided that the public would be the guinea pigs for the automobile with its internal combustion engine? In fact, the public is only recently becoming aware that automobile manufacturers are daily experimenting with "their atmosphere" by continuing to produce the internal combustion engine.

And is the same not true for new laws? Aren't they all social experiments? Are legislators better predictors than anyone else? Do they know what the final and total outcome of a law will be before it is placed in action? Who would have guessed that the Eighteenth Amendment, rather than controlling alcoholic indulgence, would actually create a generation of lawbreakers who flaunted their contempt for that social experiment by drinking at the speakeasy. Thus (people are) forever being subjected to experimentation. (Their lives), however momentarily secure, are risk-taking adventures in which there is never absolute—only relative—certainty. The industrialists who manufacture detergent soaps, cars, and drugs and the legislators who are continuously passing new laws are establishing experiments under which the people live as experimental subjects. Would it not be more humane if a group of humanistically oriented scientists tried, in collaboration with the elected officials and the public, to find better ways in which people could live—particularly if the scientists had been educated to place the highest value on improving the quality of human life? After all, the industrialists are motivated by the search for short-term profits and the politicians by political power. Surely with our current survival problems someone should be attempting to improve the general quality of human life. Since experimentation occurs as a process of living, it cannot be escaped. The real question now, as it has always been, is: toward what ends will experimentation be carried out? And who will decide to what uses knowledge will be put? What legacy will be left to our children as a result of such experimentation (pp. 15–16)?

While we will leave the details of scientific theory and methods for later chapters, it is important for the reader to understand that in the contemporary problem-solving arena combining scientific theory and methods is important and necessary (Jeger and Slotnick, 1982).

The Humanitarian Dimension

But this judicious use of science alone is only one dimension of an alternative problem-solving mechanism. Another basic parameter of a useful and beneficial change mechanism is that *it must be humane.* What this essentially means is that any social program must represent the humanitarian values that historically have served all societies of the east and the west. The great philosophers and religious leaders of the east and west have been concerned throughout recorded history with the humane treatment of individuals within a society. The importance placed upon human life is incorporated in most laws and tribal customs by assessing severe penalties for homicides and genocides and stressing love of one's neighbor as an important value, including concern for equality of individuals. These and other socially responsible values must serve as the background and as the guiding force behind scientific inquiry and its accompanying social action (Fromm, 1968; Bermant, Kelman, and Warwick, 1978; Monahan, 1980).

Current scientific work that creates nuclear contamination and toxic chemicals that can degrade the environment dramatically presents the need for a humanitarian value-oriented scientific program. Thus, when the changes that might occur as a result of a scientific inquiry could be harmful to individuals, either from a social or naturalistic point of view, those inquiries are not supported by a humanitarian value-oriented position and are, therefore, not permissible researches. To take an extreme example, overpopulation of the planet could easily be regulated by infanticide (a common practice in some early cultures). It is quite clear that such an approach to the problem is inhumane. Such inhumane social practices are excluded as possible solutions for that reason. Thus, scientific inquiry that is used to sharpen the decision-making processes of a society must consider only alternatives that it is believed will improve the human condition.

While there have been arguments and discussions among scientists, philosophers, and theologians for years—in fact, many of the current sciences historically grew out of philosophy—it has only been since the advent of atomic weaponry that the very clear need for *humanitarian values* in scientific work has been broadly entertained. Prior to the atomic bomb only a few scientists expressed concern about the effect of scientific findings on society's members. One was the social psychologist, Kurt Lewin, who believed that "research must accomplish some social good" (Bickman, 1980). Other scientists, particularly those engaged in atomic bomb development, began to show their concern when the first bomb was exploded. One of the clearest statements showing the origins of a concern for value-related scientific activity was expressed by Oppenheimer (1954) who remembered:

> There was, however, at Los Alamos a change in the feel of people. . . . This was partly a war measure, but it was also something that was here to stay. There was a great sense of uncertainty and anxiety about what should be done about it (p. 33).

Shortly thereafter, in the early 1960s, Bertrand Russell was one of the first few scientists to attempt to organize scientists against nuclear war. His activist position stemmed from his notion that most lay people, including politicians, did not have sufficient knowledge of nuclear fission and its positive and negative consequences to be able to make an adequate judgment about its use in war. Accordingly, he spearheaded a movement to organize scientists against nuclear war. This position also was concomitantly taken up by Einstein and some of his colleagues, who advocated an antinuclear war stance. In recent years, the relationship between humanitarian values and unbridled scientific activity has become more and more pronounced as groups have organized against nuclear plants that could defile the environment and endanger the lives of residents, as the Three Mile Island accident showed. The current reaction against nuclear war is a swelling social movement to which a large number of organized groups belong, not the least of which is a group of professional persons—the Physicians for Social Responsibility. This action illustrates that the public, since the days of the Bertrand Russell protest movement, has become more and more aware of the danger that currently exists with the destructive potential that science can now create.

This is not to suggest or even to imply that science itself is a negative human force. It is not—witness here the immunization techniques that have virtually stamped out mass dying from communicable diseases, and so on. But what this does indicate is that humanitarian values must be considered in the use of science so that a nuclear holocaust or other inhumane uses of scientific research, such as those used by the Nazis, will not recur.

There is yet another reason why humanitarian values must be incorporated into the scientific effort (Moos and Insel, 1974; Rappaport, 1977; Jeger and Slotnick, 1982). And that is that scientists create knowledge, and knowledge itself is power. When scientists gain new knowledge it is important to the future of our democratic society to know that the information will be used to improve the quality of life of the individuals in our society (Rappaport, 1977; Murray, 1982). There is, of course, the constant threat that unscrupulous or naive individuals (and some of them will be scientists since scientists are no more immune from human frailties than anyone else) will use information to enhance their own social and economic positions at the expense of others. It is for this reason that scientists must approach scientific inquiry recognizing that they should value the living creatures on this planet and the environmental qualities that support and enhance that life. For it is unquestionably true that scientific information can be used for destructive as well as constructive purposes. One of the most eloquent statements made about the possible misuse of scientific information came from the former head of the Atomic Energy Commission, David Lilienthal (1945) who wrote:

> ... it is by no manner of means inevitable that scientific research and technology will work for good. It is equally possible that they may yield a harvest of bitter fruit. When those speak who imply that our problem is only one of securing more and more funds for more and more scientific workers in private or public research, we need constantly to remind ourselves that, in terms of human happiness and freedom, such a conclusion is far from true. Unless research and technology are consciously related to a central purpose of human welfare, unless research is defined and directed by those who believe in and who have faith in people and in democratic ends and means, it may well be that the more money we spend on research the further we miss the mark. It is like trying to reach your destination in an automobile that is going in the wrong direction; the faster you drive the farther away from your goal you will be (p. 186).

It is for this reason that community experimentalists must take humanitarian democratic values very seriously. It is also for this reason that *no* solution that could theoretically or practically harm the population for which it is designed can be entertained in a humane scientific approach aimed at solving human problems. As will be mentioned later, from a scientific perspective we are dealing with a one-sided equation which proposes that any newly planned social program theoretically will be more beneficial to society or the problem population than was the program it has been designed to replace.

A Problem Orientation

But before a humane science can be helpful in social policy research it must become problem-oriented (Bickman, 1981; Oskamp, 1984). Thus, it is necessary that the solution to any particular problem such as unemployment, impure water, mental illness, and the like, be the focus of an evaluative research effort. Often, scientific research concentrates upon a single discipline, such as psychology, sociology, or biology, and thus *not* upon the whole of the problem. But human problems usually go beyond the boundaries of a given academic discipline. Let us take the human fertility problem as an example. It is at one and the same time a problem involving religion, psychology, sociology, political science, geography, and biology, and we could add several more. The point here is that focusing on the problem allows identification of the many fields we must consider in problem solving and permits the scientist to select from them those precise variables that are important in fashioning a contemporary solution for that problem. Even if the fertility rate issue is addressed as a disciplinary problem, such as the psychology of birth regulation, it still must be understood that the psychological aspects of fertility rates are operative in the real world and *only* in the context of some of the other fields just mentioned, such as politics, religion, biology, and the like. It is for this reason that problem-oriented research needs to be done so that when solutions are found they apply directly to the problem at the level of daily living.

Eventually, a problem orientation may lead to development of an *integrated* science. Such an integration means simply that the methods, theories, and techniques used by the different sciences are combined into a whole and are used as they become a necessary part of the problem inquiry process. This is similar to the position adopted by several scientists and is epitomized in the writing of Hare (1970):

> The answer, I suggest, is that the study of a problem such as we have been discussing is not simply interdisciplinary in the sense that it involves several of the old disciplines. Instead it demands a new kind of discipline, basically synthesizing in method. I am sure that the university will have to answer more and more calls to solve social problems, and that, if we do not answer these calls, we shall be bypassed by the creation of new kinds of institutions more flexible and realistic in outlook. I conclude that we must learn to develop these new disciplines of synthesis, and make them as rigorous as the older analytical disciplines. I can hear the scoffers scoffing—but, if we do not tackle this, we shall deserve to be counted out. By all means let us encourage interdisciplinary ventures—but in the hope that they will indeed become disciplines of the new kind (p. 355).

Hare suggests an integrated, problem-solving scientific approach. Not only does this require that theories be integrated but it also means that methods must be integrated. Thus, techniques as well as the theoretical ideas that emanate from the many different disciplinary fields such as biology, sociology, political science, and the rest need to be integrated into the problem-solving mechanism.

Perhaps the research teams that are the most visible problem-oriented group of scientists are those involved in space flight. In this endeavor, various scientific ideas and methods are borrowed from numerous fields such as astronomy, physics, geography, botany, biology, medicine, and so on, and are integrated into the plan for each flight. In addition, persons from the different disciplines combine their efforts. Thus, individuals have to perceive the particular space flight in which they are team members as more important than their own individual goals or particular disciplinary point of view. In this way goal-oriented action is achieved.

Other problem-oriented research needs to move forward in the same manner. In such a way research teams bring knowledge from separate disciplines to bear on a broader issue than the discipline itself—the solution of a human problem. Whether or not this results in a new discipline as envisioned by Hare or a series of role characteristics that permit individuals on research teams to devote their energies to finding a solution of the problem is a moot question at this point in history. What is obvious, however, is that regardless of disciplinary training persons participating in human problem solution must have an appreciation of the need for a research team that can engage in goal-directed activity organized by an understanding of the concepts and methods of all the disciplines involved.

A Multilevel Focus

This brings us to another issue, that of whether human problem-solving programs should be aimed at individuals, groups, organizations, or society at large

(Kiesler, 1980). Generally, to have long-term merit social programs must be aimed at all four audiences (individuals, groups, organizations, and society). To take one example, programs designed to help people learn to read cannot help when the reading materials needed are unavailable because of lack of funds. Under these conditions, such programs are not available to those who need to learn to read unless budgetary support is considered to be as important as the actual reading program. This is especially pronounced when programs are aimed at broader areas of adjustment, such as finding appropriate positions for such persons in the community after an inadequacy (such as a reading deficiency) has been eliminated. Such complete programs, aimed at improving the social position of the clientele, necessarily must focus on the individual and society at the same time.

While a multifocus approach is needed to solve any problem, the focus of some problems is more individualistic than social or organizational. For example, a poorly functioning kidney is a very individualistic problem in which a system within a person's body may need to be modified for the kidney to function properly. On the other hand, attempting to provide aid for chronically unemployed individuals may require reorganization of the labor force. In such a case, industrial organizations, such as the automobile industry and the housing industry, may need to create new positions and in this and other ways change their traditional practices to provide a broader range of employment. Thus, problems can be of such a nature that their solution requires a greater or lesser degree of individual change, group change, organizational change, and societal change; but most complex social problems ordinarily involve change at all four of these levels (Kelly, 1971).

An Action Orientation

For scientists to become involved in human problem solving they must adopt an *active* role in this process. Historically, science has developed roles requiring much thought and little action. This was apparently based on the notion that private thought and individual and group discussion would somehow lead to social change because new ideas that were invented would be incorporated into the body of knowledge and eventually into societal practices. This idea has also been the basis for much of the scientists' role behavior and in the belief that scientific information will eventually lead to problem solution.

Unfortunately, social change does not occur simply by cognitive awareness. Being aware of a particular problem, which is an essential first step, does not guarantee that a problem will be solved. In fact, a great deal of current research shows a very low relationship between verbal statements, attitudes, and actual behaviors (Fairweather, 1964, 1969, 1980; Bandura, 1969; Wicker, 1969; Fishbein and Ajzen, 1975). Persons who have been the victims of a social problem (unemployment, for example) know from their own experience that a social remedy ordinarily comes from some action designed to alleviate that problem at the level of everyday experience. Since valid solutions to human problems require action, scientists involved in problem solution will have to get involved in social programming at a workaday level.

This is not to say that attitudes and feelings are not important. Of course they are. However, it is important to realize that simply expressing an attitude and having personal feelings about a problem that requires change does not necessarily bring about the needed social reform. Unfortunately, there is a great schism between cognitive awareness, verbal behavior, and actual performance. It is this discrepancy that must be surmounted if scientists are to deal directly with human problems.

The action component has its roots in both the early work of the psychologist Lewin (Bickman, 1980) and the service tradition of many professions. It is also a central part of the community scientist's role. The problem-solving scientist in the community necessarily becomes more than a passive observer of social events or an implementer of existing social policy.

The community scientist's role also involves considerable time commitment to a particular human problem. Given the complexity and multidisciplinary nature of most human problems, attempting real-life solutions by the community scientist usually means a multiyear commitment to the problem area.

In this action-oriented role, the community scientist also should be aware of the need to be a social advocate for marginal problem populations who typically are without advocates in a majority-ruled society (Tyler, Pargament, and Gatz, 1983). Thus, in presenting scientific results to program administrators, legislators, and the like, it will be necessary for the community scientist to be an advocate for marginal populations as well as integrating scientific methods in the decision-making process (Kiesler, 1980; Seidman, 1983).

Thus, the community scientist role involves active humanitarian problem solving taking place within the framework of the tenets of scientific logic and methodology.

Innovation

To be realistically involved in solving human problems the problem solvers must have a conceptual grasp of the process of change itself. There are two major ingredients in this process, which represent two additional parameters: the *creation* of a problem-solving innovation and the *spread* of that innovation (dissemination) throughout the society so that it becomes part of the normative functioning of that society. This process of change was first proposed by Barnett (1953) and later elaborated by LaPiere (1965) as follows:

> . . . social change is worked by the efforts of individuals—functioning in various capacities as innovators, advocates, or adopters—who have in some small measure and in some respect been freed from the conventionalizing effects of social ideology and of organizational membership. . . . (pp. VI–VII).

The basis for change in any society is the creation of an innovation, a process to advocate its adoption by others, and the dissemination of the innovation throughout the society by this adoptive process. Thus, social change occurs in a society through creation and development of new programs that are then adopted by some segment of the society and finally, if dissemination continues, they become programs for the entire nation. Ordinarily, innovation occurs in a society as the result of the early recognition of a problem by one or two individuals within the society who attempt to create something new to solve that problem.

The first step in conceptualizing social change is to understand what an innovation is. Even though today there are several definitions of an innovation (Daft, 1982; Rogers, 1983; Blakely, Emshoff, and Roitman, 1984), probably the clearest definition of an innovation is still that given by LaPiere (1965):

> An innovation is an idea for accomplishing some recognized social end in a *new* way or for a means of accomplishing some new social end. The idea or pattern of ideas may become manifest as a new kind of tool or mechanical device, as a new process or technical procedure, as a new material or substance, as a place or terrain previously unknown to man, as a new mode of human action, or as a new concept or belief. Whatever the manifestation, the innovating consists of the creation of a unique and to a significant degree unprecedented mental construct, the idea that makes possible the "thing" (p. 107).

The new way of thinking that is required to create an innovation is also described by LaPiere (1965):

> The power of established beliefs, preconceptions, and ways of thinking over the mind of individuals is much easier to illustrate than it is to analyze. During the fifteenth century there were many men who recognized the desirability of finding a new water route from Europe to the Orient, but it was not until well toward the close of that century that any one of them was able to escape the socially imposed logic of going east to get east. So for a century and more, Spanish and Portuguese explorers worked their way down the west coast of Africa seeking a channel eastward; eventually they rounded the tip of that continent and reached Madagascar, which for a time was mistaken for the Orient. Only Columbus was able to ignore the traditional idea of how to solve the problem of getting east and to seek a solution to that problem in an entirely new way and direction (p. 120).

Basic, therefore, to the creation of an innovation is the perception of a problem for which the innovation is typically a perceived solution. Very often the process involved in creating such solutions requires approaches that differ from those that are culturally acceptable; at the very least they are not perceived by most members of the culture as ways of solving a problem at the time they are invented (Tornatzky, 1983).

With this definition of an innovation in mind, let us now turn our attention to the innovator. Technological innovators are easy to recognize after the fact—Edison and the electric light, Watts and the steam engine, and so on. But it is very difficult for us to identify social innovators. Looking at social processes historically we ask ourselves: Who invented the public school system, the legal system, the corporation, the conglomerate, etc.? All these are innovative social organizational structures that affect the lives of everyone in west-

ern societies and many in eastern societies as well. The difficulty with identifying a single social innovator is that while an individual may have an original
idea it is impossible for one person to carry out the social innovation alone,
and therefore it becomes necessary for a large number of people to be involved.
And to make matters more complex, after the original idea and the creation of
a social innovation, the innovation itself begins to spread and eventually is
adopted by such a large number of people the innovator is often lost in the
shuffle. Despite this identification difficulty, however, it appears that the same
process—a new idea as the perceptual basis for a solution to a given problem—
is as essential in social innovation as it is in technological innovation.

It is also quite clear that innovations go through a trial-and-error period of
development in which different solutions may be tried and found wanting.
This trial-and-error phase may be called the *developmental phase*. It is the
period between having the idea and arriving at the end product or solution.
During this time various new ideas are tried and the new technological or
social innovation is completed. For example, a great deal of time was spent by
Edison after he had the idea of the electric light bulb in trying to find filaments
that would convert electricity into light. This same development process seems
to occur with social innovations.

Perhaps the most puzzling part of understanding the innovation process,
particularly from a psychological point of view, is understanding why and how
people become innovators. This is at best a poorly understood process,
although some of the characteristics of such individuals seems fairly clear.
How is it that the innovator can go through the socialization processes required
to reach adulthood, and yet retain ideational freedom? Understanding this process itself is a puzzle of immense proportions. Some sociologists would insist
that this happens because the individuals belong to a subgroup that itself is not
well acculturated—such as a family group which perceives discovery and independent thought as an important event—and who, through identification with
family members, themselves become creative (Becker, 1963). On the other
hand, LaPiere (1965) and others (Rogers, 1983; Tornatzky, 1983), who have
given a great deal of thought to the developmental aspects of an innovator's
life, point out that most innovations are begun by one individual whose innovative thoughts and actions are a deviation not only from cultural patterns but
from the small group to which the individual belongs.

Regardless of how or why some people become innovators, there appear to
be certain characteristics which seem to be essential to the development of
innovations. First, there is the perception of a problem that the public has not
noticed. This recognition is followed by an idea about how the problem can be
solved. And finally, a strong belief develops that the product embodied in the
idea will solve the problem. From a personality perspective, the innovator
must have what is sometimes called "dogged perseverance," an "obsession,"
or even a "delusion." By whatever term such behavior is identified, what it is
necessary to understand is that innovators have a way of clinging to an idea
that appears to be a solution to a problem even when the idea is not culturally

approved. Thus, innovation requires the formulation by a particular individual of a new idea which is not culturally acceptable at the time, or at least not culturally used. It requires a developmental period of trial and error during which the idea becomes elaborated as a problem solution by the innovator. This time-consuming process usually occurs with little, if any, social reward and if successful results in the creation of a new product or program that bursts upon the scene without fanfare and usually completely without social support.

Dissemination

But if the process of innovation development is a difficult one, the second parameter of the change process—spreading the innovation so that it may be used by others—is even more so. It is almost an inevitable consequence of daily living that persons resist changing their behavior. From such simple tasks as tying one's own shoes to complex mathematics people learn certain behaviors and perceptions that are constantly reinforced. Through this process they become indoctrinated into ways of behaving, perceiving, and feeling that take a great deal of effort to change. The whole notion of individual change is a process that is poorly understood today, despite attempts of personality theorists, sociologists, cultural anthropologists, and others to explain it.

While all the facets of resistance to change are unknown, it also seems clear that a *fear of the unknown* is central to maintaining the status quo. LaPiere (1965) describes this fear (often called uncertainty) in the following way:

> People always and everywhere accept with considerable complaisance what is familiar to them, whatever it may be and however disagreeable it may seem to members of another, different society, apparently because almost anything familiar is less disturbing emotionally than is something unknown. It is an over-simplification to say that people fear the unknown; it would be better, perhaps, to say that what is designated as fear (or apprehension, dread, or the like) are those emotional disturbances that are induced by the contemplation of or exposure to what is unknown or unfamiliar and hence unpredictable (p. 177).

Thus resistance to change is a relatively normal human reaction. It is even embedded in the folklore of our culture in such cliches as "ignorance is bliss," and "curiosity killed the cat." For these reasons the acceptance of a new idea as the basis for a solution to a problem is so difficult to achieve. All the forces of socialization are arrayed against finding new solutions. The entire socialization process is one of indoctrinating individuals into culturally accepted ways of perceiving and behaving. These cultural forces make accepting an innovation extremely difficult.

Beyond individual resistance to change, there appears to be organizational resistance (Scheirer and Rozmovic, 1982; Radnor, Feller, and Rogers, 1978). If the discovery of a new innovation is to have national significance there is no alternative but to begin a major effort at disseminating the model to other groups and organizations which should be able to use it within the society. It may come as a surprise to the naive reader that even social innovations whose actual benefits have been scientifically established are no more readily accept-able to organizations than are innovations that have no validity whatsoever. The adoption of new programs does not appear to be based upon rational deci-sion processes at all (Fairweather, 1974; Tornatzky et al., 1980). Since dissem-ination itself is central to the processes of change there can be no general social change without wide-scale adoption of an innovation.

Thus, in addition to individuals' resistance to change, organizations also seek to maintain whatever operation is ongoing at the moment (Berman and McLaughlin, 1978). For social programs there are a wide variety of causes of resistance to change, not the least of which is a form of vested interest. Any organizational structure which is intact and operating in a society acrues cer-tain benefits to those at the top and fewer benefits, if any at all, to those at the bottom. Whether we are speaking about a health organization, a university, a union, or any other organization, social stratification exists so that those at the top of the organizational structure tend to get greater rewards than those at the bottom, and thus they have a special interest in maintaining the status quo.

There are other reasons why change often does not occur through the bureaucratic process (Goodman, Bazerman, and Conlon, 1978). Social pro-grams usually must also be carried out under the guidance of professional per-sons who often reinforce the status quo by supporting programs with which they are familiar. The mere act of having to be certified and licensed means that there is an accepted way of behaving that is perpetuated over time since individuals must learn and practice *particular* perceptions and behaviors as part of their professional role to obtain the certification or license. While the intention of providing qualified persons to the public is admirable, the social price is the continuation of services that may become invalid over time.

There are broader *societal* reasons for perpetuating the status quo. Change appears to be cyclical—spurts of change followed by status quo periods. In our society, for example, the 1960s were a period of discontent as shown in the reaction to the war in Vietnam, the emergence of civil rights issues, and the forceful emergence of the feminist movement, to name some of the most pub-licized social movements. In this period rather rapid social change occurred contrasted with the early 1970s when the war in Vietnam was over and a con-servative trend began to appear.

In addition, there may be an historical accident involved in the readiness of a society to change, because at the time when change can be accomplished advocates need to be attracted to the promotion of the innovation. Many inno-vations have not been accepted in a society because no advocate for the inno-vation happened to be present. Advocates differ from innovators in that they recognize some advantage of an innovation for themselves and for this reason they try to persuade others to accept it (LaPiere, 1965). Without an advocate or advocates to become involved in spreading the innovation, the culture will have no access to it and will therefore remain static.

If a society is in a change cycle, as in the 1960s, and an innovation is present, *and* advocates are available at the same time adopting individuals can be found, change will likely occur.

This chapter has presented the key parameters that need to be considered in creating beneficial social change. Properly integrating them should provide an action-oriented, problem-solving device based upon scientific and humanitarian thought that should provide beneficial social change to a society. Our attention now turns to this integration.

CHAPTER 3

DYNAMICS OF THE PROBLEM-SOLVING PROCESS

This chapter will integrate the ideas presented separately in the first two chapters into a sequential process linking theory and operations that will result in problem solution. Given the assumption that creation of change depends on social innovation and innovation dissemination, it follows that a problem-solving process would have the following general outline: First, it would identify the problem from a scientific perspective, i.e., find and identify the variables important in solving a particular problem. These identified variables then would be used as the basic elements in creating an innovative solution to the problem, thus arriving at a logical plan for a prospective innovative solution. Once the planned innovation is in place, new innovative solutions would be scientifically compared with the existing program or programs so that the validity of the new innovation could be ascertained. This step should assure program validity. Therefore, the process of social innovation must be carried out in an evaluative framework. To accomplish this the researcher begins planning an experimental design to compare the new innovation with an existing program or programs (Fairweather, 1967; Campbell, 1969; Fairweather and Tornatzky, 1977).

Up to this point all the processes have been cognitive in nature. Now, the research must move from planning to action. The innovative model is implanted in the community and is activated so that it can be compared with the existing model(s) in the framework of an experiment. It is during this phase of the problem-solving process that data are collected from which the innovative model can be evaluated. Following the operation of the models participating in the experiment for a prescribed period of time—an agreed-upon experimental period—the collected data are then analyzed and an evaluation of the innovative problem solution is made. If it is determined that the innovative solution is no more helpful than those programs currently in existence, there is no dissemination of the innovative program. Rather, a new model is created, sometimes with some of the same components as those in the first innovative model, and this second innovative experimental model is again contrasted with existing program(s). This process continues until an innovative program has shown significant beneficial improvement over the contemporary model or until it becomes clear that the contemporary program is as good as can be expected at this time.

When a significant improvement is scientifically demonstrated, dissemination activity begins by creation of a dissemination experiment. During the dissemination experiment the community researcher attempts to discover techniques that can encourage acceptance of the new model in the society. Once the dissemination tactics have been validated through experimental interventions, the verified techniques are used to further disseminate the new models throughout the society. In such a fashion, scientific techniques are integrated into social change.

THE PROBLEM-SOLVING PROCESS

The problem-solving processes and their sequential relationships are shown in Figure 3-1. This figure represents the activities that are linked sequentially together in a dynamic fashion to bring about a solution to a human problem. It should be obvious that stopping any one of these processes during their sequential, longitudinal operations would end the general process of social change. Since activating and carrying out these six processes is lengthy and does, in fact, involve many people over a prolonged period of time, it should also be clear that scientifically valid social change is a slow process which can only occur over a period of time. Nonetheless, as with so many activities in life, it is this commitment to long-term problem solution that is essential in solving human problems, particularly those as complex as the ones discussed in the first chapter.

Although each of these six activities will be operationally defined and discussed in considerable detail in subsequent chapters, it is important here to describe briefly each one so that the contribution of each to social change can be understood. Let us start with problem identification.

Problem Identification

Observing the problem in its real-life setting as well as searching the literature about the particular problem from many different disciplinary perspectives—sociology, psychology, biology, etc.—eventually brings about complete definition of the problem. In addition to literature and observation, discussing the problem with professionals, and the persons suffering from the problem, leads

PROBLEM IDENTIFICATION →	CREATIVING INNOVATIVE → SOLUTION MODEL(S)	PLANNING MODEL EVALUATION →
Understanding the problem from a number of different viewpoints so that potential determinants can be identified and possible solutions outlined.	Making educated guesses about the manner in which these central variables can be combined so that a problem solution can theoretically result.	Designing an experiment in which the innovative model(s) will be contrasted with the model(s) that society is currently using to solve the problem.

FIGURE 3-1
The six problem-solving processes.

to further understanding of the problem itself and aids in isolating those variables important to its understanding and solution.

Creating an Innovative Solution

Here, information gathered from problem identification is incorporated into a plan for a model that will, in the experimenter's judgment, solve the problem. The creation of models is a technique used by many sciences to assess the validity of a proposed solution—mock up models for new cars or small-scale models of proposed bridges are examples. Let us assume that the problem is unemployment and that it was discovered during the problem identification phase that older people were having more difficulty than other age groups in finding jobs. Let us further assume that during the problem identification phase it was learned that many older people lacked information about jobs that were available. The innovative solution, therefore, might be the creation of a program that would bring older people interested in jobs together with potential employers who were looking for persons with their abilities. It is this act of creating a problem-solving innovation that is most difficult to achieve.

Planning Model Evaluation

Planning for model evaluation refers to the series of concepts and actions necessary to establish the new model in an actual community setting so that it can be compared with traditional model(s) that exist there. This process requires planning a comparative experiment that will be carried out in the community. In addition, the experimental procedures of sampling, measurement, and the

ACTIVATING THE COMPARATIVE → MODEL(S)	EVALUATING THE PROBLEM-SOLVING → MODEL(S)	DISSEMINATING BENEFICIAL PROBLEM-SOLVING MODEL(S)
In this phase the model(s) move from the planning board to the community setting. All experimental models and comparative models, including control models, are activated on the same date in a community setting so that their effects can be scientifically evaluated.	Continuing to operate the model(s) for a period of time—from several weeks to several years depending on the problem(s) and the model(s)—during which time repeated measures are taken to assess relative effectiveness of models. Constant monitoring of models occurs so that program constancy is maintained.	This phase concerns replication of models that have been evaluated to be beneficial in Phase 5. Replicates are established in an experimental design so that tactics of dissemination can be thoroughly evaluated and outcomes of replicates carefully scrutinized.

like discussed in later chapters will need to be planned here so that they can be carried out in processes 4 and 5 (see Figure 3-1). This is necessary so that the new program can be accurately compared with traditional one(s) while they are in operation.

Activating Comparative Models

The processes now move from planning to action. This phase requires actual development of the new model in the community and its establishment there as a functioning unit. Thus, in the example given earlier about employment prospects for the elderly, model(s) bringing potential employers and employees together would be established in some arranged location in the community, meeting times established, measurement begun, and so on, so that the programs could be activated as an experiment and ensuring that all models to be compared were actually operating. Moving from cognition to action as planned is difficult to achieve, as will become obvious in later chapters.

Evaluation of Problem-Solving Model(s)

After the model(s) has been operative for a considerable period of time—usually from several months to years—the data that have been conscientiously collected throughout the course of the experiment are then analyzed. The analyses of data should yield definitive information about the degree to which the new model actually improves outcomes contrasted with other approaches to the problem. Should statistical comparisons show clearly that the innovative model is very likely to be significantly superior to the traditional model(s), the innovative model is presumed to be worth disseminating.

Dissemination of Beneficial Problem-Solving Model(s)

A new experiment is set up where replicates of the beneficial model are established in a county, state, region, or nationally. Each new replicate is compared with the original program to discover the degree to which it yields the same results as the original program. As more and more replicates indicate that the program is successful, the probabilities increase that beneficial results will accrue from further dissemination. In addition, information is also learned about the dissemination processes—how to help people adopt the new model and put it in operation. Successful completion of this process should establish the new innovative model in a number of community programs where the problem population, social administrators, and service professionals will have access to it.

These six basic processes need to be completed in sequential order so that a valid problem solution can be found and implemented. It should be obvious that if all six sequential processes are not carried out, by failure of any one of the six processes (problem identification through dissemination), there will be no scientifically valid solution to the problem for society to use. It is for this reason that, for beneficial change to occur, each of the processes not only must be completed but must be completed in sequence, including understanding what the basic processes of an innovative social model(s) are. To accomplish this, community scientists need to identify the variables that impinge upon the innovative social model as it winds its way from inception to community acceptance.

THE DYNAMICS OF SOCIAL MODELS

To understand what a social model is and the factors that might affect it we must first define it and explore its functions. A limited review of human, group, and societal behaviors should accomplish this task. People in all societies live their lives out in relationships with a given number of other persons, groups, and organizations. It is the interaction of each person with these others as well as with the physical and social environment that results in a person's particular perceptions and behaviors. Since each of us is also an individual with somewhat different biologies it is reasonable to assume that each person's personal and social definition results from his or her interaction with the total environment. Thus, as socialization occurs, an individual's personality is formed not only from that person's biological inheritance but also from his or her interactions with others and with the total environment.

Because of the totality and complexity of such experiences, an integration of variables normally considered the province of several different disciplines is required in the problem-solving process. To clarify this issue, it is necessary to discuss briefly some of the variables that may impinge upon an individual and thus determine behavior and attitudes. First of all, there are several disciplines and subdisciplines that deal almost exclusively with the individual. These include, for example, biology, biochemistry, medicine, and psychology. But individuals are also usually members of groups and what happens within these reference groups can also determine behavior and attitudes and even, perhaps, some of the biological functioning of that individual. So, for example, an individual is a member of a family, a sports team, a school class, and so on. Other disciplines such as anthropology, sociology, economics, and the various family sciences now need to be considered.

These groups operate within a broader society, and in a particular geographic region. One may live in an African, Asian, or European culture or in a subculture in a section of these land masses, such as the southern, eastern, western, or northern United States. Within these regions one may live in an urban or rural environment. In such cases, regional differences emerge which affect urban and/or rural environments and also group and individual behavior.

The particular geographic area in which a group lives, therefore, can affect the functioning of the members of that group and the group itself. So additional disciplines such as local geography, ethnology, ecology, and the like must be considered. But regions of the country are located in social climates related to some extent to their particular geography. For example, the social climate created by the American culture is quite different in many ways from that of India, the Soviet Union, and other countries. Each national situation also affects the regions, groups, and individuals within its borders. Here the concern is with a nation's impact that results from the national ecology, geography, political science, sociology, health care, law, and the like.

And all the countries belong to the planet earth. What happens in one country may affect others; witness here the events that created World Wars I and II and the pollution of the oceans which is causing considerable distress to all countries that lie along the shoreline of those oceans. This macrogeographic area (our planet) must be considered as having a definite effect upon all of us on this earth. Thus, there is international weather, law, a world food crisis, world overpopulation, etc., each of which incorporates a large body of information from the various sciences that is integrated at this global level. There is, for example, world ecology as distinguished from local ecology, regional ecology, and national ecology.

Thus, each individual lives in a group or groups within a geographic region which is within a nation which is within the international community. The various disciplines that will have to be studied in such a situation, of course, involve all the known disciplines that have been created, since at the global level all phenomena are functional. As we review a particular problem some of the variables at the broader levels—such as those at a regional level—may have little impact in determining a specific behavior or attitude. Nonetheless, this generic manner of viewing problems emphasizes the theoretical integration required for problem identification and solution.

Since each person lives in a particular social system at different times in his or her life, it seems only logical that all the roles that individuals have experienced throughout their lifetime will influence their personality characteristics. For example, each old person has been a child, an adolescent, a young adult, a middle-aged adult, and now is an aged adult. At any moment in that person's lifetime he or she has a propensity to respond to a given situation which is based upon his or her particular biology as well as all the past person—situation interactions that have formed the person's personality. Each of us throughout our lives has lived in a particular social subsystem that interrelates us with the broader culture and it is through these relationships that our identity is formed.

Since the interaction effect of person and environment is what appears to determine the propensity to perceive and act, a more general formulation of what a particular individual is likely to do at a given moment can be stated by the following hypothesis: A person's perceptual and/or behavioral responses are a function of his or her biology and all the social roles the person has experienced throughout his or her lifetime. Viewed from a social systems perspective, it appears reasonable to assume that the outcome of any total social system would be a summation or a product of individuals' responses and their interactions at a particular moment. Such responses are individual and also collective. For example, the outcome might be quite individualistic, such as brushing one's teeth, or quite collective, such as the action of a football team. Whether or not the individual scientist wants to concern himself or herself with individual behavior (brushing one's teeth) or group behavior (a winning or losing football team) depends upon the problem and the scientist's interests. Nevertheless, and regardless of whether the response is individual or group, the outcome of any social subsystem to which an individual belongs is a collective function of the behavior of the individuals who themselves are affected by the immediate and past situations in which they have participated.

For our purposes here we will define a problem-solving social model as any social system designed as a problem solution that can be implanted in the natural environment. From this definition it should be readily apparent that models can be designed as a solution for any human problem whether it is one of the natural environment, one internal to the person, or one involving society as a whole.

It should also be clear that a model as the vehicle for change can be affected by a wide variety of variables, some of which are internal to the model itself while others are external to it. First, there are the participants. Given the biological and personality differences that can exist among a random sample of people it seems only reasonable to assume that the persons who participate in the model—whether they are professionals, persons suffering from a given problem, or both—will interact with one another, having an impact on the way other people behave, and, therefore, how the model functions. To take some extreme examples, it seems only logical that one would get quite different results from a program if all the participants were noncommunicative, contrasted with a model where everyone is able and willing to talk; or in a model where all persons suffered from some disturbing physiological ailment such as brain dysfunction, contrasted with persons participating in the same model who were considered "normal." Thus, the participants themselves can affect the product or outcome of a model and the model in turn can affect the individuals.

But the model itself will have to be implanted in the natural environment and therefore can have a different product or outcome if the environments in which it is implanted are dissimilar. For example, while the neighborhood in which a model can be implanted will affect its outcomes, the neighborhoods themselves are influenced by what happens at a national level, and national reactions may be influenced by international events. Thus, there is constant interplay between the model which encompasses the participants and their interactions (internal processes of the model) and the external environment, varying from those in closest geographic proximity to the model (the neighborhood) to those a great distance from the model such as other nations. An attempt to capture this interaction network is presented in Figure 3-2. The dot-

FIGURE 3-2
Social model dynamics with processes internal to the model (participants, internal social processes) and social processes external to the model.

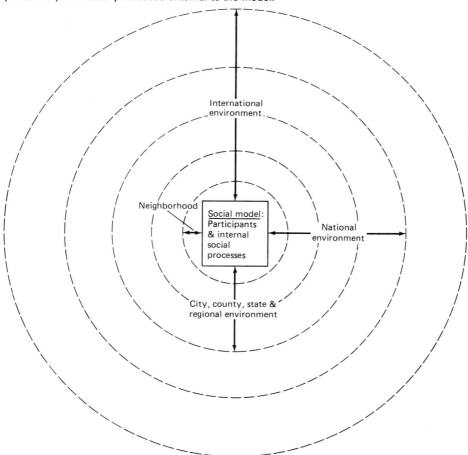

ted lines are intended to show that forces outside the model and from any geographic area (local, national, etc.) can affect its operations and outcomes.

Viewing the problem from a social perspective, the general formulation that predicts the behavior of a social model is a formula which states that *the outcome of any social model is a function of the participants and the internal and external social processes operative at that time.* This generic formula can be stated in an equation which takes the following form:

$$O_{SM} = (P_n \div (\overline{SI_n}) \div (\overline{SE_n})$$
$$+ \quad\quad +$$
$$\times \quad\quad \times$$

where O_{SM} is the outcome of the social model, P is the participants, and *n* is the number of them, SI are internal social processes and *n* the number of them, and SE are external social processes and *n* the number of them.

Components of Social Models

New social models designed to solve human problems can be defined by the aforementioned equation. With this general equation in mind, let us now turn to a description of outcomes, participants, and internal and external social processes. Since the general equation just presented expresses the basic relationships among crucial social model variables, a more detailed examination of them is necessary.

Outcomes

Every social model will yield outcomes as a result of the activities of its participants and environment. The outcomes that social models yield that demand special attention need to be explored, but first it is important to recognize that any model created to solve a particular problem will yield *a number of* different outcomes (Kaswan, 1981). One or more of these will represent the beneficial goal of the model. For example, the goal of a drug treatment model might be abstinence from drugs *and* improved interpersonal relations. To be successful both would have to occur simultaneously. Thus, persons participating in a program might change their attitudes, their expectancies, their fantasies, and/or their behavior. In addition, there are usually outcomes that relate to general social concerns such as the cost per person and the like. It is important to understand that every social model will yield a variety of outcomes, all of which may be more or less important depending on the particular problem. For example, the central goal of a program for energy conservation could be a direct outcome, such as a reduction in the use of electricity. In addition, it might be important to discover the degree to which peoples' attitudes toward energy conservation have changed as well as the degree to which such individuals might attempt to persuade others to reduce their use of energy. In a similar vein, a social program aimed at criminal behavior might be concerned primarily with a reduction in criminal behavior, but it might also be important to know the changes brought about in the person's use of leisure time, social behavior toward others, and so on.

It is also important to understand that outcomes vary over time so that measurement of outcomes in naturalistic experiments must be *longitudinal* in nature. For example, the introduction of the new energy conservation program mentioned above might not initially—let us say within 6 months—affect energy consumption by the group at which the program is aimed. However, it is possible that by the end of 18 months differences might begin to appear. Because of the time it takes for a new program to begin to affect the problem population it is necessary to measure outcomes over an extended period of time.

Even though there are many outcomes for every social problem, all of which should be measured, it is important to understand that there is usually *one* outcome that is most important to a society. In energy research in this day and age it is typically a reduction in use of energy; in the creation of new programs for criminality it is usually a reduction in criminal behavior; in drug addiction it is usually a reduction in the use of drugs, and so on. It is, therefore, necessary to understand that for each problem there is a criterion *that is reserved by societies' agencies as a solution to the problem and that is considered of primary importance. This single criterion is designated as the social change outcome criterion.* Its centrality in the change process exists because society is mainly interested in that particular aspect of the problem, and for the problem solution to have meaning for society the model must address the issue—such as energy reduction—as a primary aim of the research project. This should not be interpreted as meaning that other measures such as other attitudes and behaviors are not important. They certainly are and they can be evaluated along with the social change outcome criterion. But the importance of the social change outcome criterion is that it is the communication link between the researchers and administrators responsible for social policy planning. In Table 3-1 we have listed some general and specific outcome criteria that have been used in solutions to some selected problems.

Participant Variables A number of variables that independently can influence the outcome of social models describe the characteristics of the people who participate in them. Participants affect the models and the norms and processes of the models affect them so that persons and social situational variables interact in the model and these interaction processes determine outcomes. There are many different participant characteristics that can influence outcomes of a social program. Several key participant variables that have been found in past researches to influence behavior and attitudes of persons participating in many different social programs are presented in Table 3-2.

Age Age is a variable that can affect the interactions persons have with others and hence the outcome of a social model. Persons of different ages, often categorized as childhood, adolescence, adulthood, middle age, and old age,

TABLE 3-1
SOME GENERAL AND SPECIFIC OUTCOME CRITERIA IN EXPERIMENTAL SOCIAL
INNOVATION

| | Criteria specific to problems of: | | | |
General criteria	Mental health, criminality, delinquency, drug addiction	Education	Poverty, race, urban development	Energy
Satisfaction	Recidivism	Academic achievement	Employment	Conservation attitudes
Self-regard	Behavior control	Social adjustments	Living standards	Persuasive behavior
Morale	Employment		Family development	
Cost of maintaining model				

Source: Fairweather, G. W., and Tornatzky, L. G., *Experimental Methods for Social Policy Research,* New York: Pergamon Press, 1977, p. 50.

TABLE 3-2
PARTICIPANT VARIABLES

Demographic
  Age
  Economic status
  Education
  Employment history
  Family history
  History of institutionalization (prison, mental hospital, etc.)
  Marital status
  Medical history
  Membership organizations
  Military history
  Race
  Religion
  Sex
  Social class
Personality Characteristics
  Behavior description
  Ratings
  Test scores
Special Abilities
  Abilities tests
  Educational achievement (grades and awards)
  Test scores

Source: Fairweather, G. W., and Tornatzky, L. G., *Experimental Methods for Social Policy Research,* New York: Pergamon Press, 1977, p. 58.

have different needs and different physiologies. For these and other reasons the same person may respond differently at age 65 than he or she did at age 20. It is for this reason that age becomes a possible contributor to the manner in which a social model operates. To take an extreme example, a social model should operate quite differently if the persons participating in one model were 15 years old and 70 years old in the other. If physical work was the product or outcome it should be quite clear that these age differences would probably be very marked. For this reason, age is an important variable that must be considered in evaluating the participators' role in a social model.

Education Education is related to socioeconomic status and hence cannot be completely divorced from employment history. Nonetheless, each is presented independently here so that the reader can perceive the potential each has for influencing social model outcomes. Persons who have attained higher educational degrees frequently have different perceptions of themselves and society than persons who have had little education. While it is perfectly true that education alone is not sufficient to determine income and life's benefits, it is equally true that without considering it as a variable the experimenter can be in the position of making inferences about outcomes that might be due solely to education. To compare social models it therefore becomes important to consider the educational attainment of the participants.

Employment History Recent studies have shown that current employment is an excellent predictor of future employment (Worrall and Vandergroot, 1982). Persons with an excellent employment record tend to perpetuate that record, which brings with it the attendant benefits of income and the possibility of planning for a relatively stable future. In a capitalistic society such as America, full-time employment in a high school status job helps to define an individual's social position and, therefore, his or her worth—the benefits one will derive from the society. For this reason, employment, just as education, must be considered in evaluating the participant's contribution to social model outcomes.

Economic Status Economic status is related to employment and education but is not identical with either one. Persons can inherit wealth, achieve it through fortunate investments, and by other means so that accumulation of wealth does occur in some cases irrespective of employment and education. On the other hand, economic status is most often associated with education and employment so that persons who are the most well-educated have the highest social status employment positions and also receive the greatest economic income. Since economic income in America is highly related to the social position one has in the society, it is an important participant characteristic that needs to be evaluated for its effect upon outcome.

Social Class Social class is a category usually comprised of education, income, employment, cost of dwelling, and so on. It is a combination of the variables just discussed separately and is often used as a participant's defining characteristic. It is clearly a variable that has to be considered when participants are described and evaluated (Warner, 1960; Tumin, 1967; Burckhart, 1981).

Marital Status While the classic differentiation between married and unmarried persons has been blurred in recent years in American and some other societies, it still remains a variable that needs to be considered because of different participant responses that may result from the marriage relationship. Distinct differences, for example, still exist between married and single persons in tax laws and other legal processes which, from a social point of view, suggest that married persons may have had different life experiences than those who are single. Accordingly, it is a variable that needs consideration in defining and evaluating participants in a particular social model.

Medical History This variable probably is to some extent a reflection of the affluence of a particular culture. In some cultures medical histories are usually kept from birth on and may play a role in differentiating individuals who participate in social models. To take some extreme examples, persons who have chronic sugar diabetes, heart conditions, brain damage, and the like may very well have extensive medical histories which may differentiate them from persons who do not have such health problems. Accordingly, such individuals could behave differently in a social model, which could be directly attributable to their health problems. For this reason, the medical history of individuals should be obtained and its effects upon individual behaviors and outcomes of social subsystems evaluated.

History of Institutionalization In American society and other western cultures, it is quite common for people to be institutionalized for a wide variety of deviant behaviors—some mentally ill, criminals, etc. Many social scientists (Hollingshead and Redlich, 1958; Goffman, 1961; Fairweather, 1980) have pointed out that there appears to be a residual long-range effect upon persons' social participation and activities associated with institutionalization. It is important that this particular variable be given attention and that knowledge about any participant's history of institutionalization be taken into account when evaluating effects participants can have upon social models.

Military History Many persons in America and other countries have been in military service. The effect that military experiences may have on the future of individuals and their participation in social models is unknown for any particular individual. However, there is a distinct possibility that a history of military experiences may predispose a person to particular behaviors—for example, physical and emotional illness as attested to in the recent claims of Vietnam veterans about the defoliant Agent Orange. A poor military history may give some evidence that the person has difficulty in adjusting to highly controlled situations. Since it may be an experience that could affect a person's behavior, perceptions, and health as well as interactions in a social model, it is an important participant variable to consider and explore.

Family History Historically, psychologists, psychiatrists, sociologists, anthropologists, and others have written extensively about the effects early family life may have upon particular family members. The family has been explored and described in a wide variety of cultures. In almost all cultures it is a major contributing factor to the growth and maturity of the individual, so it seems apparent that the family's social structure and activities themselves may influence future behavior and perceptions of individual family members. Therefore, it is important to know the family history of those participating in the different social models so that outcomes that are influenced by family history can be explored and evaluated.

Race   Racial characteristics are dominant definers of a person's social position in many different societies. Skin color has been a major factor in American society, often determining or partially determining the life benefits that accrue to persons from birth on. Many articles, books, and documents attest to the fact that in American society—in fact in almost all known societies—the racial majority often places persons who do not fit its classification of color in a subordinate social position. For this reason, the effect on outcomes and social processes of different racial groups who participate in social models needs to be evaluated. Different racial groupings might account for different social interactions and outcomes of social models.

Sex   Another area of concern, particularly in terms of social discrimination, is the different life opportunities of men as contrasted with women—particularly in employment and occupations. As with race, many current articles and books attest to the notion that clear differences exist from birth on in the roles that men and women are permitted to play in different societies. As with race, sexual discrimination is ubiquitous. Accordingly, the effect of the sexual composition on the outcomes and processes of social models needs to be evaluated.

Membership Network   Membership in organizations is to some extent a definer of a person's participation in the community at large. Very often highly active social participants will belong to several community clubs, fraternities, and civic groups which will differentiate them from less socially active persons. Since social activity, including the willingness to talk to others, may be an important variable in the degree to which a group functions properly, it is important to discover the membership network of each particular person.

Personality Characteristics   This is the oldest and probably most overworked aspect of participant definitions from a scientific perspective. Going back many centuries, people have been categorized by various kinds of personal characteristics. For example, the terms *introvert* (inner living) and *extrovert* (outer living) have been around for a long time. These and many other terms (psychotic, neurotic, etc.) categorize persons who behave in particular ways. Many hold that such personality traits influence a person's relationships with others.

Special Abilities   Special abilities and intelligence are also categories that psychologists have given to people. A wide variety of intelligence tests exists. Many tests for special abilities such as mechanical abilities, aptitudes related to mathematics, creativity, and so on have been used to identify and categorize individuals. Vocational aptitudes and interests have been given predominance in the psychological testing literature. Accordingly, it should be recognized that various skills and aptitudes as well as some measures of intelligence may be important in determining the participant's contribution to the social processes and outcomes of a social program.

Religion Religion is given as a variable to be considered because of its particular historical relationship in most cultures. In America, for example, the Catholic church has taken a very strong stance against abortion. Other religious groups and organizations (the "moral majority," for example) have also taken positions on social, political, and personal issues of many kinds. When creating a solution to a particular social problem it is important to know what the religious background of the participants is so that any effect the participants' own beliefs have upon the functions of the social model can be explored.

In this section we have attempted to elaborate a number of individual variables that have been shown by experience, theory, and research to affect the processes and outcomes of various social groupings. These variables must be considered as possible contributing factors to the functioning of participants in social models and hence the models' outcomes.

SOCIAL SITUATION VARIABLES IN SOCIAL MODELS

While a social model operates over a period of time there are many processes that will affect its outcomes that are not evident from a description of the participants. Some of these are inherent within the models themselves. For example, the people who participate in a social program may themselves form a group which might have its own leadership, cohesiveness, and other dynamic group processes. In addition, there may be ways in which the decision processes of the social model are structured (hierarchical or flat) that affect the models' decision making. Those processes that are internal to the social model, consisting entirely of the manner in which the social model is organized and the manner in which individuals interact, are called *internal social process variables.* A list and discussion of them is now presented.

Internal Social Process Variables

Internal social processes are the aspects of social models most likely to be manipulated in an attempt to solve a social problem. It is important, therefore, to keep in mind that all internal social processes established in an experimental model must have the general goal of enhancing personal growth and individuality within the context of democratic processes. This issue was addressed earlier under the parameter of humanitarian values in Chapter 2.

Organizational Components

Organizations have different attributes that often determine the roles individuals play and ongoing interpersonal relations (Scott and Mitchell, 1976). Some of the most common variables are mentioned below.

Hierarchical Structure *Hierarchical structure* is one variable that defines the bureaucratic nature of organizations. *Hierarchy* can be conceptualized as the degree to which decision making occurs at the top of the organization and filters down to those below. In some organizations decisions are made by top management—the military, for example. In other organizations, decision making is diffused among many different groups. Some organizational structures combine both decision-making types so that communication flows both up and down and across the organization.

The hierarchical structure of organizations is one of the important variables to consider when social models are created within organizations or related to them. Some indices of hierarchy are: (1) number of discrete levels in the organizational chart, (2) the sharing of decisions, and (3) the number of units involved in the decision process.

Size *Size* of an organization is related to outcomes in a number of ways. It is usually significant in meaningful interpersonal relations—larger organizations are usually more impersonal. Size includes such measures as the number of personnel, the amount of budget, the number of clients the organization has, and the like.

Complexity Organizational *complexity* may have some relationship to change and innovation (Hage and Aiken, 1970). Complexity refers to the number of subunits within the organization, the number and different types of jobs, and the use of professional persons.

Formality or Informality The type of communication utilized within the organization is another separate but important indicator of the bureaucratic or nonbureaucratic nature of the social unit. *Informality* or *formality* of communication patterns refers to face-to-face communications as differentiated from organizations in which communication is accomplished via formal methods such as memorandums, letters, etc. Although the formality or informality concept is somewhat related to that of hierarchy, it is more applicable to communication processes.

Group Dynamics

Group dynamics refers to the processes that go on in groups as they function (Paulus, 1980; Shaw, 1981). Each group can be treated as an entity because its performance can change rapidly with time and with changes in other group properties. Usually, dynamics are measured longitudinally because of their changing qualities. This is particularly true in real-life groups where membership is frequently transitory.

Group Cohesiveness Many studies have shown the importance of an individual's acceptance by and desire to belong to a group. Individuals participate in quite a different manner when they share a group's goals. Athletic teams, military groups, social clubs, and other groups have demonstrated this as an operating procedure since organized groups were first studied. Many social psychologists have discussed the importance of group cohesiveness and group goals.

Norms *Norms* are behaviors which guide the activities of group members. Early studies by Asch (1956) showed that some group members were affected by the judgment of their peers even when they believed them to be wrong. Norms of each group need to be known and measured so that an understanding of the individual and group action itself can be assessed.

Leadership A number of studies have shown that *leadership* affects the performance and attitudes of the group. Fairweather (1964) showed that leadership was extremely important in the functioning of autonomous groups—groups without strong leadership very often showed poor performance. Fiedler (1967) developed a theoretical rationale supporting a contingent theory of leadership depending upon task demands. Thus, a relatively authoritarian leader was more effective when the "task environment" was either extremely good or extremely bad, while a democratic leader was more effective in the midrange of task demands. Lerner and Fairweather (1963) showed that directive leadership resulted in much more rapid improvement in performance but at the expense of group cohesiveness.

Composition The individuals that comprise a group have been shown to affect the performance of that group. For example, Katz and Cohen (1962) showed that biracial groups can give quite different responses than groups comprised of only one race. And Sanders, MacDonald, and Maynard (1964) showed that groups performed better when they were comprised of individuals who were heterogeneous with regard to social activity—groups comprised of all individuals who were socially active or inactive did not perform as well as a mix of the two types of persons. Numerous other studies have shown that the composition of a group is an important determinant of group processes.

Morale The *morale* of a group refers to the group members' satisfaction with the group, its leadership, and its membership at any given moment in time. Morale is another attribute of group process that needs to be considered when defining and describing the characteristics of a group. Fairweather et al. (1969) found that morale was unrelated to performance, i.e., it was independent of performance so that groups could perform well or poorly whether or not they had high or low morale. Morale is an important group process and should be considered a parameter of group functioning relative to but more global than cohesiveness.

Reinforcement System Every group must have a reward system. Its members can be rewarded for performing group tasks well so that the group itself may continue to function. Good group performance needs to be rewarded so that people will strive to belong to the group and perform its functions better. Very often the reinforcement system is money. On the other hand, there are sometimes rewards in simply being a group member in certain organizations quite beyond any monetary returns. For example, some groups bestow considerable prestige on their members and are, therefore, sought after by some people. It is essential that a continuing group establish a reward system through which it can reinforce the role behavior of individual members.

Fiscal Processes

Another of a social model's internal functions is the manner in which it handles monetary matters *within* its organization. These are operations which are purely internal to the model and which do not directly involve the wider social environment.

Certain operations of budgeting and accounting are necessary to make financial decisions and dispositions within certain social models. Budgeting usually allocates certain monies to purchasing food, buying equipment, and leasing property. Accounting operations are simply means of ensuring that the budget is followed by the persons responsible. All these operations are carried out by members of social models who take on these tasks as part of their statuses.

The defining characteristic of *internal fiscal processes* is that they all deal with monies handled within the model. Monetary transactions between the model and its social environment (including income from work and supporting institutions as well as output into the economy of the wider society by spending) form the *external economic processes.*

Income Income is the total amount of money available to the social model from whatever source it comes. An industrial organization's income is usually derived from production as well as from investments. On the other hand, a social organization may be a nonprofit corporation and only have income from donors or investments made by the organization. This is an exceedingly important parameter of social models, particularly in American society.

Costs Costs are the expenditure per unit within the organization. Costs might be related to the expenditure on the production of an item or personnel costs in a service organization, and so on. In the case of the latter, the costs might be the cost per client, which is often a central issue when one is computing the costs of health care, rehabilitation, or education.

Rate of Pay Rate of pay is the pay per person usually based upon the percent of time (hourly wage) within the organization. It is often desirable to know how the rate of pay is determined, since it may be simply by management fiat, collective bargaining, or agreement among workers in the case where they are also owners. Rate of pay is an important variable in a social model.

Bookkeeping Procedures   This is a general term for the deriving of profit and loss statements from the keeping of books. It includes accounting systems in large organizations, auditors, and various other business personnel. It involves the manner in which the financial records of an organization are maintained.

Membership

Voluntary-Involuntary   All persons have membership in one group or another and this membership can affect outcomes. The manner in which individuals belong may have an important effect on outcomes. This concept concerns the degree to which membership in an organization is voluntary. In grade school, students are involuntary members of an organization, as are prisoners and some persons in mental hospitals or rehabilitation centers. On the other hand, membership in a social or industrial organization is usually voluntary. As social programs move further and further into community settings they depend more and more upon persons to participate voluntarily in them. There still will probably remain, however, involuntary assignments, such as assignments to rehabilitation houses by the courts, and the like.

Turnover   Since turnover in group membership is typical in functioning groups, it is important to know whether membership in a group is permanent or temporary. Members of a family usually have relatively stable group membership. Rapid turnover in membership is demonstrated by surgical patients on a hospital ward. Thus, some memberships are relatively permanent and others last only for brief periods of time. Turnover can affect model outcomes.

External Social Process Variables

While the social model operates in a naturalistic setting there are a number of external social factors that impinge upon the organization during its own operation. Figure 3-2 shows that local, regional, national, and international environments can impinge upon a social model and affect its outcomes. For this reason, careful attention must be given to a number of external factors. Some selected variables representing these external forces are presented in Table 3-3. These variables are called *external social process variables.*

Natural Environment   A social model may be implanted in any geographic location for experimental purposes and, therefore, may operate in many different types of external natural environments. Attention to the natural environmental forces that might impinge upon the external model have been discussed in Chapter 1 but for our purposes here we will briefly list a few such as smog, air and water pollution, overpopulation, noise pollution, and so on. The experimentalist must give careful attention to the effects these environments may have upon the implanted model.

TABLE 3-3
SOCIAL SITUATION VARIABLES

Processes internal to the model	Processes external to the model (local, state, regional, national, and/or international)
Organizational components	
Hierarchical structure	Natural environment
Size	Social climate
Complexity	Socioeconomic indicators
Formality/informality	Measurement obtrusiveness
Group dynamics	Geographical location
Cohesiveness	Folkways and mores
Norms	Publicity and media exposure
Leadership	Relationship to other organizations
Composition	Legal constraints
Morale	Time
Reinforcement	
Fiscal processes	
Income	
Costs	
Rate of pay	
Bookkeeping	
Membership	
Voluntary/involuntary	
Turnover	

Source: Fairweather, G. W., and Tornatzky, L. G., *Experimental Methods for Social Policy Research*, New York: Pergamon Press, 1977, p. 70.

Social Climate of the Society The social mood of a nation, state, or community can fluctuate over a period of time. A number of dimensions are involved here, such as liberalism-conservatism, optimism-pessimism, etc. Models which are particularly sensitive to fluctuations in public mood may display rather quick changes in outcome success. Thus, indicators of social climate should be measured. For example, the conservatism-liberalism of electoral results in a given location is sometimes used as an index of social climate.

Socioeconomic Indicators Some social models are sensitive to fluctuations in the state of the economy. Programs that involve finding employment for a certain clientele are especially affected. Since the economy fluctuates over the course of a longitudinal experiment, socioeconomic indicators and their effect upon social model outcomes should be monitored. Sources for such data often include departments of labor and other local, regional, and national economic data-gathering organizations. Possible indicators would include gross national product, rate of unemployment, consumer optimism, interest rates, etc. Outcomes can be greatly affected by economic conditions of affluence or depression.

Measurement Obtrusiveness No social model can be evaluated without systematic collection of data. Often this creates some intrusion into the ongoing processes of the social model. Assessment techniques impinge upon the normal functioning of a social program since once the initial research is completed it is highly doubtful that all the assessment devices used during the evaluation of the prototype model will be used in future replications. Accordingly, the use of measurement techniques must be clearly documented and attempts must be made to assess their impact upon the social program.

Geographical Location As with all other external forces, location may or may not be an important factor affecting a model's outcomes. In some cases it could have a significant effect. For example, social models requiring racial integration might have different outcomes if implanted in geographic areas where racial strife is rare contrasted with areas where racial strife is continuous. Or an urban or rural area may be better or worse for the location of a particular social model, depending upon its function and use.

Folkways and Mores of the Institution or Community Normative behaviors will affect any social model implanted in an institution or in a local community. If the social model is perceived as violating the norms of the institution or of the community, its operation might be impaired. For this reason, the mores and folkways of the model's locale must be clearly understood and planned for in the social model-building process.

Publicity and Media Exposure Media sources such as TV, newspapers, and radio are ever-present components of contemporary life. Such information may have some effect on attitudes or perceptions. This publicity may affect the success or failure of a social model.

Relationship to Other Community Organizations Social relations with other community organizations may affect program outcomes. Thus, a social model may be involved in transactions with other social programs. This is part of the general problem of interorganizational relations involving contact among persons in different social models. The effect on social models of such interorganizational linkages should be evaluated.

Legal Constraints Experimentalists should be cognizant of legal constraints that impinge on the establishment and continuous operation of a social model. Differences between models may be a function of zoning practices, bonding regulations, contractual agreements, etc. To the extent that these can be related to social model outcomes, they should be evaluated empirically.

Time Since all social phenomena vary with time, this is an important major variable that interacts with all other social variables. Differences of many types—socioeconomic level, size of population, political power, and the like—are different at different moments in time. For this reason, time itself must be accounted for in any social experiment.

This chapter has presented two types of dynamics involved in solving human problems. The first described the sequential processes of problem solution going from problem identification to the process of disseminating valid problem-solving models throughout the society. The key element in each of the six dynamic problem-solving processes was described as the vehicle of change—the problem-solving model. Because of the central role of the innovative model in the change process, the second part of this chapter described and defined the dynamic aspects of the model itself. The basic proposition was made that the outcomes of the created social models will be affected by the characteristics of persons who participate in them and by social processes operating in and outside the model itself. Therefore, the three attributes of any social model which should be clearly defined, described, and measured are those of its participants, the social situation in which the social model operates, and the outcome criterion on which it is evaluated. The degree to which any social model can be replicated depends upon the degree to which these dimensions are clearly understood, defined, and measured. In addition, the value to society of any social model depends upon the degree to which the outcome criterion upon which it is evaluated represents a consensual solution to a pressing social problem.

CHAPTER 4

DEFINING A PROBLEM

After reading Chapter 1 it should be clear that there is no dearth of human problems that need solutions in contemporary societies. Every day we read in the newspaper, hear on the radio, and see on television news the problems of crime, mental illness, energy depletion, drug addiction, environmental degradation, and the like. It is, therefore, not difficult to recognize that problems exist, but defining the problem in a scientific sense is much more difficult. Such a definition can be made in terms of the participant and social process variables presented in Tables 3-2 and 3-3. There are several types of information that can be used to aid the scientist who is seriously interested in defining a problem, and in understanding the problem in all its complexities. Let us now turn our attention to those methods that scientists have found to be the most helpful in problem definition.

TYPES OF INFORMATION

Personal Experiences

It is important to recognize that there is a considerable difference between standing by as an uninvolved observer and being a participant in an ongoing social process. It is one thing to observe the process of poverty; it is quite another to live the process of poverty (Fairweather, 1972). Personal experience is one of the best sources of information about an actual problem. Racism, for example, is commonly perceived in America as a different type of problem by those whose skin color is not white simply because those individuals have had minority experiences since birth (Tucker, 1974). Likewise, it has been found that those who have experienced mental illness often have quite a different view of the process than a professional person (Fairweather, 1980). Thus, for example, in the case of the mental patient, such issues as citizenship rights, personal reaction to medication, unemployment, and the like very often have a central significance, whereas the professional mental health person is often more concerned with issues such as keeping adequate clinical records, proper diagnosis, and so on.

For this reason it is important to recognize that *experiencing* a problem gives an individual insight and knowledge unobtainable elsewhere. It puts a person in the unique position of understanding the problem more fully from the perspective of the participant. The knowledge gained from those who live with a problem daily is central to a full understanding of it. For this reason all persons engaged in research in a given area should experience problems as a participant as much as possible and at the very least seek out those who have experienced the problems to gain their perception of them. Participants' perceptions should be treated as one of the most valid forms of scientific data and not as extraneous information that comes from a biased source (Davidson, Redner, and Saul, 1983).

Descriptive and Theoretical Treatises

Usually, descriptive and theoretical treatises present a broad view of a particular problem, how it emerged, and what might be done about it. Representative of such works is Myrdal's (1944) *An American Dilemma,* a descriptive book about the social and economic position of blacks in America. Another historical treatise that has gained considerable fame in the scientific community has been Goffman's (1962) *Asylums.* He discusses the social positions of inmates as well as personnel who find themselves in a controlled four-walled environment such as a mental hospital, prison, or the like. This work raised many questions about the use of these institutions as "rehabilitative centers." Another example can be found in the work of the economist Galbraith (1958), who wrote about the social problems that accrue to a wealthy society. In the 1960s, a rash of monographs about problems raised by excessive population appeared, beginning with Ehrlich's *The Population Bomb* (1968) and Borgstrom's (1969) book, *Too Many.* More recent books having to do with the population and environmental situation present considerable information and draw conclusions from them that are meant to influence policy decisions. Current examples include *The Global 2000 Report to the President of the U.S.* and *The Global Perspective Quarterly* (Barney, 1980; Barney and Maiman, 1983). They give broad descriptions based upon multidisciplinary information concerning environmental and population problems. *The President's Commission on Mental Health Report* (1978) discusses contemporary treatment programs and their validity. Works such as these are important primarily in problem identification and planning for an innovative solution.

Observations

Since the beginnings of recorded science, one of the primary tools of the scientist has been observation. Although this method has not received as much publicity in recent years as more sophisticated technological approaches, it still remains the most basic technique that scientists use—observation of the problem in its naturalistic setting. Observations of social phenomena are typically more difficult and complex than those of the biological and physical world, even though some of the observational methods used for one apply to the other.

One of the first scientific observers was Mendel, who in 1866 observed that different generations of peas consistently yielded the same colors (Sinnott, Dunn, and Dobzhansky, 1950). From these observations he began to develop some basic ideas about genetics. We are all aware of the observations of the scientist Darwin and the profound effects his theory of evolution has had on science since 1859. We are also acquainted with the explosion of the first atomic bomb at Alamogordo, New Mexico, and the scientist observers who saw the first mushroom cloud and gained some insight into the atomic bomb's potential destructive consequences (Oppenheimer, 1954). From time to time, all of us study phenomena by observing them, be it botanical, biological, psychological, sociological, or whatever. Such observations occur in our daily routines. What is important to grasp here is that the observations all of us make can be improved so that scientific information can be obtained through our own observations and those of others.

In more controlled situations, scientists observe the movement of bacteria under the microscope and thus make medical diagnoses. Observing through the microscope is also used to study feeding patterns, migration, and strengths of very small living organisms. Behavioral scientists in animal laboratories observe what happens to animals after biological damage has occurred to them, or when they are fed a certain amount of food as reward for behavior, such as a right turn. In the controlled setting of the laboratory, scientists have created many devices to make various phenomena easily observed. For example, the electron microscope allows us to see molecular and submolecular events unobservable to the naked eye. Similarly, the electrical activity of animal nervous systems is translated to observable events through electrode implants. In the final analysis, each is reduced to a format which allows human observation.

Field experimenters may observe the more macrotype of behavior of animals and plants in a larger environment. In recent years many films have been made about the observations of anthropologists studying animal life from birds to apes in their natural environment (Altmann, 1980). Ecologists have observed fish and plant life in rivers, creeks, and lakes and have tried to gain some understanding of the impact of the total environment upon these animals and plants (Richlef, 1980).

Social scientists have also studied problems by observation. The behavior of youths in classrooms (Keith, 1974), decision making by juries (Bray and Kerr, 1982), and street gangs in urban areas (Whyte, 1955; Sullivan, 1983) are some examples of such studies. In these last two studies, the scientists lived with the street gangs as participant observers.

It is important to recognize that the central technique for studying these real-life processes has been observation. Some technology has been introduced in recent years so that videotapes of behavior in situations can be made and studied later. However, many naturalistic observations are not amenable to being videotaped, particularly with the current need to obtain participant approval. Trained observers thus can provide one source of problem identification information.

The idea of direct naturalistic observations cannot be overemphasized. It is difficult, if not impossible, to understand a real-life situation simply by looking at statistics and graphs. Furthermore, few individuals (if any) can grasp the true meaning of a situation without having at least observed it directly. Many mistakes in interpreting scientific data in the past have been made in the fields of mental illness, criminal behavior, energy depletion, and the like because scientists have lacked an experiential understanding of the processes involved in the problem. One important method of gaining such an understanding is through direct observation.

In social programming, furthermore, it is important to understand the problem from the observational perspective of three different groups, all of whom are important contributors to problem identification. These three groups are the participants, the social administrators, and the researchers. Often these three groups look at the problem from quite different perspectives. Most often the participant is concerned about survival and "getting by" from day to day, especially when the problem is one related to poverty or a lowly social position. On the other hand, most administrators are interested in the effectiveness of their program, how they can keep their administrative unit funded, and what the goals and opportunities are for the persons working under their jurisdiction. Thus, the administrator may pay much more attention to cost-effectiveness, whereas participants may have much more interest in what a particular social program provides for survival and daily needs such as food and the quality of life. The researchers, on the other hand, are interested in understanding the views of both these groups as well as understanding some of the more basic elements that pertain to the problem. The characteristics of the participants and the social situation in which they find themselves have been described in Tables 3-2 and 3-3 and are areas of essential concern. Thus, researchers are not only interested in the totality of the problem in its naturalistic setting but in placing it in some kind of an explanatory context or theoretical framework which will provide the background for later work.

Regardless of where or when naturalistic observations take place, it is necessary for the researcher to view them holistically and understand the totality of the variables that might be impinging upon those experiencing the social problem. One source of such information is naturalistic observations.

Surveys

Surveys consist of a series of questions asked either on questionnaire forms or by interviewers from which data are compiled to give quantitative information about a particular human problem (Rossi, Wright, and Anderson, 1983). The most common example of the survey method is the United States census. Its primary purpose is to determine the population of the United States and what the attributes of that population are—wealth, residence, etc. A further example of the manner in which surveys are used to give information describing social problems can be found in such books as *Social Class and Mental Illness,* by Hollingshead and Redlich (1958). In that classic document information was presented about the wealth, employment, and other demographic characteristics of different types of mental patients. This book showed, for example, that psychotic persons were more likely to be found in lower socioeconomic classes, and by virtue of their lowly social position would receive treatment in publicly supported mental hospitals, compared with more wealthy persons who sought out private help. An historically early examination of the heroin problem appeared in Chein et al.'s (1963) book, *The Road to H.* In it Chein presented survey material showing basic information about persons who became heroin addicts.

Surveys are often used in today's society to assess contemporary economic and political climates. A common use is political opinion polls. Seldom does a week pass in the United States without the results of a political poll being described in the national press.

The information obtained from surveys gives data that often elaborate human problems from a more quantitative perspective than that found in descriptive theoretical information. It is a commonly used technique for problem identification and in planning an innovative solution. The main function of the survey is to elaborate the problem and to get additional information about problem solution and dissemination that may not be obtained from any source other than through questions answered by a particular audience.

Case Studies

When researchers want in-depth information about a particular individual, group, organization, or even a society the case study technique is often used. The case study can also be used in problem identification. Historically, case studies have been perhaps most often presented in the mental health literature, where they have even become popular books such as *The Three Faces of Eve* (Thigpen and Cleckley, 1974). Another well-known case study, involving several criminals, was *My Six Convicts* (Wilson, 1951). During World War II and more recent conflicts in which America was involved, case studies were done of combat groups which traced them from their arrival in countries such as Vietnam until they left.

Tribal societies such as those with different social systems than those in the United States have been studied through the case study method by anthropologists. Some examples are cultures where the dominant role is played by the women in the society (Ortner and Whitehead, 1981). Case studies provide information that more clearly illuminates the problem and the possible effects that different kinds of interventions might have. Case studies typically represent one individual's or group's perspective.

Case studies of a society can also point out broader culturally supported behaviors, such as child-rearing practices, that may have an impact upon the manner in which adulthood is achieved and the type of person—passive or aggressive, for example—normally produced in a particular family structure in a given society. Child-rearing practices such as Margaret Mead's (1971) *Coming of Age in Samoa* is an example. Case studies have been found to be valuable in describing what happens in actual experimental models, for example, in describing several different lodge societies that had been created (Fairweather, 1980). In a dissemination experiment, a single hospital (El Dorado) was selected as a case study of "bureaucratic entrepreneurship" (Tornatzky et al., 1980). This case study presented actual events that occurred when a mental hospital adopted the lodge society as part of its treatment program. These last two illustrations show it is not uncommon in naturalistic field experiments to use the case study technique to elaborate variables important in problem definition.

Laboratory Research

Psychologists particularly have developed laboratory methods where problems are isolated from the real world and translated into an artificial setting. Here various aspects of a particular problem are explored by studying them in highly controlled situations. Studies of biracial work groups by Katz and Benjamin (1960) and Katz and Cohen (1962), and juries by Bray and Kerr (1983), are examples of the use of this method. Another specific example can be found in the work of Zimbardo and his associates (1975). They created a simulated prison setting in which students participated, either as guards or inmates. Many behaviors observed in actual prisons began to appear in the simulated setting. Such information is useful in understanding the dynamics of prison behavior.

In recent years much discussion among social psychologists has concerned the use of laboratory and field research in solving human problems (Cialdini, 1980; Proshansky, 1981; Mook, 1983). While a distinction between laboratory and field research is clearly recognized (Bickman, 1980), different uses in social problem solving of both types of research are perceived by the different scientists. Nevertheless, the laboratory experimental technique, particularly if it addresses issues that emerge from naturalistic observations, can demonstrate the importance of particular variables in the problem-solving process. Isolating and verifying the importance of these variables under laboratory conditions can be an important first step in understanding the function of variables that might be important in understanding the problem in its naturalistic environment. Thus, laboratory experiments can identify crucial variables that need to be manipulated in the problem-solving process. But it should be clearly understood that moving experimental conditions from the laboratory to the naturalistic setting is a difficult and time-consuming task (Wortman et al., 1980).

Pilot Demonstrations

Pilot demonstration projects ordinarily are set up to identify difficulties that may arise when a plan is transferred to a naturalistic setting. Usually, *single* programs are observed. There are many historical examples of pilot demonstration studies such as the Synanon House for Drug Addicts, described by Yablonski (1964). In addition, sheltered workshops have been established for persons with physical and emotional handicaps; pilot demonstrations of this type are described by Olshansky (1960). In the early 1950s Jones (1953) created the therapeutic community, a classic example of staff and patient participation in decision making. It stands even today as a singular example of a pilot study involving changes in the mental health system. It is important to notice here that pilot demonstration projects typically use only *one* innovative solution for a particular social problem. Thus, they are not established to gain comparative information, i.e., to compare the pilot model with any other model(s). Pilot studies are very helpful in problem identification, planning the solution, and planning the experiment, and are sometimes used initially to activate a model prior to the establishment of an actual experiment. Thus, pilot demonstration studies can contribute to the first three phases of the change processes as shown in Figure 3-1.

Quasi Experiments

Another type of information has been called *quasi experimental* and traces to the work of Campbell and Stanley (1966), who maintain that quasi experiments are done only when actual experiments cannot be carried out. Quasi-experimental techniques have some of the features of an experiment, such as comparing social programs, but they are not actual experiments and should not be substituted for them. The researcher usually compares two or more programs already in existence by taking a sample of participants from each of the programs and comparing them on various measures. An early study of this technique was an analysis of traffic fatalities in Connecticut before and after the police had instigated a crackdown on speeding (Campbell and Ross, 1965).

There are many advantages to quasi-experimental methods. A few of the most important are: (1) usually the researcher does not have to innovate a new program or be responsible for programs or participants, (2) random sampling does not have to be performed, and (3) attention to control of a large number of variables is not the responsibility of the researcher since many of them are out of his or her purview. Unfortunately, these advantages can also turn out to be disadvantages when inferences must be made from information collected.

Inferences that can legitimately be made from such studies are subject to much greater error than inferences that are possible from more highly controlled experiments. Quasi experiments, however, do provide information for problem identification, planning an innovative solution, and planning the experiment. They can define selected variables that may be crucial in problem solution in the actual field settings.

Field Experiments

Probably the most valid source of information available to the community researcher is other field experiments (Boruch et al., 1979). Although they are currently few in number, these experiments evaluate the effectiveness of selected variables in a community setting under conditions that provide the most valid scientific information possible. Once one problem-oriented experiment is completed it becomes a source of information for a second experiment, the second for a third experiment, and so on. In this way a database of valid scientific information is accumulated.

A field experiment requires comparison of two or more social models or programs under conditions where the scientist is involved in and responsible for the creation and monitoring of the social program, using a randomized experimental design. The value of field experiments as a background for new experiments is threefold: (1) they improve the scientific validity of the information collected through the experimental control of extraneous variables and research supervision of the programs and data collection; (2) they involve the scientist in the creation of the actual innovation and therefore increase her or his knowledge about a program's day-to-day operation; and (3) this operational understanding, along with information gained from experimental data, permits the scientist to make the most informed inferences possible about the effectiveness of the models.

Since problem-solving scientific information is incremental in nature—it accrues slowly over a period of time—the completion of one experiment is typically the signal for the beginning of another. Through a series of successive experiments valid scientific information is gathered that permits an understanding of the basic parameters of a particular problem at a specific moment in history. While all the previously mentioned sources of information are important and should be used in planning, creation, and development of new models, it is the experiment which provides the soundest scientific information. Unfortunately, few field experiments on specific human problems actually have been completed, so that a body of experimental knowledge is usually not available for specific human problems. Nevertheless, the few that have been completed show clearly the social policy decision-making advantages of field experiments.

To clarify these inferential benefits, seven experiments or different human problems have been selected for presentation throughout the remainder of this book. While the information for planning each of these experiments came from many of the sources mentioned above—experience, surveys, case studies, participant observation, laboratory studies, and the like—the experiments themselves provide specific information which can be used in the future for the development of additional problem-solving experiments. Knowing the techniques through which to gain information is only one aspect of developing background knowledge for program design. The second aspect of problem definition is to know where such information can be found.

LOCATION OF INFORMATION

The types of information the researcher needs to seek out have been reviewed. We will turn our attention to the sources where the researcher can get information. The first place to look is in the articles and books written about the problem.

Theoretical Literature

Typically, several disciplines will have developed theories about a particular human problem. This is because a problem may be viewed from several different perspectives, depending upon where one sits. The question of energy depletion, for example, may be viewed by the engineer as a matter of creating new techniques to obtain more sources of energy; by the ecologist as a problem of shrinking fossil fuel sources and what that means to the planetary system as a whole; by the sociologist as a cultural and social matter where norms or values might be changed, bringing about greater conservation of energy; and by the psychologist as an individual matter where each person needs to become an energy conserver. In all these perspectives there is truth. The important point for the field researcher is that he or she must bring these various elements together in an approach that theoretically could, in these times, reduce energy use.

Thus, it is important to look at the variables that come from many different disciplines and perspectives when we are attempting to understand a particular problem. Researchers need to understand the problem in its most complete context. For any given problem, therefore, different facets might be found in the literature from different disciplines. Thus, it is necessary to review the literature of several different disciplines for variables that might affect the outcomes of social models. In most instances there are some political variables, some economic variables, some sociological variables, some biological variables, and some psychological variables which will have impact on social problems and their solutions. The researcher should not shy away from important variables simply because they are outside the scope of the discipline in which he or she may have been trained. As far as scientific literature is concerned, variables from several different disciplines may be involved in a human problem and the researcher must understand what they are to define the problem adequately.

Technical Literature

Quite aside from the theoretical literature which one finds listed under the different disciplines of political science, sociology, biology, and psychology, there is a very rich literature which often can be found in technical manuals. These documents are usually multidisciplinary in their orientation and problem-focused. For this reason, they have considerable meaning and importance to problem-oriented researchers. A great source of technical literature is maintained by the federal government. For example, the National Institute of Mental Health prints periodic manuals and reports dealing with various problems of mental illness. Probably the most visible are reports to the President from appointed commissions. In Chapter 3 a report to the President entitled *Global 2000* was mentioned (Barney, 1980). It presented the problems (environmental, population, etc.) that the nation faces and is classified here as technical literature. The President's Commission on Mental Health, which completed the *Commission on Mental Health Report* (1978) during President Carter's administration, is another example. An earlier report on racial issues by the Kerner Commission for President Johnson (National Advisory Commission on Civil Disorders, 1968) is another example of a technical report that presents information about a particular social problem. In addition, there are many research institutes that publish technical documents about human problems.

It is also possible to obtain information about such technical reports from computer searches such as those sponsored by the Smithsonian Institute, the National Institutes of Health, professional associates, and others. Thus, there is a wealth of problem-oriented technical information constituting a body of literature beyond the disciplinary literature, which yields important information about problems in our society and the potential variables that might contribute to a problem solution.

Information from Peers

Another source of information about problem-solving variables that may be important in defining a particular problem scientifically stems from other scientists working in the same area. While information from peers may be published in technical manuals or the theoretical literature, frequently current information is still being developed and has not yet been published. Thus, the most recent information about a particular problem can often be gained from talking with other researchers who are currently engaged in their own research on one aspect or another of the selected problem. Frequently, these may be unconfirmed hunches or ideas that are only beginning to be supported by scientific documentation, but this is information that should not be overlooked.

Researchers' Own Investigations

Even though the reader may not have come to this conclusion yet he or she probably soon will understand that longitudinal research on problem solution typically requires a series of researches aimed at defining a solution to the problem. An individual researcher in an area such as crime, health, or energy may create knowledge not available from any other source. In fact, it probably is accurate to say that the more one is in the forefront of research on a particular problem, the more likely it is that his or her own research will generate new information that tends to spell out rather specifically the variables related to a particular problem. It is even more important to recognize that if the researcher is using experimental methods and is, therefore, contrasting different approaches to problem solution, the generation of information is likely to be accurate even though it may be time-consuming to generate. Nonetheless, it appears that successive experiments aimed at problem solution will put the researcher on the edge of problem solution so that information from his or her own researches may become a primary source of information for the generation of future researches.

By taking all these sources of information and combining them into an information pool the perceptive experimentalist should then be able to select the major variables that appear to be central to the problem and whose manipulation might result in problem solution. The logic of this approach is centered upon a rather artistic aspect of science which is difficult to define but which exists for the scientist as much as it does for the artist. The art comes in integrating information from these various sources, which permits the researcher to select variables that can be put together in such a way that they can help solve a serious national or international problem. It is to this aspect of problem definition that we now turn.

EXAMPLES OF PROBLEM DEFINITION

The following section should make the reader aware that most human problems can be defined in a scientific manner. To present this process in as much detail as possible we have selected seven examples of problems from different areas. Five of these—those immediately following this section—were created from definitions arising from the scientific literature, observations, and personal experiences. The last two include those aspects and add the authors' own experiments as an information source in defining a solution. For this reason, the last two examples—the problems of chronic mental illness and juvenile delinquency—include rather extensive longitudinal definitions of the problems based upon consecutive experiments and, therefore, are presented in considerably more detail than the first five problems. This is because the authors believe it is essential for the reader to understand that it is often necessary for a series of research projects to be completed before a final definition of the problem is clarified.

Citizen Participation in Health Planning

While working as a researcher and health program implementer in a health agency, Beck (1973) became concerned about the roles that providers and recipients of health services had in decision making at an agency level. Her experiences and review of the literature about citizen participation resulted in her defining the problem in the following manner:

> Research has demonstrated that participation in the decision-making process by the recipients of the decision often leads to greater acceptance of the decision, and hence, more successful implementation (Coch and French, 1948; French et al., 1959; Gilmer, 1966; Tannenbaum, 1968). In governmental planning agencies the basic task is decision-making and the recipients of such decisions are the consumers of the programs planned. In such agencies, citizen participation in the decision-making process plays a vital and powerful role in "monitoring" professional plans and making sure that the planning professionals and technical experts do not design programs with either disregard for citizen interest or simply for the interests of certain power groups (Altschuler, 1970; Dubey, 1970).
>
> While the concept of citizen participation as a valuable contribution to the decision-making process may have been accepted by many, incorporation as an operating concept in most planning agencies has been, on the whole, slow and ineffective. . . .
>
> A recent effort has been made to involve citizens in decisions affecting their health care. In 1966 Congress recognized the problems of multiple health care delivery mechanisms and soaring costs by creating Public Law 89-749, the "Partnership for Health" Act. Section 314 established a mechanism for resolution of some of these difficulties—comprehensive health planning (CHP), at the federal, state, and local level. Recent years have also brought a heightened social awareness of equal rights; among them, that health care is a right of all people and not a privilege of the fortunate. Congress also recognized this right as shown in community participation in health planning decisions, and, therefore mandated that health care consumers be included in all policy making and advisory boards in comprehensive health planning (National Commission on Community Health Services, 1967; Ready, 1972). The secretary of the U.S. Department of Health, Education, and Welfare in promulgating the guidelines for Section 314 further stipulated that consumers be the majority on these boards. Thus, a planned mechanism was established for partnership between health consumers and providers where providers were specifically prevented from numerical domination (Andrejewski, 1972).
>
> Formal membership does not, however, automatically lead to effective participation. Many have complained that, like other social action agencies in the past, CHP has basic problems in consumer participation, primarily little participation by a relatively uninformed, ineffective citizen group (Andrejewski, 1972). Citizens themselves have also complained of being marginal rather than central to the decision-making process (Strauss, 1972) (pp. 1–3).

Jobs for the Elderly

Gray (1980) spent several years working with elderly people in nursing homes and other locations. His own experiences and knowledge of the literature led him to believe that many of the elderly wanted to be employed but were unable to find employment. Gray defines the problem in this manner:

> There has been very little research focused on the circumstances which foster unemployment among older workers and retirees nor on possible avenues of reducing it.

Although such neglect may have seemed benign during a time when federal mandatory retirement laws and social security rules attempted to encourage older individuals to get out and stay out of the workforce in deference to new young job force entrants, such neglect can no longer be viewed as benign. Current circumstances, including a smaller and disproportionately older labor pool, [and] ... a critically overtaxed social security system, evidence which documents the productivity of older workers (Meier and Kerr, 1967), evidence that involuntary and reluctant retirees suffer untoward personal and medical repercussions from job loss (National Council on Aging, 1975; Streib, 1956; Cobb and Kasi, 1972), and increased advocacy on behalf of older individuals in general, dictate that we take a fresh look at the employment related needs of our older citizens and possible mechanisms of promoting employment in this group. ...

Unfortunately, the traditional avenues of facilitating employment have not been very responsive to the employment needs of old people. For instance, based on the reports of Sheppard and Belitsky (1966) and others (NCOA, 1975) state employment services offer fewer services to and make fewer referrals for older registrants. In the area of subsidized employment and training options, the older job seeker fares no better. There is evidence to support the following: older job seekers are underrepresented in Manpower Development and Training Act (MDTA) training slots (NCOA, 1975; Riley and Foner, 1968), are underrepresented in CETA slots and are ignored as a high risk employment group in discretionary programming by local manpower boards (Schram and Osten, 1978). As Schram and Osten (1978) have pointed out, diminished allocations and fierce competition for limited funds among already funded groups will probably preclude the older job seeker from making any inroads in these program areas (pp. 3–10).

Poor Readers

Tucker (1974) was interested in the problem of poor readers, particularly in reading difficulties experienced by black children who essentially had lived in two different cultures and, therefore, could be considered bilingual in their reading habits. In reviewing the literature and from his own life's experiences Tucker described the problem in the following way:

Most teachers and school programs are oriented toward the middle class student. The teachers speak and read standard English. Middle class children know, more or less, when they enter school why they have to learn to read and that they were going to learn to read (i.e., they have a model). They have at least a passing acquaintance with the alphabet. They engage in discussions in standard English, ask questions, and have been asked questions by adults in their standard English environment.

Most teachers mistakenly assume that all children are very much alike, and more particularly, that they are very much like they (the teachers) were when they were children. Even further, they assume that if children do not have the teachers' learning skills when they enter school the children's abilities are suspect (Tucker, 1970). The teachers falsely label these children as being "culturally deprived or disadvantaged." They often overlook the basic fact that much learning occurs in the child's environment external to the school, before the child enters school, and concurrently while s/he is in school.

The black child on the other hand, has learned to follow a set of rules that are different from the set rules that middle class teachers learned by, learned to teach by, and that dictate their behavior in the classroom. Although there are similarities in the two learning situations, there are nevertheless distinct differences. Failure to recognize and adapt teaching approaches to these differences often inhibits formal classroom learning.

Most ghetto children develop two sets of verbal skills that can come into conflict. Verbal skills which are necessary for ghetto children to negotiate successfully through their environment outside of the classroom differ from those required for her/his ultimate success in the school environment. These verbal skills are often unknown to teachers, and are considered by them to inhibit formal learning. Children of the ghetto with highly proficient verbal skills in their natural environment are discouraged from using these skills because they are often considered to be vulgar, backward, wrong, or irrelevant to learning in the classroom (pp. 4–6).

Energy Depletion

Leedom (1980) spent a considerable amount of time reading about and discussing the energy problem with persons involved in energy conservation research and actions. As a result of this information, she became convinced that a major effort toward energy reduction could and should occur in American society through conservation. She described the problem in the following manner:

> It was not until the international oil crisis of 1973–74, and the attendant long lines and rationing at the gasoline pumps, that most Americans realized the United States had an energy problem. The Arab oil embargo did not cause the energy problem, but it did serve as a demonstration that a problem existed in the United States.
>
> The roots of the problem are related to patterns of consumption and the use of nonrenewable resources. America is an energy-intensive society, consuming more total energy than any other country. While the U.S. population only accounts for 6 percent of the world's poupulation, Americans consume 30 percent of the world's per annum total energy production (Koenig, 1979). This high demand, coupled with the fact that America's energy supply is based largely upon dwindling fossil fuels (petroleum, natural gas, and coal), clearly poses a problem. . . .
>
> A summary of findings from existing social scientific studies of energy conservation attitudes and behaviors (Olsen and Goodnight, 1977), in general, showed that the American public has thus far adopted a minimal number of conservation practices (e.g., turning down home lighting and heating). During a crisis period (such as the oil embargo), the results of various surveys indicated that from 63 percent to 93 percent of families did engage in these minimal conservation practices. However, once the crisis had passed, the percentages of families engaging in conservation dropped substantially. In addition, proportionally fewer individuals adopted any significant conservation measures, such as insulating their homes or purchasing smaller cars. The conservation efforts generally reported via survey studies have involved minimal effort and no significant change in lifestyle on the part of American energy consumers (Rappaport and Labaw, 1975) (pp. 1–2).

Smoking and Health

Coelho (1983) became concerned about the effect of excessive smoking on health. After working on a project in a medical school whose purpose was to persuade individuals to quit smoking for health benefits he arrived at the following conclusions:

> As increasing evidence has been reported concerning the connection between cigarette smoking and many serious physical disorders (U.S. Department of Health and Human Services, 1981) . . . research efforts to help the chronic smoker break the tobacco habit have been intensified . . . In 1964, 52.8 percent of the United States males over the age of 21 smoked (U.S. Public Health Service, 1964). When reassessed in 1975, a decrease of 13.5 percent in male smokers was noted. During the same period, smoking among U.S. females 21 years of age and older declined from 31.4 to 28.4 percent. Although a significant percentage of the U.S. population had quit the smoking habit, there still remained approximately 53 million smokers in 1975 (Schwartz, 1979).
>
> Most people agree with the scientific evidence that smoking is harmful to one's health and many chronic smokers express a desire to give up cigarettes, but cannot do so of their own accord (Schwartz and Ride, 1978). A national survey sponsored by the Department of Health, Education, and Welfare in 1976 reported that six of ten smokers had seriously attempted to stop but failed; another three said they would try to stop if there were an easy way. Many smokers need help in attaining abstinence, which is the reason smoking cessation methods have proliferated during the last 20 years (pp. 1–3).

Juvenile Delinquency

Davidson's approach to the delinquency problem began while he was a graduate student. His first task became one of defining juvenile delinquency. To accomplish this he examined the social and historical context of the term, reviewed the theoretical literature, and gained personal experiences in the juvenile justice system. He found that historically the specific phenomenon called juvenile delinquency was created around the middle of the 1800s. Two particular events occurred that led to difficulty in defining the delinquency problem. In 1824, legislation created child-rearing institutions for juvenile delinquents and other young persons felt to be in need of residential care (Rothman, 1971). These alternative families became widespread and proliferated rather quickly. But by the end of the nineteenth century there was considerable dissatisfaction with the refuge home tactic of dealing with delinquency, particularly the use of children as cheap manual labor in these refuge homes.

It has been argued that juvenile delinquency was formally created as a social phenomenon in 1899 when separate juvenile courts were established in Illinois. As with refuge homes, the mission of the juvenile court was to provide for the care of children in a manner which would approximate care provided by natural parents and which also would protect society. Essentially, it was suggested that juveniles exchange their constitutionally derived rights to due process proceedings for the parentlike treatment of the courts.

The creation of juvenile courts and, hence, juvenile delinquency in an official sense, began with all the fervor of a publicly supported social movement. By 1907 the Illinois juvenile court had jurisdiction over uniquely juvenile offenses (status offenses), had been given judicatory as well as dispositional powers, and had been provided with a paid professional staff. After the intensity of the social movement which resulted in the creation of juvenile courts subsided, concern over the problem of juvenile delinquency also subsided. The courts conducted their business through most of this century in a rather dormant fashion. By 1928 all but two states had adopted similar legislation relying heavily on principles of humane treatment and parentlike settings (Sarri and Vinter, 1976). However, 65 to 70 years after its initiation, this method of handling juvenile offenders again became the focus of considerable debate. The juvenile justice system, like many other social institutions, became the target of a great deal of criticism. Three major types of criticism emerged.

The first concerned the juvenile courts' operation and philosophy. The intention of informal judicial handling in combination with parentlike treatment was criticized in the Supreme Court (review of the case of Gerald Gault). The Supreme Court held that the juvenile court failed to provide either sound, effective, or humane treatment and cited as well its roughshod handling of constitutionally guaranteed procedural safeguards. In its majority opinion, the Supreme Court concluded that "the condition of being a boy does not justify a kangaroo court." The Gault decision provided a major impetus for a more extensive and critical examination of the juvenile justice system and a concerted effort at finding alternative approaches.

The second criticism focused on the ineffectiveness of correctional institutions for juveniles. Recidivism rates for juvenile correctional institutions were running as high as 50 to 80 percent (Scarpitti and Stephenson, 1971; Jesness, 1975). In addition, a series of national media exposés called attention to the poor conditions which continued to be present in correctional facilities for juveniles.

A national moratorium on the construction of correctional institutions was espoused (Nagel, 1973; Nagel, 1977). In a similar vein, Irwin (1974) argued that the current correctional system had become so malignant that any attempts at reform were doomed to fail. Other authors characterized this society's juvenile justice process as a way of throwing away unwanted youth (Richette, 1969), providing a forum for regimenting the poor (Polier, 1973), isolating undersocialized youths (Feldman et al., 1972), punishing youths reacting to social inequities (Jordan, 1974), and providing a judicial example of the discriminatory handling of the nation's youth (Sarri and Vinter, 1976).

A third and somewhat more controversial criticism of the juvenile justice system occurred in the early 1970s. It addressed the apparent insistence of the authorities to view the problem of delinquency solely from a statistical point of view. Specifically, this view assumed that delinquency was defined by official delinquency rates, which led to the conclusion that delinquency was primarily a lower-class phenomenon and suggested that these delinquency rates were an indication of individual deficits prevalent among the poor (e.g., Mednick and Christiansen, 1977). However, studies of delinquency which had used self-report definitions rather than official delinquency rates indicated that unlawful behavior by young persons was apparently equally spread over all social strata (Erickson, 1973; Williams and Gold, 1972). A similar position was presented by Polk and Schafer (1972). They suggested that delinquency in schools had to be viewed from a broader perspective rather than being concerned only with youths in official legal jeopardy. Finally, it was suggested that official delinquency rates reflected considerably the visibility of youth and the activities of law enforcement officials rather than behavior of youths (Lincoln et al., 1977).

In addition to these major issues of procedural formality, ineffectiveness and inhumaneness of the justice system, and controversy over the definition of delinquency, American society was very concerned with skyrocketing crime rates. These rates were kept in the forefront of publicity by intense media attention to quarterly and annual crime rates as reported by the Federal Bureau of Investigation. In the area of juvenile crime, the message was similarly worsening. Official crime rates for youthful offenders were escalating even faster than overall crime rates, which were rising at a previously unexperienced pace. Different crime reports throughout the early 1970s pointed to massive increases in the juvenile delinquency rate. The rates increased even though the federal government's war on crime was by the early 1970s in full swing through the ever-increasing funding of the Law Enforcement Assistance Administration. Each component of the juvenile justice system tended to point to other components to solve the problem (citizens were unhappy with police responsiveness to the problem, police blamed "soft" juvenile courts, and the juvenile courts argued that resources were insufficient to effectively deal with the problem). The young people labeled delinquent also believed that the current system was failing because they were not receiving the employment or education they desired. Thus, at the time of the planning of the Adolescent Diversion Project, there was an unparalleled search for alternatives to the justice system, particularly as it concerned juveniles (Gold, 1974). Almost everyone seemed to agree that a drastic change was needed.

Chronic Mental Illness

In 1949, Fairweather was working in a veteran's administration hospital where the emphasis was on diagnosis and psychotherapy for the mentally ill. Those admitted to the hospital were mostly World War II veterans who were, at that time, usually in their early twenties and who had either a neuropsychiatric diagnosis before discharge from service or had developed symptoms of mental illness following service. What became noticeable to the author was the number of patients who returned to the hospital after it appeared that they had been "cured" and also the number who did not leave at all. In 1949 very little was written about chronic mental illness, although it later became the subject of widespread investigation and speculation (Stanton and Schwartz, 1954; Freeman and Simmons, 1963; Scheff, 1963, 1966). Because of the dearth of scientific information about hospitalization and mental illness at that time, the senior author began paying particular attention to this situation through observation and discussions with persons who repeatedly entered the hospital or who never left.

What became evident during this period of observation and discussion was that some persons left the hospital and did not return, some left and returned periodically, and some never left at all. Whether or not those who did not return had actually been "cured" no one knew, but they did not return to the particular hospital where the senior author worked. On the other hand, there were a number of persons who came in rather routinely, very often showing the same symptoms they had shown on previous admissions. Most often these were acute psychotic symptoms such as disorientation about who and where they were, and frequent hallucinations and/or delusions. They often complained that they could not find work, that their parents or spouses did not want them, and so on.

Another group, those who never left the hospital at all, often hallucinated and deluded openly in the hospital setting. Upon interview they frequently said they stayed at the hospital because "no one wants me." It also appeared that contemporary treatment programs were not working well for these chronic patients. This raised an issue about treatment: Did those who constantly returned or never left the hospital need a different type of treatment than those who did not return?

Following up this hunch about short-term and long-term stay groups, the senior author attempted to discover information that might differentiate the long- and short-term patient groups upon admission to the hospital. If this could be done, it might be possible to prevent revolving admissions and permanent stay by placing these at-risk persons in a program designed to prevent repeated or long-term stay when they first arrived at the hospital. In searching the literature, a survey by two psychologists, Giedt and Schlosser (1955), was found. The Giedt and Schlosser study raised some particular questions about the identifying characteristics of individuals who stayed for a long or short term. To look into the problem further, a great deal of information was taken from the clinical files of patients who had previously been discharged. Some information was available when the patient entered the hospital and other information was available about adjustment after discharge. A quasi-experimental comparison showed that individuals who had short-term stays differed from those who had long-term hospital stays in some clearly defined characteristics (Lindemann et al., 1959). Long-termers were significantly more often single, diagnosed as psychotic; were considered severly incapacitated upon interview at entry; were typically declared legally incompetent; and did not use alcohol as excessively as short-termers. But most important, the analysis showed that those who remained 1 year were likely to remain 2 years and so on until the individual had stayed so long that there was virtually no probability of leaving the hospital. Thus, this study raised serious questions about the validity of the treatment programs available to potential long-termers, particularly in regard to leaving or remaining out of the hospital.

It was therefore decided to establish a randomized experiment comparing the different types of treatment available to hospital patients and to compare them for different types of patients. The treatments compared were individual psychotherapy, group psychotherapy, participation in a Maxwell Jones (1953) type of therapeutic community, and a work only (control condition). Three groups of patients—two short-term groups identified as neurotics and short-term psychotics—were contrasted with a long-term group of individuals diagnosed as psychotics who had been hospitalized for over a year with one or many admissions. This division of patient groups was considered necessary since the study just mentioned had indicated that time spent in the hospital was associated with follow-up adjustment.

This comparative study showed that the long-term chronic psychotic patients did not respond well to any of the traditional forms of treatment—return rate to the hospital was 75 percent within 18 months for all conditions. The return rate for the short-term psychotics by contrast was only 20 percent in the same period of time while for the neurotics it approached 50 percent. This study also showed that measurements taken in the hospital concerning the patients' hospital behaviors, attitudes, and test scores were not related to what happened to them in the community. For example, adjusting well behaviorally in a hospital ward did not predict that a person would adjust well in the community, and working well in a hospital job did not predict work success in the community. In addition, test scores, behaviors, and attitudes were found to be relatively unrelated. This made the researchers aware that a proper outcome would have to involve a number of different dimensions of measurement broadly conceived as attitudes, fantasies, and behavior. Since these domains were unrelated, measurements in all three dimensions would have to occur. Furthermore, the 75 percent return rate in 18 months was very similar to the return rate shown on the earlier survey for the most chronically hospitalized ized group. From all this information it was decided that a new and more valid program needed to be created.

Reading the literature, talking with others, and reviewing the researcher's own findings and observations, raised a central question: How could community adjustment be accomplished by this chronic group? These diverse sources of information showed that persons who constantly returned to the hospital or remained in the hospital, in addition to having psychotic symptoms, also had high unemployment rates and often had no place to live in community settings. Creating a socially supportive living situation for these individuals appeared to be the central problem. Accordingly, the idea was spawned in the minds of the researchers that a supportive living and work program in the community might be an attractive and meaningful solution for individuals who found themselves constantly in mental hospitals.

In the last section of this chapter, seven programs have been defined and the definition process has revealed some common characteristics. In each case, but with different intensity, direct observation, personal experience, utilization of available research literature (professional and technical), and previous research by the scientist have contributed to the process of problem definition. Once the dimensions of the problem are defined, the process of creating an alternative social innovation(s) can begin. Specifically, the experimentalists need to understand what dimensions of the problem can be altered to achieve a more beneficial approach. For example, what type of reading situation would be more effective with minority group children? What type of alternative to the juvenile justice system appears most promising? What kind of community support is necessary to reduce the rehospitalization of chronic mental patients? In the next chapter we will discuss the planning of alternative social interventions as attempts at social problem solution.

CHAPTER 5

PLANNING AN INNOVATIVE SOLUTION

As mentioned earlier, new techniques for handling problems which confront society are necessary when existing procedures, programs, or policies are ineffective. As presented in Chapter 1, a strong case can be made for the need for innovation in almost every human problem area including crime, poverty, education, health, housing, and the like. This is not for any lack of effort toward solution of these problems, but rather because a variety of obstacles have stood in the way of scientific attempts to improve the human condition.

While these obstacles have included a number of impediments to beneficial change at the political level (Chapter 1), they have also included the historical inability of social science research to solve such problems (Berger, 1976; Kohn, 1976; Cook, 1979).

Procedures presented in this book represent an attempt to rectify these deficiencies through creation of life-enhancing, small-scale social models, their careful evaluation, and extensive examination of their dissemination. In planning an innovative solution to a human problem, it therefore is necessary to understand the use of models as the change vehicle. First, it is important to understand the uniqueness of social models.

Social models are often compared to technological models, but this analogy appears to be inappropriate so far as solving contemporary human problems is concerned. Dating at least to the "space race" approach of the 1960s, the major approach to social problems in this society has drawn heavily on the technological analogy of the physical sciences. As our society responded to the "Sputnik scare" through a massive infusion of federal funding and technological innovation, the space race to the moon was eventually won. During that time, and to this writing, it is common to hear politicians and even social scientists expounding the virtues of applying the technological analogy to human problems. The typical quote proceeds in the following manner: "If in one decade we could land a man on the moon, in 10 years we should be able to alleviate _____" (fill in your favorite social problem). This scenario has provided a good deal of political energy for appropriating many program dollars aimed at ameliorating human problems.

Unfortunately, a number of processes operate in the social problem domains that are not present in landing a spacecraft on the moon. First, the environment in which social programs must function does not possess the constancy of space. Second, it is not clear that social problems are amenable to a technological approach in a physical sense—that simply providing greater educational thrust (faculty and curriculum) will provide the theory and methods for social problem solution. Possibly the most critical point at which the technological analogy breaks down is in implementation. We often assume when dealing with social problems that if the appropriate "silicone chip" could be developed it could then be plugged into social program circuitry nationwide. Research on the dissemination of social programs strongly suggests that new programs are not implemented in exactly the same manner (Havelock, 1979; Rogers, 1983; Tornatzky et al., 1983; Blakely et al., 1984). What is apparent is that social programs are very complex phenomena operating in a dynamic and ever-interacting way with their environments. Thus, both the problem population and the social situation have a major impact on their effectiveness and can change with time.

As community scientists become involved in implementation, operation, evaluation, and dissemination of new social models they gain a greater understanding of the interaction of such variables in their naturalistic, dynamic environment. They also begin to understand that there are limits to the size of social programs that can be evaluated from a scientific perspective (Weick, 1984). It is for this reason that innovative social programs should first be implemented as small-scale models.

THE LOGIC OF SMALL-SCALE MODELS

The first question that might occur to the reader is: Why small-scale models? One of the answers is that small-scale models have several advantages for the problem-oriented scientist that are not found when one attempts to implement a new program at the state or federal level. While there appears to be little argument that advocacy for the impact of scientific information at all governmental levels is desirable and needed (Keisler, 1980), it is also necessary that scientists intervene on a small scale at the problem site for a number of important reasons that pertain to establishing the scientific validity of any new social program.

Their Administrative Value

In Chapter 2 the social model was described as the vehicle through which change occurs. Let us now examine in more detail the characteristic of such models. The first aspect of social model innovation that we must understand is the need for a naturalistic community setting for the model's operation. This approach is logically similar to the traditional scientists' laboratory except that the problem-solving social scientists' laboratory is the community. To examine this thesis more closely, let's compare the analogy of natural scientists using the laboratory and see if it resembles that of social scientists using the community. To take several examples: Chemists might look very closely at chemical reactions in the laboratory; physicists might look at force from a very small model of a lever created for use in the laboratory; archeologists might look at rocks of various kinds in a laboratory setting. From a logical sampling point of view it is important to understand that what is examined in the laboratory is usually the *exact* object that exists in nature—a piece of quartz is a piece of quartz whether one looks at it in the laboratory or in the field; chemicals are exactly the same whether they are in the field or in the test tube; and force is the same in the laboratory as in the field. For this reason, the natural scientist can bring the actual physical sample into the laboratory for examination.

However, in social processes the total social situation to which the experimentalist wishes to generalize often exists only in the community. Thus, the actual situational sample exists only in the naturalistic setting of the community and it is this exact situation to which the scientist will need to generalize. For this reason the only realistic laboratory for evaluating new social models is the community (Proshansky, 1981). In this way, the community resembles the laboratory of the natural scientist. Since an actual sample program in a real-life situation provides the most valid scientific information, a small-scale social model operating in the naturalistic setting is the logical research situation in which to evaluate a social innovation.

If social scientists have learned anything from the past, it should be that implementation of large-scale national interventions without first evaluating empirically what the outcomes of such programs might be can lead to disastrous consequences. Some consequences are that once the program is put into effect on a national scale it gains a large number of constituents. The constituents perceive the program as essential to their future and it is, therefore, very difficult to change such national programs. One advantage of small-scale models is that if evaluation shows that the new model is not producing the expected outcomes, only a small number of people are involved and terminating the model is much easier.

It is also true that small-scale models can be placed in existing organizations for evaluation with a minimum of organizational disruption. For example, in a mental hospital it is usually possible to establish a small-scale program on a ward. In a prison, it might be established in a cell block. In the broader community it might be established in one energy corporation, one school, and so on. For this reason, activation of the small-scale model program so that its outcomes can be evaluated can be accomplished without destroying the organization itself. It is only after the program has been evaluated and found to be beneficial that major changes in the organization would be required. Another advantage of small-scale models, therefore, is that they make possible gradual as well as valid social change.

Another helpful aspect of small-scale models is that a much smaller staff is required to implement and evaluate the program. Since there is typically a dearth of money available for social problem researchers, it is important that the costs of operating a small-scale model, which include hiring a staff, creating and evaluating measuring instruments, and the like, is kept low so that creation and evaluation of the model is economically feasible. Smallness, therefore, contributes to the economic feasibility of establishing the model. Thus, small-scale models have a number of characteristics that make them highly desirable as the change vehicle. They can be implemented with a minimum of organizational disruptions, they are economical, their vailidity can be determined, and they can be readily disseminated if valid, or terminated if not.

Their Fit with the Community Scientist Role

The act of implanting small-scale social models as a first step in a scientific approach to human problem solution requires that the scientist be active in the community as outlined in Chapter 2. Active rather than passive approaches are needed because the scientist becomes involved in planning and operating the small-scale model programs designed to address a selected area of human concern. Thus, alternative approaches to such issues as crime, poverty, mental health, excessive drug use, and energy conservation are operationally defined, constructed, and implemented. The behaviors needed to carry out activation of small-scale social models require community activity—a central feature of the field experimentalist's role.

Creating alternative social models is also congruent with innovation planning. We have seen that contemporary approaches to the human condition are falling short of effectively attaining their goals in a variety of situations. Hence, the need for new approaches is a basic consideration of the scientist. Since small-scale models permit creation of new programs with a minimum of disruption to the environment, it is often possible, from a practical point of view, to create small-scale models when large-scale interventions would be impossible.

As will be highlighted in the next chapter, creation and operation of small-scale social models also fits well with the researchers' scientific need to control the social program for the purpose of scientific evaluation. Recent social history is replete with examples of programs such as Head Start, the Job Corp., Alternative Income Maintenance, etc., in which major debate still continues over exactly "what" was implemented (Fairweather and Tornatzky, 1977). Since the activist scientist is primarily interested in gaining scientifically valid information concerning the processes and effectiveness of the new social model(s), the use of small-scale programs permits scientists to control their operation so that an understanding of "what is happening" is possible. Thus, scientists' ability to control the operation of social models for scientific evaluation is enhanced by the use of small-scale model(s).

Activating small-scale social models so that real-life evaluation is possible requires creation of a receptive interpersonal and organizational environment. This demands that the activist scientist understand and measure the interpersonal and organizational components (see Tables 3-2 and 3-3) to evaluate their impact on the effectiveness of the small-scale social model. Conceptualizing innovative interventions as social models rather than as global social policy opens the models' creation and maintenance processes to theoretical and conceptual understanding. It also provides a research technique that helps scientists remain problem- rather than discipline-focused.

We have also seen in Chapter 1 that one of the major shortcomings of scientific attempts to ameliorate human problems has been an overly narrow conceptual framework. Our society's typical strategy has been to identify a problem of human concern, specify those individuals in whom that problem is most prominently displayed, discern statistically reliable differences between the specified population and society, and implement programs that it is believed will reduce those differences. What has been lacking from the scientific perspective is (1) a multifaceted view of the problem population and the social context in which such problems occur, and (2) scientifically valid information about the effectiveness of the implemented programs. Use of the small-scale social model demands that scientists consider all aspects of social problem solution. It requires attention to all levels of research and innovation from intra- and interindividual variables to those of societal impact.

Creating Small-Scale Models for Research

As can be seen from the examples given in Chapter 1, there is no dearth of human problems extant in our society and there probably will not be a shortage as long as humans inhabit this planet. But knowing that a problem exists is quite different from planning a solution for that problem. The knowledge created from personal experiences, literature review, and the like, as mentioned in the last chapter, helps us to find a problem and gives us the background for creating a problem solution. But this information alone does not create a solution for us. Assuming we have identified a problem of interest to us, it is now necessary to turn our attention to the process of planning a solution for the problem we have defined.

There is difficulty in doing this because of differences in individual perception. It seems to be a fact in the pursuit of scientific answers to problems that some people have the ability to ferret out the essential characteristics of a problem and then combine the elements of that problem into a new solution. Other persons appear not to have that ability, motivation, or whatever is involved in program creation. It is akin to two persons looking at the same object when one is an artist and the other a layperson. A discussion with the artist might show that he or she understands a great deal about the object simply by observing it—its density, texture, form, color, and so on. On the other hand, the naive observer simply sees an object—an object with some particular form. It is this perceptual difference that appears to be central to planning an innovative solution. While observational ability and cognitive know-how are fairly easy to describe; they are extremely difficult to define. In many ways it's similar to birds flying south—we can see them, but we're not exactly certain what mechanism compels them to go south when the weather begins to get cold. Nonetheless, we shall attempt to construct the act of model development in as much detail and with as much insight as we can muster.

IDENTIFYING THE BASIC CHARACTERISTICS OF THE INNOVATIVE MODEL

In Chapter 3 we proposed that the outcome of any social model is a function of the participants and the internal and external social processes in which the model operates. When the experimentalist has determined the participant and/or social processes that need to be varied to solve a particular problem, the planning process then turns to creating a social model where this occurs. To explore this part of the problem-solving process, we will examine models that focus either upon the participant or the social situation or both and their innovative characteristics.

The logical process goes something like this. With information derived from the several sources of information defined and described in Chapter 4, the scientist mentally attempts to write the equation showing that the outcome is a function of the participants and their social situation (pp. 40). He or she decides that the outcome of a new model will need to be of a particular type (increased employment, improved social adjustment, etc.) and that certain participant and internal and/or external social processes need to be changed or rearranged for the outcome to occur. Thus, personal characteristics or social processes or both will then be used in particular proportions in the problem-solving equation and translated into a new social model.

Let us take urban unemployment as an example. Let us assume that after examining all sources of information we find that the unemployment problem is greatest with persons between the ages of 18 and 22 (selecting a participant variable). Let us further assume that additional information shows few organizations willing to hire this age group. Having this information permits us to plan several different models for 18-to-22-year-old youths. All models would serve this population. One model might teach persons to search for jobs, based on the premise that these persons cannot find work because they do not know where to find work (varying internal social processes). A second model might teach work skills, based upon the idea that people in this age group lack desirable work skills (varying internal social processes). A third model might create a small industry to hire such persons, based on the idea that discrimination against this age group is so intense that few if any 18-to-22-year-olds can find work in the industrial system regardless of where they look or what skills they have learned (varying external social processes). Comparing these three models on an outcome of participant employment should determine or help to determine the validity of these three different approaches to the problem of urban unemployment.

The Human Dimension

Looking back at the outcome formula on page 40, it is very clear that the researcher can come to the conclusion that only participant variables need to be varied to solve the problem. The question may now become: What participants will respond in what way to the social model? To find answers to this question, the experimentalist can vary the important participant variables of a model so that the outcomes can be attributable solely to the participants in that model. For example, it would be possible to investigate age differences in one education program. To accomplish the participant age comparison, the experimentalist might establish four models of the same education program in which the participants would be adolescents, young adults, middle-aged persons, and the elderly. This would require four equivalent models, each serving a different population. All four models would have the same program but be composed of different age groups, thus comparing the participant dimension of age. Theoretically, since all models are the same and the participants vary only in age, the effectiveness of the outcome of the model can be attributed to the age differences.

There are, as the reader can see from Table 3-2, many participant variables that could be varied by such a scheme. For example, one might try the same educational system with different racial groups, different socioeconomic groups, groups with different educational backgrounds, groups who live in different-size homes, and so on. The logical point to be made here is simply that it is possible to create a unidimensional model where the only variables compared are those defining the participants. It must also be recognized that to accomplish this comparative goal not only must the persons participating in the different models be equivalent on all participant variables other than those that are varied, but the internal and external social processes must also be equated for each comparison model.

Internal Social Process Variables

Reference to Table 3-3 suggests that the internal social process variables can be varied in an attempt to discover the degree to which they might affect outcomes. Take, for example, hierarchical structure as listed in Table 3-3 and described on page 51. Two models, each having the same program, could be managed in different ways. For example, one might have a very "tall" hierarchical structure where all decisions are made at the top and eventually filter down to participants at lower levels. On the other hand, a "flat" organizational structure might be developed for the same program which would give every participant an equal voice in the program. In this organizational structure matters might be decided by vote rather than by one person at the top making all decisions. These different types of organizational structure might yield different kinds of outcomes.

To take another example from the internal social processes in Table 3-3, it might be that the experimentalists would want to vary some of the group dynamics processes. They might have the same program and the same types of individuals in the groups participating in each program, but different types of leadership might be established. One program might have a democratic leader and the other an authoritarian leader. If there was a performance or attitude difference due to these leadership variables, it would be revealed when comparing the outcomes of these models.

Referring again to Table 3-3, it becomes apparent that many different types of internal process variables could be varied and their outcome effects ascertained. To take some additional examples, experimentalists could be interested in the same program having different kinds of financial arrangements, such as one where all income is oriented to the individual and another where the group itself gets the income which it could then later divide. Or, the turnover of the group might change so that one group would agree to stay together and the comparative group might have the freedom of entering and exiting the group when they wished, thus creating potential membership turnover. Different outcomes might result from different types or amounts of group turnover. The point to be emphasized here is that a program can be created where the central variables of the program that is to be varied is one or more of the internal social process variables. When evaluating one or more internal social process variables, however, all participant, external social processes, and remaining internal social process variables must be equivalent.

External Social Process Variables

By contrast, it is possible to vary the external social processes while keeping the internal social processes and the participants equivalent. For example, experimentalists might wonder what would happen to the model's outcomes (for the sake of the example let's assume it's employment in a work-training program) if the model program were implanted in a poor economic area contrasted with a wealthy economic area. In such a case, the program would be implanted in two different socioeconomic areas, and if all other participant and social situational variables were equivalent for the two models, the outcome effects of these different socioeconomic areas could be ascertained. Or again, experimentalists might decide to implement two employment programs, one in high areas of unemployment, comparing it with the same model implanted in low areas of unemployment. Or a program for criminals might be initiated in a prison setting, and be compared with the same program implanted in a community setting. The difference in the manner in which two equivalent models might function due to their external environment could greatly affect their outcomes. Thus, it is important to recognize that the situation in which the model is implanted (external to the model) can affect the model's outcomes.

Multidimensional Models

So far we have discussed models where only the participant variables are varied, internal social process variables are varied, or external social process variables are varied in one model. Under certain conditions it is possible to vary several of these variables at once. For example, we might have different forms of psychotherapy administered to different types of patients. This creates a design where both participant characteristics and the programs themselves—in this case the internal social processes of different roles for patients and therapists—are varied. We can all think of several different types of more complicated models where all three dimensions might be varied. For example, different racial groups might participate in three different types of skill-training programs located in three different geographical areas—urban, suburban, and rural. This yields a design where participant variables, internal social process variables, and external social process variables are all varied in the same design.

While multidimensional comparisons may yield significantly more information than unidimensional comparisons, it is nonetheless often more advisable to complete several unidimensional experiments rather than one larger complex experiment simply because of the logistical and experimental difficulties involved in implanting and administering social programs in community settings. As experimentalists become more and more multidimensional in design, the number of researchers and service persons as well as the number of participants begins to increase geometrically. Because of the difficult and time-consuming nature of designing, managing, and evaluating models, it is often wiser to use several simple comparisons rather than one large multidimensional model.

EXAMPLES OF PROGRAM INNOVATIONS TO SOLVE PARTICULAR PROBLEMS

In Chapter 4, Beck's (1973) concern about the lack of social influence and political power that consumers of health procedures had obtained was presented. In an attempt to bring the consumer into a more meaningful decision-making role she concluded that the following innovation might improve health planning:

> For alleviating the multiple difficulties to marginal consumer status, the most advantageous alternative to the typical workshop method of individual interaction might be an autonomous small group training approach. According to Palmer et al. (1972):

Didactic presentation for rational planning issues is not likely to reach and modify the personal barriers to group functioning. The contribution of behaviorists in structural techniques of group process to achieve full participation as well as ability in problem analysis and decision making offers a valuable approach which may be used both in initial orientation and continuing development of participatory skill.

Collins and Guetzkow (1964), after an extensive review of the literature, summarized the major advantages of group products over that of individuals. They report that, in general, group members may achieve collectively more than most superior members could alone and that face-to-face groups have a profound inpact on the motivations, knowledge, and personalities of the participants. . . .

The creation of a group could allow for more varied information, more creative suggestions on the promotion of consumer legitimacy and division and duplication of effort in solving consumer problems. Social motivation could come from other consumers so that the participants might become effective consumers rather than merely well-informed ones.

As a group, consumers could take valuable risks which they as individuals might have been afraid to do. If, in the past, they had conformed too quickly to the professional experts' opinion, they could learn that this was not necessary and was also unproductive. They might realize that they have their own unique expertise as community representatives which providers do not have. Such a group could also utilize all three information sources: (1) verbal reports, (2) personal investigation, and (3) observation of other members' investigation. Most importantly, however, group members might overcome a major problem which Collins and Guetzkow (1964) caution against—dependency on others rather than thinking or learning on their own (pp. 15–16).

Jobs for the Elderly

It will be recalled from the last chapter that Gray (1980) was primarily concerned about the unemployment problem that many older workers face in our society. His own work with elderly people and the review of literature from several different fields led him to the following conclusion about a program that might rectify the high unemployment rate among the elderly.

Since older job seekers experience very long periods of unemployment, confront discriminating hiring practices, often lack saleable skills, and frequently want to access a very small, part-time job market, it seems reasonable to conclude that they represent an inordinantly problematical and unique population of job seekers.

In general, the body of research just reviewed presents a pattern of findings which appear to support the efficacy of a behaviorally based approach to improving job search competence and placement success . . . through the organization of a job club. The job club will attempt to facilitate job seeking knowledge and skill in job search activities through training and support of group members (pp. 35–42).

Poor Readers

You will also recall that Tucker (1974) was concerned about the reading deficiencies shown by younger people in our society. He was particularly concerned about young black students who had learned "black dialect" prior to entering school and then attempted to substitute standard English for their earlier learned language. In defining a solution to that problem which grew out of his experiences and literature review, Tucker concluded that a new approach might be quite beneficial. He stated his problem-solving innovation in the following way:

> The basic notion of this proposed (model) is that the language abilities brought to school by ghetto children can be used to complement and facilitate the learning of the "new" dialect, standard English. This study represents an attempt to use the learning of the child outside of the school situation to enhance her/his learning in school. Formal learning in the classroom and learning outside of the classroom could then complement—not oppose—each other. This may be accomplished by means that I have chosen to call associate bridging. This involves having the student proceed from the familiar (her/his dialect) to the unfamiliar (standard English) in small steps (p. 9).

Energy Depletion

As presented in Chapter 4, Leedom (1980) decided that energy conservation behavior should begin at an early age and in the school system. Her extensive review of the literature in several fields and her own experiences led her to draw the following conclusion about the program innovation that would address that problem.

> It appears that an educational approach which involves the student in actual energy conservation tasks is more likely than a traditional, "passive" approach to lead to the development of: (a) more pronounced pro-energy conservation attitudes, and (b) more intensive energy conservation behaviors in the future (pp. 30–31).

Smoking and Health

It will also be recalled that Coelho (1983) had identified the problem of the cessation of smoking as a health problem of great significance in this society. As with other researches presented here, his extensive study of the problem from the literature and from working in a smoking clinic led him to conclude that a multiple-treatment method, including individual contracts, group support, educational procedures, and psychotherapy components needed to be created.

> Acknowledging the pressing need to develop procedures and programs to assist smokers in the cessation process, researchers have increasingly turned their attention to the problem. To date, single treatment techniques have not yielded very beneficial results (Bernstein, 1969; McFall, 1978). Such strategies and techniques include but are not limited to the following: Stimulus control (Gutmann and Marston, 1967; Bernard and Efran, 1972); aversive conditioning (Whitman, 1972); systematic desensitization (Pyke, Agnew, and Ropperud, 1966); contingency contracting (Lawson and May, 1970); covert sensitization (Sachs, Bean, and Morrow, 1970); rapid smoking (Lando, 1976) and self-monitoring (McFall and Hammen, 1971).

The smoking cessation strategies noted above have shown varying degrees of short-term success, but minimal long-term success. Reviews of the smoking cessation literature (Bernstein, 1969; Leventhal and Cleary, 1980; Hunt and Matarazzo, 1973; Lichtenstein and Danaher, 1976; Keutzer and Lichtenstein, 1968; McFall and Hammen, 1971; Schwartz and Ride, 1978) have produced the following conclusions:

1 Essentially any treatment will decrease smoking levels by as much as 30 to 40 percent of baseline.
2 Approximately 3 to 6 months after treatment ends there is usually a return to about 75 percent of baseline smoking levels.
3 The percent of subjects abstinent at 3 to 6 months follow-up is seldom more than 13 percent.
4 Less than one-third of those subjects abstinent at end of treatment manage to maintain the non-smoking behavior 3 to 6 months later.

Lichtenstein and Danaher (1976) have suggested that single component techniques may be more useful if used in combination. Multiple treatment or "package" programs have been employed by a variety of researchers (Best, 1975; Delahunt and Curran, 1976; Hamilton and Bornstein, 1979; Lando, 1977; Pederson et al., 1975; Powell and McCann, 1981). The basic argument for the multiple treatment approach is that the complexity of smoking behavior and the variety of functions that cigarettes can serve for each individual requires it (pp. 24–25).

Juvenile Delinquency

The diversion project for juvenile offenders drew heavily on information which was available in the early 1970s on some potentially promising directions.

The creation of the diversion project for juvenile offenders grew out of major dissatisfactions with the operation of the juvenile justice system. From these dissatisfactions the idea arose for using community-based preventive intervention strategies. The idea emerged in part as a result of the apparent ineffectiveness and inhumaneness of institutional programs mentioned in Chapter 4 (Empy, 1967; Goldenberg, 1971; Wright and Dickson, 1977) and the general move toward community-based service prominent in social service fields at the time (Cowen, Gardner, and Zacks, 1967; Spergel, 1973; Rubin, 1977). Theoretical and empirical support for the community-based preventive intervention recommendations came from two rather divergent lines of thought. The first placed heavy emphasis on the role of social structures and social milieus as critical factors in producing delinquency (Merton, 1957). Using official delinquency rates as a data base, early studies such as those by Shaw and McKay (1942) had demonstrated a disproportionate number of social problems among the poor. Combining such information with the propositions of anomie theory, it was believed that delinquency was a result of differential access to means of attaining personal and material goals (Cloward and Ohlin, 1960).

In addition, a second area of thought emerged from the "individual difference" ideas then prominent in the field of psychology. The classic work in that area was carried out by the Gluecks over four decades ago (Glueck and Glueck, 1950). Their research indicated that five critical factors, essentially descriptive of differential parenting modes, were predictive of delinquency. A great deal of effort had been put into demonstrating the difference between delinquent and nondelinquent youths based on a variety of personality, social, and other individual characteristics (Waldo and Dinitz, 1967).

From these two theoretical perspectives it was only a short logical jump to perceive the need for intervening in community settings. If social structures were a central element in creating delinquency, intervention by placement in long-term institutional care away from the very community which produced delinquency was not likely to be successful. Similarly, if youths who were likely to become delinquent could be identified early in life, preventive community-based interventions had some merit.

In retrospect, it probably was not only the theoretical or scientific merit of either of these two positions which led to the push for community-based preventive interventions, but rather that these two positions provided an alternative to traditional treatment. Thus, the intense search for alternatives to traditional programs for juvenile delinquency at that time enhanced the impact of these arguments. Since innovations often arise in the face of a crisis (Rogers, 1983), the suggestion for community-based alternatives was given credence because of the perceived crisis in the institutional care of juvenile offenders.

Another response to dissatisfaction with the delinquency system was the widespread acceptance of nonprofessionals and volunteers to provide less expensive interventions for delinquent youths. Two primary factors provided the thrust of this second social force. It was argued that juvenile courts had been ineffective in preventing or correcting delinquency and that there were insufficient public funds available to update court procedures. The use of nonprofessionals was also enhanced by evidence that traditional individual psychotherapeutic techniques and casework services were ineffective for adolescent delinquent groups. The basic "talk therapy" modes of intervening in the lives of delinquent youths were found to be particularly ineffective (McCord and McCord, 1959; Levitt, 1971; Grey and Dermody, 1972; McCord, 1978). Levitt concluded that, in general, "conventional psychotherapy methods appear to be least effective with delinquents. The reported improvement rate is more than a standard deviation below the mean for all treated groups."

This information and concerned social forces produced a nationwide volunteer movement. Judge Keith Leinhouts, one of the early leaders of the volunteer movement, claimed that volunteer programs "may well be more than an answer to the crime problem; they be *the* answer" (Raskin, 1971). In the early 1970s, it was estimated that well over 1000 juvenile courts in the United States had formal volunteer programs, and similar efforts had been initiated in Europe.

A third outgrowth of the upheaval in the juvenile justice system was a suggestion that whenever possible youthful offenders should be diverted out of the sphere of influence of the court. The general argument was that the functioning of the courts had become so ineffective that alternatives for social control had to be undertaken. It is in this area, more than any other, that the direct recommendation of the President's Commisssion on Law Enforcement and the Administration of Justice (1967) had an important impact. Theoretically, proponents of the diversionary alternative found instant allies among social labeling theorists (e.g., Becker, 1963; Lemert, 1971).

Diversion policy recommendations drew their theoretical support from a group of sociologists generally linked to the Chicago school, who had for some time been suggesting nonintraindividual explanations for deviance. Basically, they argued that if most youths drifted in and out of the legal system they would receive a negative social label of delinquency from the formal proceedings of the juvenile court, and such labels could have an adverse effect on the future incidence of delinquency. From this perspective, keeping young people away from the influence of juvenile courts, diversion seemed to be indicated (Matza, 1964; Schur, 1969; Faust, 1973; Schur, 1973; Lemert, 1974; Rutherford and McDermott, 1976).

From all these sources of information the plans for an innovative adolescent diversion program emerged. The evidence indicated that such a program should provide (1) community-based alternatives to institutional treatment, (2) the use of nonprofessional persons working with delinquent populations, and (3) an alternative community setting to the juvenile justice system (diversion).

Chronic Mental Illness

A review of the results of the failure of the chronic psychotic person to make adjustments in the community was presented in the last chapter. These findings led the research group (Fairweather, 1964) to perceive the problem more broadly—as one in which these persons had no role in society once they left the hospital because they appeared to have no community support group. The more information that was accumulated from discussions, readings, and researches the more it appeared that for the long-term hospitalized psychotic entering the community was very similar to survival for persons in situations of conflict. As thinking and discussion proceeded in this manner, a great deal of attention was paid to the group dynamics literature, particularly those studies involving field research. Some studies indicated that groups can survive if their members form a cohesive problem-solving unit, whereas the members might fail as individuals. This also seemed to have some relationship to the early history of immigrants to the United States where different ethnic groups worked in the greater society, but usually lived among persons who had similar backgrounds and who provided a social support system for them. The researchers therefore concluded that they would try to create groups of problem-solving mental patients who might then be able to take care of one another and help each other solve their own problems.

But roadblocks appeared. Most of the literature indicated that these partic-

ular individuals were too irrational and preoccupied with their psychotic idea-
tion to attend to other group members and their needs. Nevertheless, Lerner
and Fairweather (1963) decided to explore the possibility of group formation
in research organized in a mental hospital ward. They compared groups who
operated autonomously without staff leaders with staff-led groups. While there
were many findings from this experiment, the most important for innovation
creation was that cohesive groups of problem-solving patients could be organized, could solve their own problems, and could complete tasks in routine
living. Even though autonomous patient groups took longer to reach the same
level of performance as the staff-led groups, they eventually did develop similar efficiency in task completion and, in addition, showed an interest in belonging to their group.

Fairweather (1980) and others then decided to follow this experiment with
another experiment which would organize an entire ward of about sixty
patients into patient-led groups. Patients and staff on this ward were then contrasted with a similar ward that was staff-led. The differences between these
two wards was perhaps best summarized in the following description of the
programs developed in a Veterans Administration hospital:

> To highlight the differences, one must trace the events in a patient's life for the first
> few days on the small-group as compared to the traditional ward. A patient arriving
> on the traditional ward was interviewed by the ward psychologist. Historical infor-
> mation was gained during this interview, and an attempt at establishing rapport was
> made. The patient's clinical file was studied. After the patient was informed of the
> treatment program, including job assignment, ward regulations governing money
> and passes, and other policies, he was seen by the nurse and a bed assignment was
> made. Soon after, the patient was sent to be interviewed about and to receive a job
> assignment. After the first day, the patient followed his assigned schedule and he
> could request an appointment with the appropriate staff members for discussion of
> money, passes, problems, and the like. A roster on the bulletin board was available
> for indicating which weekend days he wished passes and how much weekly money
> was requested. The roster was then given to the ward psychiatrist for approval or
> rejection. Every day the patient attended the large-group meeting, where free discus-
> sion was encouraged. The patient remained on the ward following this meeting for
> the recreation hour, when he could engage in a chosen activity. On this traditional
> ward, a list of regulations governing passes, money, and medication, among other
> things, was posted on the bulletin board.
>
> By contrast, a patient arriving on a small-group ward was briefly seen by the psy-
> chologist and informed that he was now a member of a particular patient task group.
> The task group was responsible for orienting him to the ward and explaining the
> program to him. He was shown the bulletin board, which displayed only the list of
> requirements for each role advancement that he must fulfill to complete successfully
> the program, and the rewards associated with them, as well as a list of patients who
> were members of his newly assigned task group. A note was placed in the group's
> box informing them of their new member, and it now became their responsibility to
> orient him to the program. On the first day the patient met with the task group and
> was introduced to the ward procedures. The introduction included an explanation
> of the treatment program, the handling of passes and money, and what he should do
> about personal and other problems. At this point he became a group member (p. 8).

The findings from this experiment led directly to a proposal for problem solution. This information is best summarized in the following quote from the aforementioned book:

> In comparison with patients in traditional treatment, those in the small-group program demonstrated a heightened social activity in all situations, with even the most chronic patients participating. Members of the program displayed higher morale and more frequently perceived their fellow members as socially desirable. Patients participating in the task groups demonstrated a pronounced personal involvement in the adjustment of other members to their group, and perceived the increased responsibilities required by the program as difficult but rewarding. Their expectations about the future were brighter. Community adjustment by former task group members was better with regard to employment and social adjustment in the community. In addition, many of the most chronic patients were active participants in the small-group program. Some became group leaders.
>
> In playing the roles required of them, the various staff members themselves became a cohesive group. The social atmosphere of this staff group was one of respect for each person's judgment and individuality. The staff perceived the change in patients' behavior and this, in turn, raised their morale and increased their interest in the task groups. The equal vote held by all staff members became a symbol of the responsibility given to each individual and of the value placed on his judgment. This feeling of togetherness was transmitted to the patient groups and was reflected in their behavior.
>
> The patients' increased social activity, the increased self-involvement of the more chronic patients, and the increase in staff morale occurred concomitantly with a shortening of the time patients required to complete this hospital treatment program. But despite these advantages of the task group approach—and they were considerable—the problem of recidivism still remained. Fifty-six percent and fifty-eight percent of the non-psychotic and most chronic psychotic patients, respectively, returned to the hospital within six months following discharge. What then had been learned from this experiment that could be used to reduce or attenuate the high recidivism rate, particularly among chronic patients, even when hospital treatment conditions appeared to be excellent?
>
> Information about the patients' community adjustment in the follow-up period for this study emphasized that the locus of future treatment programs had to be the community. Hospital treatment should, it seemed, be only one aspect of a total organized program that would clearly define the patients' role and status both within the hospital and the community. If what had been learned in the hospital was to sustain the person in the community, an almost direct transfer of the role behaviors he had learned had to occur. Furthermore, such a situation would have to be established with a minimum of professional personnel since any program requiring a large number of professional people would not be feasible.
>
> A look into the future . . . suggests that task groups that had been trained in decision making within the hospital might be moved as units into the community. This would provide a stable social system in which former chronic patients would have an established role and status, but at the same time, the activities of such a group of patients would, of necessity, have to be consonant with the role requirement of citizens in the community. . . .
>
> It seemed from the evidence that the ingredients necessary for the group to perform effectively would be very similar to those already developed in the hospital.

Thus, groups of predominantly chronically hospitalized and currently unemployed people could be moved into community residences, provided they were organized in the hospital into effective task groups. . . . If such groups followed the developmental pattern of those created in the hospital, they would soon develop adequate leadership. Since all group members would be employed, the system of rewards could, by and large, be determined by the productivity of each individual member. A communication system between a trained evaluation committee and the task groups could be established. This committee could evaluate the recommendations of the task groups and serve as testing ground for the group's ideas. Finally, a flexible system of role behaviors required of each member had to be instituted since this allowed for rational and systematic role changes to meet the vicissitudes of community life without allowing necessary changes to be so easily made that change itself became the accepted behavior (pp. 283–285).

This chapter has presented the development of proposed problem solutions for several different human problems. Their recognition and solution planning was the result of a series of inferences and ideas emanating from personal history, literature review, observations, and experiments leading to other ideas and experiments until finally researchers found what appeared to be an acceptable solution to the problem. How these plans are translated into an actual experiment to determine the planned solutions' effectiveness by creating an experimental design will be discussed in the next chapter.

CREATING AN
EXPERIMENTAL DESIGN

First, it is necessary to place the topic of designing community experiments in the context of the other topics covered in this section. While the design, measurement, and evaluation of community experiments have been separated into three chapters for organizational purposes, this distinction is highly arbitrary. The design, measurement, and evaluation of social research are interrelated (Runkel and McGrath, 1972) and in community experiments are inherently intertwined (Fairweather and Tornatzky, 1977); hence, many of the topics which arise in Chapter 6 will reappear in Chapters 7 and 8.

Second, it should be noted that the scientific aspects of the field researcher's role, as defined in such behaviors as designing, measuring, and evaluating, go hand in hand with the actual implementation of the models and their operation (Fairweather and Tornatzky, 1977; Davidson et al., 1981; Rossi et al., 1982). Because these activities are usually occurring at the same time, the description of scientific methods presented in Chapters 6, 7, and 8 will interface with problem definition and program operation (Chapters 4 and 8).

THE LOGIC OF DESIGN FOR FIELD EXPERIMENTS

The construction and use of appropriate experimental designs in the field research setting is a central aspect of the social problem-solving process. The use of valid research designs allows the unambiguous interpretation of outcomes (Campbell and Stanley, 1966; Cook and Campbell, 1979). Further, the relationships of outcomes, participant characteristics, and internal and external social processes can be examined (Davidson, Redner, and Saul, 1983). The selection of a research design is simply the next step in the problem-solving process, once an innovative model has been intellectually created. The value of the innovative model is best determined through activating an appropriate research design.

The primary goal of design in social experimentation, therefore, is to be able to make generalizable inferences about the benefit of the new model(s). Examination of social models' effectiveness using experimental designs allows us to draw conclusions which have scientific and logical credibility. To accomplish this, the outcomes of the innovative social model(s) are compared with the outcomes of traditional approach(es) to the problem. Comparisons with traditional approaches, which may include benign neglect, are the basis of determining the effectiveness of new social models. This comparison is necessary because the socially concerned scientist needs to know how beneficial the innovative model is in contrast with the traditional way society has been handling the problem. If significant beneficial improvement can be attributed to the new model, then and only then is broader social use of the model logically justified. For this reason the traditional model is called the *control* in community experimentation. In a sense it is the baseline against which new models may be compared in order to demonstrate their social value. To make a comparison of model benefits, it is important to know that the observed outcomes are truly a function of the model and not extraneous factors.

To isolate the effects of the model from all other effects it is important that the traditional model and the new model have their own defining characteristics. It is equally important that the effects of all other factors that could contribute to the differential effects of the models be determined. Recalling again the basic assumption that the outcome of a social model is a function of the participants and the internal and external social processes (Tables 3-2 and 3-3), it becomes apparent that the logic of the experimental design is similar to that of solving a simultaneous equation. For the sake of examining this general logical principle let us review Tables 3-1, 3-2, and 3-3. These tables give us a list of the variables that we need to consider so we can evaluate the effectiveness of the new model.

With these tables in mind, let us assume we are trying to evaluate models where the primary focus is staff leadership styles in operating shelter homes for spouse abuse victims. Let us further assume that we want to compare democratic with autocratic leadership because our problem definition information suggests that the former type of leadership is more beneficial than the latter. In the first model (Model A), therefore, we want staff who will lead the shelter democratically. In the traditional model (Model B), we want staff who will behave as authoritarians. Let us further assume that we have selected and trained a sufficient number of democratic and authoritarian leaders for Models A and B so that we have a representative sample of democratic and authoritarian leaders who can be assigned as staff of the two shelter homes. We must then equate the two shelter homes on all other participant and internal and external social process variables. This will leave leadership style the only

TABLE 6-1
THE OUTCOME EQUATION FOR MODELS A AND B, COMPARING
DIFFERENT LEADERSHIP STYLES

Outcome Model A $= P_1^* \dots P_n + IS_{LD}^{**} + IS_2^* \dots IS_n + ES_1^* \dots ES_n$
Outcome Model B $= P_1 \dots P_n + IS_{LA}^{***} + IS_2 \dots IS_n + ES_1 \dots ES_n$

Outcome difference $(A - B) = 0 + IS_{LA}^{**} - IS_{LD}^{***} + 0 + 0$

---

*P is participant.
*IS is internal social processes.
*ES is external social processes.
**IS_{LD} refers to authoritarian leadership.
***IS_{LA} refers to democratic leadership.

resulting difference between the two shelter homes. If we can accomplish this equation, we are in a strong logical position to attribute differences in the two homes' effectiveness to the leadership style. Thus, to evaluate the effectiveness of the variable of interest (leadership style), we equate both of the programs on *all other* variables. This takes the form of the following two equations as shown in Table 6-1.

The equation shows us that the outcome difference between the two types of shelter homes is a function of leadership difference ($IS_{LA} - IS_{LD}$) since all other participant and social situational variables apply equally in both Models A and B and are thus logically equated.

APPLICATION OF THE LOGIC OF EXPERIMENTAL DESIGNS

The absolute equality of two comparative models is rarely achieved in practice (Radnor, Feller, and Rogers, 1978; Davidson et al., 1983), but since it is the logic upon which experimentation is founded the closer we are to equality the more accurate are the inferences we can make from the results (Judd and Kenney, 1981). Thus, while absolute control and equality of extraneous participant and social situation variables may never occur in an actual field experiment, it is logically necessary to account for the contribution of each and every variable. For this reason, attention to all potential contributors to differential effectiveness must become the focal point of any adequate field experimental design. Unlike laboratory experiments, variables cannot be eliminated in field experiments by constructing an artificial environment where they do not exist. In fact, the purpose of most laboratory settings is to eliminate sources of variability which are not of central interest to the scientist. Since other extraneous variables cannot be "walled out" in field work, particular attention to the variables presented in Tables 3-1, 3-2, and 3-3 is essential in creating an experimental design. In addition, measurement of such variables, a topic which will receive considerable attention in future chapters, is a critical strategy for examining the equality and impact of such variables on model outcomes.

There are four domains of control which must be of primary concern in designing field experiments. These are the sampling of participants, their assignment to experimental conditions, the internal equating of experimental conditions, and the external equating of experimental conditions.

Sampling Participants: Randomness and Representativeness

The discussion presented here will treat participants as if they are individuals. Even though individuals are the focus of social interventions, the reader should keep in mind that *any* level of human behavior may be the focus of such experiments (Kelly, 1971; Rappaport, 1977; Davidson et al., 1983)— groups, organizations, or cultures. For purposes of consistency, language will be used here which indicates that the unit of analysis is individuals, but groups, organizations, or cultures could readily be substituted for individuals as the unit of analysis.

Elsewhere, Fairweather and Tornatzky (1977) have discussed participant sampling in the following manner:

> At any given moment a certain number of people experience a particular social problem in a society. The total number of individuals in the society who are victimized by a given problem represents the *population* for that social problem. Thus, for example, there are certain number of people who are chronically mentally ill, socially deprived, school drop-outs and other marginal persons in the entire country who are participants in its many social problems at any one particular time. These populations overlap and change from moment to moment as the result of several variables, such as population increases, economic conditions, and changing attitudes. Because the social innovative experimenters wish to establish social models that have *general* applicability, they attempt to select from the total problem population a sample that is representative of it.
>
> A sample that is to be representative of those individuals experiencing a given social problem—one that yields valid information about the effects of a social model in solving the social problem for the population—*must be selected at random.* To attain randomness, the experimenters must exercise no choice about the selection of individuals within the framework of the sampling procedures chosen. Exercising such a choice makes useless the probability tables from which inferences about the effectiveness of the social models will later be made. It is easy for socially innovative experimentalists to ignore the principle of random selection because random samples are often difficult to attain. Such difficulties are particularly pronounced when the research is completed in institutional settings, since appropriate sampling procedures require institutional commitments to new solutions for their problems. Experimental necessities for innovative solutions are quite often in conflict with existing institutional norms. Nonetheless, the experimentalists must strive for random selection although even with perfect cooperation—a condition rarely achieved—it is doubtful that randomness ever occurs in naturalistic settings (pp. 169–176).

Concerning random selection under field conditions, Snedecor and Cochran (1981, pp. 7–8) state:

> Randomness in sampling is perhaps never quite attained in practice. It is neverthe-

less the mathematical model on which most statistical theory rests, and since the theory must be used in drawing conclusions from work-a-day samplings, it is to the interest of the investigator to approximate, as closely as feasible, the ideal conditions. The better the approximation, the more nearly correct will be the inferences drawn.

The selection of the social problem is the first step in determining the population with which the experimenter is concerned. For example, if the experimenter chooses to study the effects of heterogeneous and homogeneous (track system) groupings of students upon academic achievement, the population has been limited to students. It may then be decided that the effects of these different group compositions on the performance of elementary school students is of the most interest. And then later there may be concern only with elementary students in suburbs around large urban communities where middle-class and upper-middle-class families reside. Subsequent data might show that homogeneous and heterogeneous groupings occur most frequently in these settings and they are a continuous source of difficulty there. The problem therefore has immediately limited and defined the population with which the experimenters must be concerned. In turn, the researchers have also limited the inferences from the results of the experiment to this selected population, a matter discussed more fully in Chapter 10.

To select a sample which meets the demands of representativeness, it is necessary, after problem selection, to define the characteristics of the population which will provide the participant sample. The experimenter defines the population by describing its attributes. The distribution of age, socioeconomic status, health, educational level, and other demographic information of the members of the problem group along with behavior and biological characteristics needs to be known (see Table 3-2). These attributes define the population.

Assigning Participants to Conditions: Matching and Stratifying

There are two techniques that are most frequently used in equating the participants. These techniques permit the experimentalist to either rule out the effects of participant variables that are not being varied or to look for differences in subgroups of participants. The formula presented in the last section showing the leadership difference in outcome between Models A and B is dependent upon equating the participants in the two models. This can be accomplished by *matching* participants and creating matched pairs *prior* to random assignment. In this case, scores on participant variables mentioned in Table 3-2 are given to each participant in the sample and then persons matched on those variables are randomly assigned to Model A and Model B. These matched pairs (if equated on such variables as socioeconomic status, age, race, to name a few of those listed in Table 3-2) theoretically should provide a relatively equivalent representative sample from the problem population who can then randomly be assigned to the two models. Thus, one means of controlling participant variation is to match persons on demographic background information *before* the experiment and then assign the matches by random sampling procedures to the experimental models so that the model samples are theoretically equivalent.

On the other hand it is sometimes important to keep some participant differences so that the model outcomes can be ascertained for different participant groups, such as those of different ages, racial groupings, and so on. For example, we might be interested in the two previous experimental leadership models' effects on two different age groups—e.g., under and over 30 years of age. This can be accomplished by randomly assigning to each model an equivalent number of persons above and below 30 years of age. If this occurred, the two leadership models (authoritarian and democratic) would be *stratified* on the basis of an age stratum—those above and those below 30 years of age.

Matching participant variables to equate the effects of participants on model outcomes, or stratifying participant variables to be able to attribute outcomes not only to model differences but also to participant characteristics, can be achieved by proper planning while designing the experiment.

Equating Experimental Models: Internal Social Process Variables

Reference to Table 3-3 shows a large number of internal social process variables listed under the headings of organizational components, group dynamics, fiscal processes, and membership. In the models discussed earlier (Model A contrasted with Model B), the one internal social process varied was leadership style (democratic contrasted with authoritarian leadership). If leadership style is the only process varied and if participant variables are matched so that representative samples of equated individuals participate in each of the models (A and B), then it is also necessary that each of the social models have equivalent internal social processes, except leadership style. To accomplish this, both models need to have the *same* organizational components, group dynamics, fiscal processes, and membership. Thus, as explained in the equation presented in Table 6-1, all internal social processes except the one varied—leadership—will need to be common to both social models. For example, take size as an organizational component. Both will have to be the same size (e.g., twenty persons per shelter home). Or consider the reinforcement component and group dynamics as a second example. Both models must have the same reinforcement system for performance (e.g., group rewards). A third example from fiscal processes could be rate of pay, which would need to be equivalent for both models (e.g., hourly wage rate). And finally, from the fourth category, membership, both models would have equivalent membership requirements (e.g., members could enter and leave at will). The perceptive student can readily see that a considerable amount of planning time will be consumed in equating programs for internal social processes. Nonetheless, this equating process needs to be carried out because it permits scientists to make accurate inferences when evaluation occurs (Chapter 10).

Equating Experimental Models: External Social Process Variables

The formula presented in Table 6-1 also shows that for Models A and B to vary only on authoritarian and democratic leadership styles, as in the earlier example, the models will have to be implanted where the external social environment is equated. Reference to Table 3-3 shows that social climate, socio-economic indicators, measurement obtrusiveness, geographic location, folk-ways and mores, publicity and media exposure, relations to other organizations, legal constraints, and time are the external social situational variables that require equating. Again, if we want to compare Models A and B and attribute the observed outcomes to leadership style, the social models must be placed in environments where external social variables are equivalent. Thus, both should be implanted in the same social climate and geographic location, both should be established under the same socioeconomic conditions, both should have equivalent measurement procedures, equivalent folkways, and exposure to publicity and the media, equivalent relationships to other organizations, the same legal constraints, and both should start and terminate at the same time.

The control of external social process variables requires a great deal of planning. Some external forces are easier to control than others. Determining equivalent social climates in different geographic areas requires extensive planning. By contrast, the control for time simply requires that the innovative and control models open and close on the same dates. Tryon (1967) created scales from census data that can be used to score different geographic areas for social climate. Using his index, equivalent scores for innovative and control models' geographic locations indicate social climate equivalency. Severy, Houlden, and Wilmoth (1982) created an instrument to predict model acceptance in the local environment. Different geographic areas can be equated on these scores for model equivalence of community acceptance of the implants.

Some physical distance between models needs to be maintained to prevent participant interactions that could contaminate results. Here, the experimenter should consider the use of different floors of the same building, if all models are located there, using different entrances and exits for the different model's participants; different areas of a city equated on Tryon's social index scores can be used to equate models on external social climate while keeping model participants from interacting. Planned properly, different cell blocks in the same prison, wards in a hospital, or classrooms in a university can be used to maintain geographic equivalence while, at the same time, they can be located in areas where little or no participant interaction is likely to occur. Publicity is usually controlled by "keeping a low profile" while the experiment is in process. During this time publicity is discouraged, usually through discussions and agreements with the press and other interested parties. In this way, the dates of the release of information can be controlled so that they do not interfere with the experiment. To control assessment equivalence and obtrusiveness, the same measuring techniques need to be used for all models (equivalence) and made as much a part of the ongoing programs as possible (unobtrusive). Thus, work behavior can be assessed by routine checklists used as an ongoing part of each job, cost-effectiveness by commonly used bookkeeping techniques, and so on.

What we have attempted to convey to the reader here is that the planning for a naturalistic experiment must be extensive and thorough and involves a large number of participant and social situational variables. Needless to say, each moment of time devoted to planning will be well repaid when inferences are attempted. Of course, it is possible that upon occasion some of the variables mentioned in Tables 3-2 and 3-3 cannot be controlled or, if they are controlled in the beginning, become uncontrolled through inadvertent events during the course of the experiment. The possibility of such an occurrence makes longitudinal measurement of internal and external social process variables critical. Even though theoretically equated, it is important that such variables continue to be measured throughout the experimental life of the models so that they can later be correlated with the outcomes. An examination of their relationship to outcome effectiveness can then be accomplished (Judd and Kenney, 1981).

Although planning an experimental design is inherently difficult, these time-consuming research activities are justified because only with adequate planning and effort can experiments conducted in real-life settings permit accurate inferences about the future. Occasionally, an experimentalist will declare that field experiments cannot be accomplished and that, therefore, it is foolish to try to control any variables since all variables cannot be totally and completely controlled. What is overlooked in such a logical position is that the statement applies to all experiments, field and laboratory alike. There are many times in highly controlled laboratory experiments where a slight temperature change, a minor illumination change, observing animal behavior at different moments in time (for example, 9:00 for one experimental group and 9:30 for another), or the expectancies of the experimenter affect the results (Rosenthal and Rubin, 1978) and therefore prevent *total* control. In other field researches such as those in agriculture, rain, sun, and other uncontrolled variables may influence differently crop growth on some experimental plots. Nonetheless, generalizations from such experiments are often valid. The truth is that the closer we approximate the probabalistic logic based upon randomness and experimental control, the more accurate are the inferences we can make from the probability tables—usually located in the back of statistical textbooks that researchers inevitably must use. Ignoring such research planning simply makes the inferences made from these tables of significance (that have been computed on theoretically accurate probabilities) that much more inaccurate. Therefore, the closer we come to obtaining representativeness in sampling and in controlling extraneous variables in field experiments, the more likely we are to make valid inferences from the results. This will become clearer in Chapter 10.

While this review of the experimental logic of field experiments has been very brief, it is our hope that the reader has understood its general nature. For a more complete review of sampling and making research conditions comparable, the reader is referred to Fairweather and Tornatzky (1977, pp. 124–200).

TYPES OF DESIGNS

There are a wide assortment of designs that can be used in field settings. A general discussion of a large number of them can be found in Fairweather and Tornatzky (1977), Campbell and Stanley (1967), and Cook and Campbell (1979). However, there are a few experimental designs that recur over and over in field research which present a picture of the types of designs that are very useful in field settings. The complexity of designs is ordinarily limited by the logistics involved in creating new programs, implanting them in the community, finding appropriate service and research personnel, and the like. Therefore, extremely complex designs, as one might find in traditional statistical textbooks such as Winer (1971) and Snedecor and Cochran (1981), are often not extremely helpful in field research.

A cursory examination of the most often used experimental designs reveals that they fall under three categories. Here, for ease of reading they will be called simple designs, complex designs, and the simple and complex designs carried out over time. Let us explore each of these in turn.

Simple Designs with One, Two, and Three or More Levels

Simple designs with one level are used when two models are compared without attempting to evaluate experimentally the impact of any other variable. For example, Model B of authoritarian-led shelter homes contrasted with Model A, democratically led shelter homes, with all other variables controlled would be an example of a simple one-level design. If the simple design just mentioned (Models A and B) also includes a second dimension, for example two levels of age (above and below 30 years of age), we would then have a *simple two-level* design. Each experimental condition (Model A or B) occurs at two levels (age over 30 versus age under 30). If we were to compare Models A and B (democratic contrasted with authoritarian leadership) for more than two levels, for example, five age levels—10–20, 20–30, 30–40, 40–50, 50 and over—we would then have a *simple, five-level* design. Simple designs of this kind are the most common in community experimentation because they keep to a minimum the logistic difficulty in fielding experiments. They only require construction, operation, and measurement of two social models. Figure 6-1 presents the three models just mentioned.

Complex Designs with One, Two, and Three or More Levels

Complex designs occur when three or more models are simultaneously compared. Assuming that another leadership condition is added, for example,

Simple, one-level

MODELS

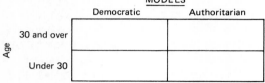

Simple, two-level

MODELS

Simple, three or more levels

MODELS

FIGURE 6-1
Simple designs with different levels.

"naturally emerging leadership," to the authoritarian and democratic models, there would then be three models to evaluate and the experimenter therefore has a complex design. Any design comprised of three or more models is a complex design. If three or more models are used and compared for different participant characteristics (for example, age levels as shown in Figure 6-1), then a complex design with different levels is used. Examples are presented in Figure 6-2.

Simple and Complex Designs Over Time

Simple and complex designs can be repeated over time and are known as time-trend or repeated measures designs. In some designs two time periods are evaluated. In such cases, measures are usually taken before the social intervention starts and after it is terminated. Such evaluations usually are applicable to

Complex design with one level

Leadership

Democratic	Authoritarian	Naturally emerging

Complex design with two levels

Leadership

	Democratic	Authoritarian	Naturally emerging
Over 30 years of age			
Under 30 years of age			

Complex design with five levels

Leadership

Age	Democratic	Authoritarian	Naturally emerging
10–20			
21–30			
31–40			
41–50			
50+			

FIGURE 6-2
Complex designs comparing authoritarian, democratic, and no designated leadership models with one, two, and five levels.

either simple or complex designs of all levels. A simple two-time measure (pre- and post-design) can be seen in Figure 6-3.

A simple or complex design of any number of levels can also be subject to periodic evaluations over a time span. In addition to model and strata comparisons, these simple or complex designs reveal time trends. For example, suppose that the complex design of authoritarian, democratic, and naturally emerging leadership models (A, B, and C) were measured every 180 days for 2½ years. This would give us the same design repeated five times as shown in Figure 6-4 and would yield model, age, and time comparisons.

There are many and varied types of designs. What we have presented here are the most commonly used designs in field experimentation. Let us now turn to some examples of experimental designs used in actual field experiments.

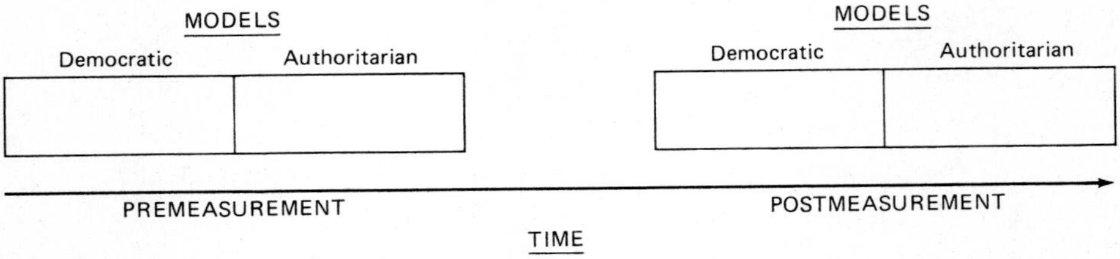

MODELS
Democratic
Authoritarian
MODELS
Democratic
Authoritarian
PREMEASUREMENT
POSTMEASUREMENT
TIME

FIGURE 6-3
A simple one-level design over time.

EXAMPLES OF SIMPLE, COMPLEX, AND TIME-TREND DESIGNS

The following are examples of designs that were established to investigate the problems identified and planned in Chapters 4 and 5. It would be beyond the scope of this book to discuss all the processes that were involved in creating the following designs. However, all experimental designs presented required the random assignment of individuals to the different models and the control of extraneous variables. As mentioned earlier, random assignment is one way of attempting to control extraneous or biased outcomes due to differences in participants. In addition, several of the following designs used preexperimental participant matching or stratification processes to further reduce variability introduced by the participants in the programs. The internal and external social processes were accounted for in the manner described in the preceding sections to eliminate or identify undesirable effects. When it was impossible to equate each model on every internal process mentioned in Table 3-3 these variables were monitored throughout the research so their effects could later be evaluated through correlative techniques (Judd and Kenney, 1981). External social situational variables were typically accounted for by locating the programs in similar (or the same) organizations, in similar locations—often the same buildings or in the same geographic areas. All were placed geographically

FIGURE 6-4
A complex two-level design over time.

MODELS
D = Democratic
A = Authoritarian
N = Naturally Emerging
LEVELS
30 years of age and over
Under 30 years of age
D A N
30 and over
Under 30
First measurement
Second measurement
Third measurement
Fourth measurement
Fifth measurement
TIME

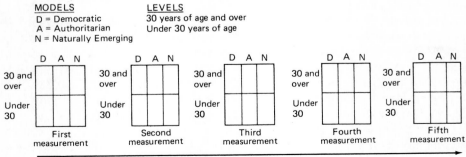

so that interaction of participants in the different models did not occur. All were started and terminated on the same dates to eliminate differential time effects. While the following examples do not represent all possible types of designs, they do offer a sample of commonly used designs.

Citizen Participation in Health Planning: Simple Design, One-Level, Time-Trend

It will be recalled that Beck (1973) had found that the citizens who were users of health services rarely actively participated in meetings where it was their responsibility along with health providers to make final decisions about the health services in their community. Rather, she found that the decisions were made by the health service providers with the citizens playing little role in the decision processes. Accordingly, she designed an experiment to find out what would happen if participants were trained in group decision-making processes prior to their participation in the meetings. To accomplish this, she established one model that she called the "autonomously trained consumer support group" and another model that she called the "traditional participant group." The participants in both of these models later engaged in a decision-making group with the health providers in which they were observed and a record made of the differences that existed in the decision-making meetings of the two differently trained groups. (See Figure 6-5.) In discussing the design of her experiment she described the two conditions as follows:

Traditional Participant Model

After being selected by a (random) sampling procedure, the comparison group had no further systematic intervention into their activities. They continued whatever degree and style of participation they had become accustomed to in whatever activities were available to consumers in the agency. This usually consisted of one committee or Board of Trustees meeting monthly. They were usually notified of these in

FIGURE 6-5
Beck's citizen participation experiment (simple one-level, time-trend design).

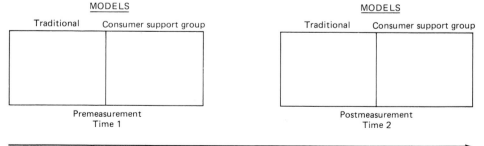

advance by mail with an RSVP card enclosed. No special measures were taken to insure their attendance. The only information they usually received was the standard packet of materials relating to matters on the next meeting agenda. These were generally copies of proposals to be acted upon but without any analytic explanation. They received no systematic help to encourage the quantity or legitimacy of their participation, either in the meeting conversation itself or in extra-meeting activites. Those who attended agency meetings generally arrived immediately before meetings, left immediately after and did not meet or talk with other consumers or providers between meetings.

They had contact with the training group members only when they attended the same agency meetings (used for experimental measurement) or when training group members contacted them for information or assistance. Contact at meetings generally occurred during the meeting proper and therefore was usually relative to the meeting topic. Contact outside of meetings was infrequent, averaging less than once per month (pp. 56–57).

Autonomously Trained Consumer Support Model (CSG)

After being selected by the random sampling procedure . . . the training group participated in the experimental program which consisted of three major phases—each of four meetings held biweekly. Phase I meetings were generally conducted in the format of a consumer workshop model. The staff coordinator actively led the group, transmitted health planning information and promoted the legitimacy of consumer participation in comprehensive health planning. The coordinator also actively promoted the development of group autonomy. Meetings were temporarily spaced to allow for the group experience acquired in one meeting to be practiced between meetings and subsequently reinforced. The emphasis of the first two meetings was on initiation of the program and group formation rather than information. While group development was still important in the last two meetings in Phase I, increased emphasis was given to task-related information. Throughout all Phase I meetings, the coordinator actively promoted the legitimacy of consumer participation where possible and reinforced conversation and behavior related to consumer legitimacy.

Phase II generally followed a developing autonomy format in which the staff coordinator assumed the role of reactor rather than initiator. She responded only with specific information requested directly by participants and only reinforced comments and behavior leading toward increased group autonomy and consumer legitimacy. During this period the members themselves assumed leadership of the group, developed their own mechanisms for further group development, began making contacts with relevant people outside of the meetings, generated information for themselves, and promoted the legitimacy of their own participation as consumers and of that of all the consumers in the agency. In the first two meetings of this phase, information exchange centered primarily around "what" questions, i.e., information relevant to specific task content. In the last two meetings the focus switched to "how" questions, i.e., information utilization through participation skills. In the first two meetings group development activities were still centered around group leadership change. In the last two meetings the focus changed with group productivity becoming more important.

Phase III generally followed an attained autonomy format. The staff coordinator had withdrawn completely from the group and the members now operated as a self-sustaining autonomous group. In addition to functioning independently of project staff, the group also displayed a strong cohesiveness, group identity, and awareness of the goals of the group itself (pp. 27–29).

Jobs for the Elderly: Simple Design, One-Level, Time-Trend

The reader will recall from Chapters 4 and 5 that Gray (1980) was concerned about the general disuse of elderly people in our society. He accordingly attempted to create a social model that would improve employment for those elderly persons wishing to obtain employment. (See Figure 6-6.) Gray described the two social models in the following manner:

Information and Referral Model

Before Older Worker-Retiree Employment Service (OWRES) began assisting older job seekers, several agencies were already attempting to assist older individuals to find employment. The Michigan Employment Security Commission's (MESC) Job-Service had an older worker specialist in their local office. The older worker specialist's role developed out of the Referral Employment Network for Elderly Workers (RENEW) program begun in Michigan and four other states. Essentially, the program uses trained older individuals as interviewers and job developers for older workers (45+) within a local state employment office. The program is intended to facilitate the placement of older workers and has been described in recent publications (Anderson and Fine, 1978; Stacknik and Stoffelmayer, 1981). In addition, several agencies offered employment to older individuals whose income fell below poverty level.

Since an innovative social model's utility is best gauged by comparison to normally available services . . . (Fairweather and Tornatzky, 1977), Control Participants were provided information about and a written referral to the above-named programs. This referral was included in the sealed envelope each participant received immediately following the premeasure assessment. It detailed who to see at the agency, how to get in touch and a target date for making that contact (which coin-

FIGURE 6-6
Gray's evaluation of two programs to create jobs for the unemployed elderly (simple one-level, time-trend design).

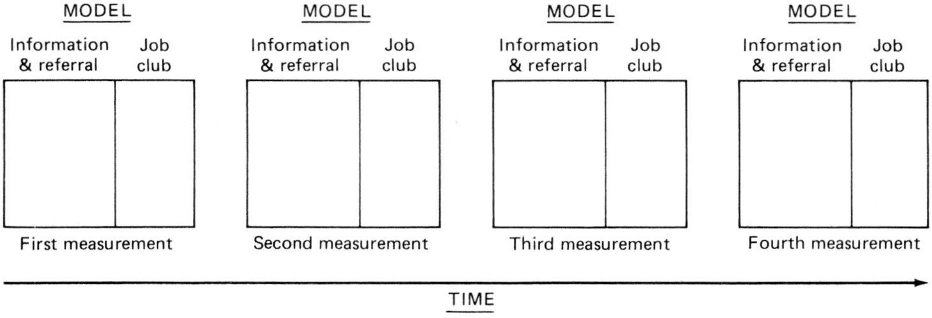

MODEL		MODEL		MODEL		MODEL	
Information & referral	Job club	Information & referral	Job club	Information & referral	Job club	Information & referral	Job club
First measurement		Second measurement		Third measurement		Fourth measurement	

TIME

cided with the start of the Job Club program). It also made it explicit that the individual would receive all future job finding assistance from these agencies and that the interviewer was not a service provider but a member of the research staff (pp. 56–57).

Job Club Model

Individuals assigned to the job club were notified in the same fashion as Information and Referral participants; after the premeasure interview, they were given a sealed envelope with a written referral and instructions on how to use their assigned program . . . a number of factors including job-seeking knowledge, skillfulness and the performance of job search activities all appear to play important roles in successful job search efforts. The job club attempted to systematically facilitate client performance in all of these areas. To achieve this, participants attended a one-day Job Club Workshop and an ongoing series of biweekly Job Club meetings. The Job Club Workshop served the following functions: orientation, education and skill training. The biweekly Job Club meetings, in addition to serving education and training functions, also serve as a support group and a task-oriented laboratory for actual job search activities.

The introductory workshop occurred on a Friday in a large meeting room at the AAA office. The workshop lasted approximately five hours including a free lunch break. The workshop was led by the Job Club trainer who was assisted by the Job Club employment specialist.

A variety of training methods and technologies were used during the workshop meeting. Participants were given a "Job Club Training and Resource Manual" which contained copies of forms and resource materials covered during the meeting. At the beginning of the workshop, members of the OWRJC were asked to participate in a "consciousness-raising" discussion of problems and advantages of becoming an older job seeker. A discussion paper was used to suggest areas for discussion. The paper ends on a very positive note describing reasons many employers give for preferring older workers and gives a short thumbnail sketch of recent Job Club members and the jobs they found.

The remainder of the morning sessions were instructional or discussion-oriented, covering the background of the program, how the program worked, membership agreements and goal setting procedures. After a lunch break, members attended instructional sessions on job lead sources and a goal setting exercise focused on obtaining job leads. This concluded the first day workshop. Materials used in all these procedures were contained in the Job Club Training and Resource Manual. . . .

The ongoing Job Club meetings followed a standard and rather simple format. The meetings occurred every Tuesday and Thursday afternoon beginning at 1:00. The meetings began with a review of goals set by members at previous meetings. Both Azrin (1978) and Pumo, Sehl, and Cogna (1966) used a similar procedure. Since positive mutual support was a rule of the Job Club, the job search goal completion was acknowledged and reinforced. If need be, this was modeled by the Job Club trainer and employment specialist. Within the context of the goal review, discussions and task-oriented problem solving occurred. The trainer facilitated group participation by using appropriate group discussion leader techniques (Fry, 1978).

If all training modules had been covered, the next part of the session was used for structured job search activities. Members were given available resources (i.e., historical job leads list, job openings called into OWRES, newspapers, telephone books, etc.). A unique and sometimes productive resource was job leads obtained from a public bulletin board at Michigan State University. The Job Club trainer copied these job leads and distributed them at the biweekly Job Club meetings. Members were encouraged to use telephones in the meeting rooms to pursue and follow-up job leads immediately. In addition, training related needs which surfaced during a meeting (for instance, someone has an upcoming interview) were handled by repeating a given module, having a member go over materials or by simply pairing off a less competent member with someone more skilled in that area, the so-called "buddy system" (pp. 57–60).

Poor Readers: Simple Design, Two-Levels, Time-Trend

It will be recalled that Tucker (1974) was concerned about poor readers, particularly those who had grown up in black communities. It was his belief that through "associative bridging" he could use the language learned in the first few years of life to help students learn standard English. To adequately measure changes over time, he used the pre- and post-, time-trend design described in the last section. Tucker was also interested in the differential effects that treatment programs might have on racial groupings so he stratified (two levels) his sample into black and white student groups. He measured participants prior to the onset of the experiment and at the termination of the experiment. (See Figure 6-7.)

To test associative bridging Tucker created a series of stories in black dialect and translated them into equivalent standard English. He also created a series of comprehension tests written in black dialect as well as standard English. Then for 1 hour each day during the regular school period the groups randomly assigned to the two models read the stories. Participants in the associative bridging model spent exactly the same time reading as those in the traditional model, but their time was spent in first reading a story in black dialect and answering comprehension questions in the dialect, and then reading the story

FIGURE 6-7
Tucker's comparison of standard English and associative bridging learning models for poor readers (simple two-level, time-trend design).

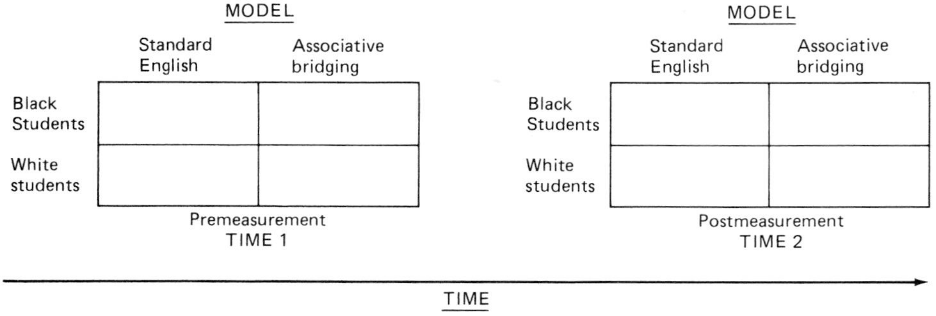

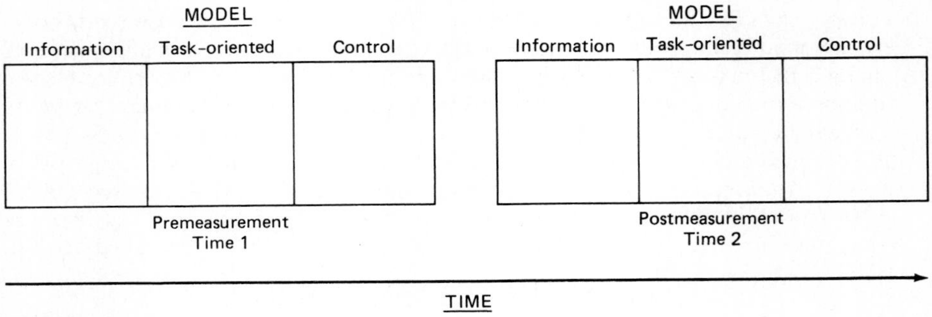

MODEL

Information	Task-oriented	Control

Premeasurement
Time 1

MODEL

Information	Task-oriented	Control

Postmeasurement
Time 2

TIME

FIGURE 6-8
Leedom's models created to reduce energy depletion (complex one-level, time-trend design).

in standard English and answering comprehensive questions in standard English. Those in the traditional model spent an equivalent amount of time but read the stories *only* in standard English and answered questions *only* in standard English.

Energy Depletion: Complex Design, One-Level, Time-Trend

The reader will also recall from discussions in Chapters 4 and 5 that Leedom (1980) carried out an experiment in which she attempted to evaluate the effects of different types of energy conservation training programs for children. (See Figure 6-8.) Nine schools were involved in the experiment, and students were randomly assigned to three different models established to persuade and train them to adopt energy-conserving activities. She described the three conditions in the following manner:

The Information [Model]

The information [model] consisted of the training workshop. . . . At [the] workshop, students received information on the United States energy situation in the form of films, lectures, and printed materials. They also participated in values clarification exercises related to their own energy beliefs and other exercises designed to increase their awareness of energy use. . . . (p. 36).

The Task-Oriented [Model]

The task-oriented [model] consisted of an optional homework assignment to be completed by students. . . . Students were asked if they would be willing to participate in a two-week energy conservation project. They were told that it would be necessary for them to keep track of their family's energy usage during that time by reading their electric and natural gas meters (or fuel or oil propane gauges, if applicable) on three separate occasions. It was explained how they would use these meter readings to compare a "baseline" week of family use when there was no attempt to conserve energy to a second week when they made an intensive effort to reduce the family's energy consumption. Emphasis was given to the fact that during the second week a major effort to conserve would be required and the entire family's cooperation would be needed (pp. 36–37).

The Control [Model]

The control [model] received no treatment of any type. The study was introduced to these students during a personal visit to each control school by the experimenter. At that time, the concept of a control group was explained to them, and they were given the same general description of the study as the [other two models] (p. 38).

Smoking and Health: Complex Design, Two-Level, Time-Trend

Coelho (1983) attempted to compare one commonly used program designed to stop smoking, a new innovative model, and a control model. He was concerned that, as suggested in some scientific literature, there might be differences between men and women in their behavior when attempting to stop smoking. He therefore created a two-level design. The program was evaluated every week for a 3-month period. Thus, the design is a complex, two-level, time-trend design. Coelho (1983) describes the three programs in the following manner:

American Lung Association Clinic [Model]

The ALA stop smoking [model] entitled "Freedom from Smoking" is based on the philosophy that smoking is a learned habit. Quitting becomes a conscious process of un-learning the habit; substituting in its place a more healthy way of living. The program offers a step-by-step reduction plan for quitting. The first phase focuses on the health consequences of smoking and offers various techniques and methods to help individuals, within a supportive group atmosphere, to gain control of their habit. At the end of this phase, smokers are asked to quit on a specified date. Phase two begins after the "quit date" and the focus of the meetings is [on] the benefits of quitting. The program utilizes films, lectures, self-recording, relaxation tapes, group support and self-enforced contingency contracts.

Innovative [Model]

The innovative model is an extension of a model proposed by Stacknik and Stoffelmayer (1981). They postulate that the most powerful relevant social influence procedures for the alteration of smoking behavior are: (1) group support and group pressure; (2) feedback through self-monitoring or surveillance by others; (3) social reinforcement from a relevant social environment; and (4) the arrangement of contingency contracts which involve reasonable amounts of money.

The proposed model is conducted in two phases. Phase one focuses on getting the smoker to quit. Through group discussion, selected films, and guest lectures, the

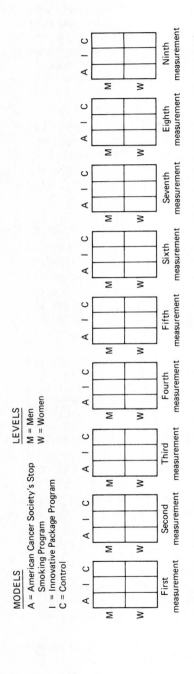

FIGURE 6-9
Coelho's experiment to stop cigarette smoking (complex two-level, time-trend design).

smoker is given an opportunity to develop a strategy to stop. Members of the group are each required to deposit a sum of money with its return contingent upon their smoking behavior during phase two. Contracts are signed by each participant and mailed to "significant others" stating the participants' pledge not to smoke and giving program staff permission to check with each recipient about the participant's smoking behavior. Phase two of the program is not concerned with smoking as such, but the benefits of a generally healthy lifestyle. This is aided by guest lectures, films, and group discussion centered around participants' lifestyles.

Control Model

Persons in the normative (control) model received no specific information about stopping smoking. They were subjected, however, to the normal attempts by friends, neighbors, and the media. For their willingness to volunteer, all participants were informed that if they were randomly assigned to this model, they would receive the most effective method resulting from the experiment after the experiment was completed.

Juvenile Delinquency: Complex Design, One-Level, Time-Trend

The creation of an experimental design for examination of the diversion project was at one and the same time both a simple and yet complex process. The basic issue of scientific concern was whether the diversion model was more effective in reducing delinquency than programs of the typical juvenile justice system. As a result, it was necessary to compare directly the official delinquency rates of youths referred to the Adolescent Diversion Project for service with those processed by the juvenile justice system. Further, the critical components of the diversion project were examined to determine causal processes that accounted for any differences observed. This required the creation of several alternative diversion intervention models, all using nonprofessional volunteers, which could be compared with each other and with the normal processes of the juvenile justice system. Thus, several specific models of diversion intervention were created to compare with the typical juvenile court activities.

The first model (action) was a combination of child advocacy (speaking up for the youth's rights) and behavior contracting (signed agreements about selected behaviors). At the time the diversion project was originally designed, advocacy (Davidson and Rapp, 1976) and contracting (Stuart, 1971) had shown promise with the delinquent population. This general intervention was divided into four segments.

1 The first segment involved a volunteer conducting an assessment of the youth's needs in the social areas of family, school, friends, employment, recreational activities, etc.

2 The second segment of the intervention consisted of implementing a planned intervention to meet these needs. This included negotiation and initiation of behavioral contracts between the youth and significant others, collection of additional baseline data on targeted behaviors, selection of a focus for advocacy efforts, and initiation of advocacy efforts to mobilize needed community resources.

3 The focus throughout the intervention was on a sequential problem-solving strategy based upon monitoring the impact of initial contracting and advocacy efforts. This specific feedback loop allowed for an ongoing refinement of intervention strategies and the inclusion of new target behaviors as needed.

4 The final segment of the action intervention involved training the youth and parents for termination.

Throughout the entire process of this model and all others the emphasis was on providing referred youths and their families with the requisite skills for avoiding further official involvement in the juvenile justice system.

The second model is labeled here the "relationship model." It was derived from the interpersonal theory of human behavior (Sullivan, 1953) and the assumptions that interpersonal relationships are the central ingredient in the therapeutic process (Rogers, 1957; Truax and Carkhuff, 1967). This model was designed so that the volunteer established a close interpersonal relationship with the youth as the basis for intervention. The relationhship condition followed the same four sequential components of intervention described in the action model except that the *sole* focus was the interpersonal relationship. The structures of training, supervision, and intervention in the relationship model were identical to those of the action model. Essentially, all variables were held constant in terms of intervention intensity except that the intervention was focused on the relationships themselves.

A third model, aimed at providing a broader intervention focus, is called the "family model." Briefly stated, the family model used the principles of behavioral contracting and advocacy, but only within the context of the family—only family issues, not school or employment issues, were addressed in the context of the intervention. Volunteers in the family model received training and supervision using the same four-tier format and intensity as presented in the relationship model and described in the action model.

One of the critical logical issues in field experimentation involves the extent to which any observed differences may be attributable simply to a specific setting (in this case diversion) and/or the amount of attention the participants receive (in this case attention from a nonprofessional college student). Hence, the fourth model (attention and setting) was designed to provide such an evaluation. The training, supervision, and intervention stages of this model did not provide a specific theory or focus for skill development by the volunteer. Emphasis was given to the "natural" intervention that college student volunteers provided. As such, low-intensity training was provided. The supervisors for this model were drawn from a local volunteer bureau. They designed three introductory lectures as a basis for training volunteers. These orientation sessions covered such general issues as theories of delinquency, history of the problem, and the role of volunteers. No specific intervention modality was provided. Supervision occurred once per month rather than once per week as was the case in the other experimental models. No training manual was developed. Volunteers in this model were required to provide 6 to 8 hours of intervention with referred youths, as were all the volunteers in the other models.

The intended effects of this model were threefold. If the same results were obtained as in the first three models, the effects of the research setting and volunteer attention might account for their outcomes.

The "court model" was a fifth experimental model. It was an attempt to examine the role of organizational settings in producing differential outcomes. It involved a replicate of the action model mentioned earlier, with one significant exception. Following training in all other models, the supervision of volunteers remained with the experimentalists. In the court model *only,* supervision was transferred to the juvenile court. This condition allowed examination of the impact of the intervention setting on program effectiveness.

To compare the effects of diversion programs using nonprofessionals with the juvenile justice system, some youths were randomly assigned back to the court for usual processing. These youths received the same treatment as was received by all youths in the juvenile justice system and constitute the traditional model.

Figure 6-10 provides an overview of the research design employed to evaluate the effectiveness of the juvenile diversion program. It is a six-model, four time-period design, as shown in Figure 6-10.

FIGURE 6-10
Davidson et al.'s complex one-level, time-trend design contrasting alternative diversion models with a traditional model.

MODELS

A = Action
R = Relationship
F = Family
S = Attention and setting
C = Court
T = Traditional

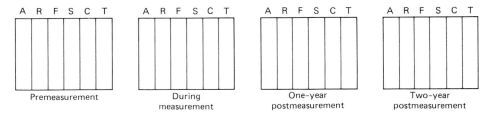

Chronic Mental Illness: Simple Design, Three-Level, Time-Trend

The reader will recall from Chapters 4 and 5 that a new innovation concerning community placement of the chronically mentally ill was deemed necessary from problem identification findings. The creation of the design for that experiment was presented by Fairweather et al. (1969) in the following manner:

> Once the research group was assembled, the research design was put into final form. There were several questions that the experiment was expected to answer which were an outgrowth of the earlier small-group study (Fairweather, 1964). The results from that study suggested that reference groups to which ex-patients could belong might be valuable as a rehabilitative vehicle to bridge the gap between the hospital and the community. But what kind of social situation could be provided the group members that would meet two conditions that the experiment just mentioned indicated are essential if small groups of mental patients are to function effectively—namely, a meaningful task for adult males and a supportive living situation? Clearly such a situation would have to provide employment, because work status is the key status for adult males in American society. At the same time, the previously mentioned study also showed the necessity for providing a supportive living situation for these marginal members of society. After exploring the type of work that was needed in the community where the experiment was to be conducted, it was decided that the most appropriate community situation would be a patient-owned and patient-operated business which was combined with a living situation for the workers. Initially, the available facilities suggested a cafeteria business, but since the geographical area in which the study was to be carried out displayed a high and possibly unfilled demand for janitorial and gardening services, eventually it seemed more appropriate to establish a business that would provide these needed services. Furthermore, a business organization could create a number of jobs that varied in level of social responsibility, thus providing the opportunity for each member to find a job commensurate with his level of adjustment. A group of ex-mental patients living together was expected to provide the needed social and psychological support in the community suggested by the earlier experimental model.
>
> To compare the effectiveness of the new post-hospital community program with the traditional community programs available to mental patients, it was necessary that all participants should have the same hospital treatment program so that any differences that might later be found between these two community programs (work–living and traditional) could be attributed to them and not to differences in hospital treatment. The hospital small-group program presented in an earlier publication (Fairweather, 1964) was selected as the hospital treatment program (pp. 25–27).

The small-group program took place on one ward within the hospital and was administered by a single staff. All patients in the study participated in this program. Thus, the hospital treatment program was the same for everyone in the study. It was the community aspect of the treatment program that was different. By comparing traditional individualized treatment (the staff selected community treatment judged best for the individual, e.g., posthospital psychotherapy, halfway house, etc.) with an innovative community working and living situation, the differential effects these two community situations might

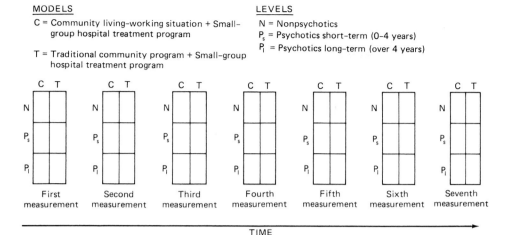

MODELS

C = Community living-working situation + Small-
    group hospital treatment program

T = Traditional community program + Small-group
    hospital treatment program

LEVELS

N = Nonpsychotics
P_s = Psychotics short-term (0-4 years)
P_l = Psychotics long-term (over 4 years)

FIGURE 6-11
Fairweather et al.'s simple three-level, time-trend evaluation of the lodge society contrasted with traditional community treatment programs.

have in reducing chronic hospitalization and improving self-perception could be ascertained.

Finally, earlier studies had shown that neurotic and chronic psychotic patients might respond differently to treatment than those persons who were less chronic (Fairweather, 1960, 1964). For this reason, an experimental design was constructed so that both the effects of posthospital treatment and diagnostic group membership could be evaluated. The final form of the design is presented in Figure 6-11.

THE ROLE OF DESIGNING STUDIES IN COMMUNITY EXPERIMENTATION

This chapter has examined the logic of experimental designs by discussing some common research designs for community experimentation. Several examples of different types of problems and designs have been discussed. In concluding this chapter, it is important to add a further comment about the process of designing community experiments. It is extremely difficult to capture for the reader the dynamic processes involved in the design of community experiments. To describe in writing the interaction of theory, experiential hunches, the prior work of the investigator, and the press of the moment in creating an appropriate design is difficult. As part of the course in which this book is being used, the reader should have the opportunity to begin experiencing the complexity involved in planning the design of community experiments as presented in the accompanying workbook.

Most problems addressed by community researchers lack an extensive history of investigations relevant to problem solution. While previous scientific work may shed some light on important variables for logical inclusion, the most important scientific information may come from researchers' attempts to examine experimentally the efficacy of new social models. In addition to the issues of scientific history, other critical ingredients which contribute to efficacy of an experimental design include issues of measurement and implementation. It is these issues which are the topic of the next two chapters.

CHAPTER 7

MEASUREMENT IN FIELD SETTINGS

Assuming that the tasks outlined in the preceding chapters have been accomplished, the next step in the scientific problem-solving process is to select or create measurement devices. Prior to actually placing the new social innovation in its experimental context in action, assessment procedures for outcomes, participant characteristics, and internal and external social processes need to be selected or developed. All fields of science use measuring techniques of one type or another. Thus, for example, thermometers measure temperature, barometers measure atmospheric pressure, and telescopes measure the heavens. Community experimentation is no different except that it typically requires many assessment techniques. Selecting and/or developing these measurement devices is the topic of this chapter.

GENERAL CHARACTERISTICS OF MEASUREMENT DEVICES

There are at least three ways in which measurement devices can vary. First, assessment devices vary considerably in the extent to which they directly measure a phenomenon. For example, having trained observers count the frequency of "laughing" behavior in a classroom is a relatively direct measure of classroom behavior. Asking the classroom teacher for weekly ratings of laughing behavior to be completed in the teacher's office is an indirect measure. "Directness" is both a characteristic of particular methods of measurement *and* a characteristic of what is being measured (Goldfried and Kent, 1972)— some concepts can only be measured directly and others indirectly. Generally, attitudes, intentions, or expectations of individuals cannot be directly seen, while actual behaviors of individuals are directly observable. As one example, attitudes toward energy conservation cannot be directly observed, but actual electricity use can be directly seen on the user's meter.

Second, measurement devices can also vary in the degree to which they are "passive" observations of a phenomenon rather than "active" interventions (Webb et al., 1981). For example, telescopes have little if any impact on the stars whose light they collect. Similarly, using historical hospitalization information from files about patients should not directly affect current hospitalization rates. On the other hand, entering a family's home three times a week with a video crew to record social interactions may dramatically affect the family's performance. While there is debate over which is the "best" way to proceed, the degree to which measures vary in their "activeness" is considerable. Both the nature of the measurement procedure and the phenomena being measured will contribute to the degree of activeness involved in a particular measurement procedure.

Third, measurement devices vary considerably in the extent to which they are intended to reflect a part of the phenomena in question or whether they reflect all the phenomena. For example, students' academic achievement can be assessed by grades in mathematics, spelling, and other academic areas. On the other hand, a global grade point for all academic areas can be used. It is most important to recognize that the theoretical perspective of the investigator, the form of measurement used, and the nature of the phenomena to be measured all contribute to the degree to which a simple or global measure is used (Wiggins, 1973).

The goals of systematic measurement in the social sciences are fourfold. First, systematic measurement must elevate information collection beyond the level of opinion. Thus, one goal is to make the information collected so accurate that the same conclusion would be reached by many individuals observing the same event. Replicability is at the very core of systematic measurement in field experimentation (Seidman, 1983; McClure et al., 1980). Second, systematic measurement devices serve to codify information into a common language, which enhances the replicability of the information. All measuring devices produce coded information in a standard format so that two or more observers can describe the same event in the same terms. This has the distinct advantage of making information concerning outcomes, participant characteristics, and internal and external social processes more understandable (Wiggins, 1973). Third, measurement devices often produce a specific type of code, namely numbers. Translating the information resulting from observation to numbers allows easy use of resulting data for statistical analyses. Finally, a fourth major goal of measurement devices is to compress information. If data concerning outcomes, participants, and internal and external social processes of social interventions were continuously recorded, particularly in longitudinal field research, an overabundance of information would be produced. Reducing information to manageable terms is one major purpose of assessment devices.

TYPES OF SCALES

When a number of items are placed together in sequence to measure a phenomenon such as anxiety, work performance, and the like, a scale is formed. Usually, each item can yield a different score, from 1 to 5 for example, and the scale score is the sum of these items. There are different types of scales that can be produced by the collected data. While information about scales is covered in considerable detail in most statistics and measurement books (e.g., Winer, 1971; Wiggins, 1973; Hays, 1981), some comment is necessary here since so many different types of scales are used in community experimentation. The type of scale that results from measuring a phenomenon is controlled by the nature of the events being measured and the type of measurement device used. Measurement scales used by community researchers involve all four major types of scales described below.

Nominal Scales

The simplest type of scale produced by a measurement device is a *nominal* or *categorical scale.* This type of scale names or labels places, things, and events and presents information in a dichotomous fashion. Such nominal scales show the presence or absence of a characteristic. They indicate membership in a class, category, or group without specifying any relationship between the classes, categories, or groups. Many demographic variables (e.g., occupation, sex, race) are assessed by using nominal scales. No quantitative or relative position is indicated between such categories except the quality of membership and exclusivity. As such, nominal scales represent the simplest form of coding information.

Ordinal Scales

A second type of scale produced by measurement devices is an *ordinal scale.* Ordinal information adds a level of complexity to the nominal scale. While nominal scales indicate membership and exclusivity, ordinal scales indicate membership, exclusivity, *and* information concerning differences among them. Thus, ordinal scales indicate differences between groups or categories as points on a continuum of a *less than, equal to,* or *more than* quantity. The relative position of groups or points on a continuum are arranged without specifying the actual distance between the points. A typical measurement procedure which produces ordinal data involves ranking procedures. For example, ranking ten classmates from the most to the least popular indicates the relative popularity of the individuals but provides no information about the "popularity distance" between the most popular individual, the second most popular individual, and so on.

Interval Scales

Interval scales go a further step in delineating information. Measurement devices which produce interval data indicate class membership, relative position of the classes, and make assumptions about the distance between the classes. Interval scales specify the distance between any two points on the scale and typically assume equal distances between any two adjacent points on the scale. As with other types of scales, interval scales indicate not only information about the phenomena being assessed but information about the characteristics of the assessment procedure being used. Scales which measure temperature are of the interval type. Specific temperatures are exclusive classes, with each degree occupying a position relative to every other degree and the distance between each degree being equal.

Ratio Scale

The fourth type of scale adds a further refinement to the characteristics of the data. *Ratio scales* satisfy all the qualifications of interval scales (exclusive membership, relative position of classes or points, specified distances between points or groups) and adds the characteristic of an absolute zero point. This means that there is an observable absence of the property measured by the scale *and* this position on the scale is a real zero point. Typical examples of ratio scales include physical measures of mass, velocity, or distance.

Knowledge about the type of scale resulting from the measurement procedures in a community experiment is critical for an accurate interpretation of results. For this reason, particular attention should be given to the type of scale generated by every research instrument.

DATA QUALITY

In addition to the general characteristics of measures and the types of scales they produce, the community researcher needs to be concerned with the *quality* of data generated. Obviously, it is desirable to use measures of high quality and avoid those of questionable quality. But how does the community experimentalist decide what criteria to use in selecting or designing quality measures? Traditionally, the criteria applied to such decisions have been those of reliability and validity. While discussions of reliability and validity have filled many volumes (e.g., Cronbach et al., 1972; Wiggins, 1973; Messick, 1980) and the relative desirability of each is debatable, both are important to the community experimenter (Davidson et al., 1983). Simply stated, the *reliability* of the measure indicates its replicability and reproducibility. The *validity* of a measure traditionally refers to the accuracy of the meaning of the data produced by the measure.

Reliability

The reliability of a measure is a term which can have many meanings, but in general reliability refers to the extent to which a measure would produce replicable results if it were possible to repeat the measurement conditions exactly, i.e., to what extent two independent measurements completed under identical conditions would produce the same results. This is a critical issue for community experiments because data from such experiments may influence social policy decisions. Accordingly, replicability of findings is critical.

There are various types of reliability which interest the community experimenter. The first involves repeating the same measure at a later time and comparing the results. This type of reliability is typically called *test–retest reliability*. By keeping the two administrations of the same instrument relatively close together in time and holding all other conditions constant (same people tested, in the same place, etc.) one would expect that similar data would be produced if the instrument was highly reliable. Similarly, examining the reliability of a measure holding everything constant except the observer or the person administering a questionnaire is traditionally labeled *interobserver agreement* or *interrater reliability*. A third type of reliability examines the consistency of data when using several different items comprising a scale. This is called a scale's *internal consistency*. Internal consistency in one sense is a specific type of test–retest reliability in which each item is viewed as a "test." In such a case, high reliability occurs when item scores remain the same on different administrations of the scale. Essentially, measures which produce highly consistent information when there is minimal variation in the conditions of measurement have good reliability.

Validity

Like reliability, the term *validity* has been given many definitions, ranging from those that are highly empirical to those that are highly theoretical (Campbell and Fiske, 1959). However, in its most global sense, whether or not a measure is valid is determined by whether it accurately measures what it is supposed to measure. Traditionally, types of validity include content, criterion, and construct. *Content validity* is, simply stated, the extent to which a measurement device covers the domain of the phenomena adequately and reasonably. Does a questionnaire addressing job satisfaction appear to reasonably cover the content of job satisfaction *and* include items reflecting the various aspects of job satisfaction? It is generally agreed that all measures must meet content validity standards. *Criterion validity* encompasses several specific methods of examining validity. In general, criterion validity addresses the extent to which a particular measure produces information consistent with a second (or several other) measures of the same phenomena. For example, suppose a physiological index of anxiety (elevated blood pressure, sweating, muscle tenseness, etc.) has been accepted as a "true" measure of anxiety. Other measures such as paper-and-pencil tests of anxiety would need to show a high relationship with this physiological index to be valid measures of anxiety. Classically, then, criterion validity indicates that some "new" measure of a construct produces information consistent with some tried and true or accepted measure.

The community experimenter adds to this list *outcome validity* (Fairweather, 1967). In most situations approached by the community experimenter in trying to solve social problems, there is an outcome variable which is of major social significance (Bachrach, 1982). Examples would include recidivism for criminal populations, rehospitalization for mental patients, energy usage among consumers for energy conservation, etc. Thus, with most human problems there is a criterion which is the society's consensually defined criterion for needed change. From this perspective, the validity of any measure is the extent to which it produces information consistent with this major criterion. Hence, the outcome validity of any other measure used in the course of a social experiment is its relationship to this consensually established criterion.

Consistency

Prior to actually fielding the measures to be used in examining the efficacy and processes of some new social model, each measure needs to be examined and its consistency delineated. This permits the investigator to establish the consistency of measurement procedures prior to conducting the actual study. While there are no hard and fast rules, the next section will provide examples of the techniques usually considered important for each type of measurement device.

METHODS OF MEASUREMENT

There are many types of measurement devices that can be used in community experiments, but only a small number that are used in almost all community experimental settings. This section will briefly describe these *common* types of measurement devices, with comments on the typical format of each type of measurement method and its major characteristics. The community researcher will usually employ most or all of these methods in any community experiment. The types of measurement will be presented in order from the most unstructured to the most structured. Thus, the degree to which the format of the measure controls the responses increases as one proceeds through the list.

Personal Histories, Diaries, Log Notes

The most unstructured methods of gaining information are personal histories, diaries, and research notes. Free responses about the phenomena in question can occur. In most community experiments it is extremely useful to have a running account of events from program staff, participants, and other observers. This method usually involves minimal experimental control of the events or perspectives to be covered. Typically, the staff or participants or both are asked to keep a record of daily events from their own point of view and in their own language (Fairweather and Tornatzky, 1977). The resulting data can be left in narrative form and important trends or events later abstracted by the investigator. Structured formats for coding responses can then be developed. This method is relatively passive in its orientation, and nondirected in its focus. It is hoped that the total population (rather than a selected sample) of events will be captured with this method. While theoretically all types of scales could be applied to such open-ended accounts, verbal summaries are the most often used codification of the data. The primary concern for data quality rests in consistency over time, observer, and method.

Critical Events

Critical event recording refers to the investigator keeping track of important events that occur during the course of the experiment (Goldenberg, 1971). This differs from the previous category in that only critical events are recorded rather than all events. Capturing critical happenings which may affect the course of the social model under investigation or the actual execution of the study itself is the major concern. Such events as staff turnover, difficulty with the assignment and use of research space, the political entanglements involved in operating the social model, and positive or adverse media coverage of the social models under investigation, are all examples of different types of critical events. The critical event record is relatively directed, passive in nature, and focused on reflecting the majority of the intrusive events that occur. Typically, the resulting data are used for descriptive and interpretative purposes only and are not scaled in any particular fashion. Agreement among different members of the investigating team is the most often used source of consistency.

Interviews

Interviews occur when two people sit down and talk to each other about a phenomenon. The interviewer asks the questions and the interviewee responds. Types of questions can vary from the relatively unstructured ("How do you feel?") to the more structured ("Do you feel happy or sad right now?"). Thus, interviews encompass a continuum of methods which range from the totally unstructured, where the interviewer and interviewee have an open-ended conversation about some specified topic(s), to a relatively structured procedure in which the questions asked and acceptable responses are specified in great detail (Wiggins, 1973). The common feature of interviews is that an interviewer presents questions to a respondent and records results in a variety of fashions from descriptions to scaled structured responses. Thus, the interview method can vary in its directedness and its relative activeness, and typically focuses on obtaining a sample of behavior. All types of scales can be used with the resulting information. Most techniques for determining data consistency can be used with interview data.

Archival or Record Data

It often happens that variables of central importance to experimental research are available from archival or record sources (Webb et al., 1981; Sechrest and Belew, 1983). For example, the cost of alternative programs (often of primary concern to social program administrators and policy makers), recidivism, employment, and other social indicators are often available from records or archival sources. The use of such data is called *unobtrusive* because such information is available from sources other than research participants, and no intrusion of the research sample is necessary. Unobtrusive techniques are the most passive methods and involve minimal directedness because the investigator is left with what is available in the records. One major difficulty with this type of method is that often its consistency with other methods and facets of measurement is difficult if not impossible to assess. Since the events in question have already taken place, other methods cannot be applied to assess consistency. Yet archival records often are the only source of critical information available to social model reseachers.

Behavioral Observations

Directly rating behavior typically requires the training of observers to record selected behaviors. Outside observers can be trained to systematically observe a performance of interest as well as staff and participants (Fairweather et al., 1969; Fairweather and Tornatzky, 1977; Wilson and Prentice-Denn, 1981). Behavioral observations usually provide ratings of selected types of behavior, frequencies of the occurrence of types of behavior, and descriptions of social interaction patterns. Typically, behavior observations are passive. They do not require participants to engage in a particular performance, but rather seek to note data occurring "naturally" in the environment. On occasion, observational methods do involve the use of contrived simulated situations (Alexander and Parsons, 1973).

Observational strategies usually require ratings at certain times. The most common rating of reliability for observational data is interrater (or observer) agreement. Other less commonly employed consistency checks include those for time and method. As with most other methods, several commonly used observational ratings exist, such as Bales' social interaction scales (1950), Fairweather's hospital ward behavior ratings (1964), and Cobb's (1972) classroom behavioral instrument.

Structured Paper-and-Pencil Measures

Structured paper-and-pencil measures are the most standardized of the measurement devices discussed here. These measures involve written items which are presented to respondents. They also include several types of available responses, from the relatively unstructured (essay questions) to the highly structured. This category includes such common measures as essay questions, psychological tests, aptitude tests, vocational preference inventories, and attitude questionnaires (Messick, 1980; McReynolds, 1982). The content of such instruments can cover a number of different categories such as personality characteristics, abilities, interests, perceptions, personal preferences, satisfactions, and social or organizational climates. Their administration can focus on the individual, small group, or organization. The types of general information can take the form of any of the scales described earlier. The paper-and-pencil measurement method is usually very directed in its focus and active in its orientation in the sense that an item is presented to the respondent which would not otherwise have been in the environment. It is a method which is almost always used to assess a sample of some domain of interest to the researcher's— anxiety, for example. The paper-and-pencil method of assessment comes from a tradition within psychology which has stressed data reliability and validity more than any other method (Anastasia, 1982). This method also has great popularity due to its relative ease of administration, low cost, and the degree to which easily usable information is produced.

Selecting a Method

The selection of a method of measurement for a program's outcomes and internal or external social processes is very critical in assessing the effectiveness and operation of an innovative social model. Once the variables of interest have been delineated, a measurement method will often emerge as correct for that variable. For example, attitudes are typically assessed through paper-and-pencil measures, classroom behavior is often assessed through behavioral observation methods, and organizational costs are often assessed through archival methods. By selecting a method which has a tradition of measurement use, the knowledge of previous investigators can be used as background experience. Too often methods are selected for their convenience rather than for the extent to which they provide accurate, reliable, and valid information. Investigators should reject this simple course and select the method which will best measure the concept under investigation, recognizing that it is essential that the reliability and validity of the method be established in the new research situation. Usually this results in encouraging the use of multiple methods of assessment (Davidson et al., 1983).

USING EXISTING MEASURES VERSUS DEVELOPING NEW MEASURES

One of the most difficult decisions the community scientist will face involves whether to use existing measures or to construct new measures for the investigation. This is more difficult when the particular human problem has already had extensive investigation and experimentalists are trying to make their experiment comparable with previous research. In such a case, equivalent measures are essential. However, many of the social problems faced by the community scientist will be in areas which do not have a tradition of measurement and, therefore, it is usually necessary for community scientists to develop their own measures for the particular research situation.

When the community scientist is working in an area that has a tradition of scientific investigation and therefore of existing high-quality (i.e., reliable and valid) measures, the investigator has an easy decision to make. More often, however, the situation is one in which several existing measures of unknown quality are available. Under these conditions the investigator must assess the quality of the measure, its practicality in the situation, and the appropriateness of the concept defined in the measure.

There are advantages and disadvantages in using existing measures rather than developing new instruments. The advantages of using existing measures include a savings in the resources that would have to be committed to their development, having data operationally identical to data used in previous investigations, and possibly benefiting from previous work in measurement and administration of the instrument. There are, however, some distinct disadvantages. Existing measures seldom have ideal quality (adequate reliability and validity), often do not fit the concepts of current interest, and may not have been used in an experimental situation identical to the one being considered.

There are some distinct advantages, therefore, in developing measurement procedures for a particular problem, not the least of which is that experimentalists can focus on the exact variables of interest and can establish for themselves the validity and reliability of such measures in the particular research situation. Disadvantages include the cost involved in constructing high-quality measures, the possibility that data quality concerns cannot be completely addressed prior to initiation of the experiment, and the risk that the constructed measures will not be accepted as credible by other investigators, either on face or content validity grounds. Although instrument selection or creation is a complex decision in many experimental situations, investigators should not hesitate to create new valid and reliable measures for investigating a human problem when none exists.

DIMENSIONS OF INTEREST FOR MEASUREMENT

As discussed in Chapter 3, there are four main areas of primary interest to the community experimenter. These are social outcomes, participants, internal social processes, and external social processes. Each is important in conducting community experiments and every community experiment should include an assessment of the relevant variables in each of these four social model functioning domains.

Measuring Outcomes

As mentioned earlier, the *social change outcome* of a social model represents a consensual societal agreement about what the program ought to accomplish to demonstrate effectiveness. For this reason, most social change outcome criteria can be stated in simple behavioral terms. For example, programs aimed at unemployment should include an assessment of employment as an outcome (Fairweather and Tornatzky, 1977); programs aimed at alleviating mental illness would typically include an assessment of psychiatric symptoms as an outcome (Paul, 1981); programs aimed at crime usually include an assessment of recidivism or criminal behavior as a program outcome (Lerman, 1975); programs aimed at energy conservation will typically include actual energy use as a major outcome (Messe and Crano, 1981).

Usually the major social change outcome criterion is a behavior which can be directly measured. Of equal importance is consideration of other major outcomes which should also be measured. For example, researchers concerned with an unemployment program should also be interested in the job satisfaction of employees, type of work obtained and its stability, wages earned, and so forth. These outcomes need to be measured and their relationships to employment as well as to participant characteristics and internal and external social processes examined. Table 7-1 presents a sample of human problems and their typically accepted outcomes.

Participant Characteristics

Since the outcome(s) of any social model can be affected by participants and internal and external social processes, it is important to assess these three

TABLE 7-1
SOME GENERAL AND SPECIFIC OUTCOME CRITERIA IN COMMUNITY EXPERIMENTS

General criteria	Mental health, criminality, delinquency, drug addiction	Education	Poverty, race, urban development
Satisfaction	Recidivism	Academic achievements	Employment
Self-regard	Behavior control	Social adjustments	Living standards
Morale	Employment		Family development
Cost of maintaining model			Integration Housing and living conditions Criminal behavior

dimensions to understand their influence on outcomes. Usually, a personal history of all persons participating in a social model is gained from them prior to participation in the experiment. Historical background information of importance typically includes demographic information such as age, education, employment history, and the like. This information is for sampling purposes (usually for modeling or stratifying) and for later correlations with process and outcome variables. In addition, it is often important to obtain personality, aptitude, and social adjustment measures from participants. Other areas of measurement, such as personal expectancies of the outcomes and attitudes toward other persons and the processes operative in the model, are typically gained from each participant through the use of selected or created scales. In addition, it is not uncommon for behavior ratings to be used to assess individual behavior while participating in the models. Archival records can be used for gaining evidence about the individual, both for correlative purposes and to check the accuracy of the participant's memory. For example, school records (archival data) can be used to check the accuracy of the educational information given by participants in their personal history. All these participant measures are important because of the need to examine the effects that particular individual characteristics might have on the processes and outcomes of any social model.

It is important to recognize here that even though random sampling has occurred, often in the context of modeling or stratifying selected variables, and thus reduced sample differences, it is still possible for randomly assigned participants in the different models to differ on some characteristics unknown at the time of assignment to the models. Thus, the participant characteristics of those involved in each model are often used to find general sample equivalence or difference. This information can play a prominent role in inferences made later when the experiment is completed. Information about sample equivalence or difference in making inferences about model outcomes can be used to check on the validity of the random-sampling procedure, and thus researchers can use it in making inferences from experimental data (Chapter 10).

Internal Social Processes

Another critical area to assess in the functioning of innovative social models is that of internal social processes (Table 3-3), which can be divided into *specific* and *general* internal social processes of the social model in question (Davidson et al., 1983). An example of specific and general internal social processes can be seen when a cooperative energy use group institutes a social model in a high-rise apartment building to control peak load demand for electricity by using an educational group that meets twice weekly. Internal social processes *specific* to this group include knowledge gained from group meetings, communication about energy matters among group members, and energy conservation skills gained by members. There are additional *general* internal social processes, however, which naturally occur whenever groups of individuals assemble. Measurement of group cohesiveness, leadership morale, norms, and social communication are general internal social processes that can occur whenever groups are formed.

Thus, there are specific processes internal to the social model which are theoretically prescribed by the activities inherent in the model, *and* there are also general internal social processes which typically occur in any social model. Both must be monitored if the operation of social models is to be thoroughly understood. By examining the relationships between these internal social process measures and social outcomes it can be ascertained whether there is any relationship among the specific or general processes and observed outcomes (Judd and Kennedy, 1981).

External Social Processes

A final category of processes that can affect social innovations is called *external social processes* (Table 3-3). These are processes and events in the social model's environment which can impinge upon it. The model can in turn affect the environment, thus establishing an interaction effect. As with internal social processes, determining the impact of the social model on the external environment, and its corresponding impact on the model, can be critical to an understanding of observed outcomes. Thus, for example, the social climate of the environment of a selected program might be ascertained by measuring aspects of its location, including the surrounding neighbors' political beliefs; socioeconomic levels; geographic location; area population density; and so on.

As with internal social processes, there will be selected variables that may be directly varied for experimental comparison (number of model linkages to other organizations might be the experimental variable) and there will be events which naturally occur in the environment (state of the economy, for example). Regardless of whether the processes are systematically varied or naturally occur, it is important that the researcher include all measures of external social processes which could theoretically be expected to affect operation of the model.

EXAMPLES OF MEASUREMENT DEVICES

Now that the general characteristics of measuring devices have been described, dimensions of information quality outlined, and types set forth, examples are in order. Consistent with the seven researches which have been presented as examples in previous chapters, one measure from each of the seven studies will be presented in its complete form and the other measures used in each study will be delineated. While this does not provide an exhaustive list of all possible types of measures for all domains of interest to the community researcher, it does provide the reader with a sample of measurement procedures from some actual field experiments.

Citizen Participation in Health Planning

Beck (1973) established two different models to train persons for participation in health decision making. A large number of measures were designed to compare and contrast the two models on the dimensions of outcome as well as their participants and internal and external social processes. The first example chosen from Beck's study is an administrative record often used to measure the conformity and interest of a particular group. The simple measure of attendance gains meaning when it is recognized that in Beck's experiment a person's attendance at a particular meeting was essential for decision making even though attendance was not mandatory.

This measure was thus archival and focused on a specific internal social process within the experimental model and also was an outcome for comparing the two citizen groups. An attendance record was kept by the group leader.

Attendance

Measurement: Attendance records were kept of all meetings for the experimental period. *Scoring:* Average frequency of attendance was calculated for each of the three group phases during the postexperimental period. Percent of attendance was computed for those eligible during each period (p. 57).

Table 7-2 outlines the measures used by Beck to assess outcomes, partici-

---

TABLE 7-2
BECK'S MEASURES

---

1 Outcome measures
   a Attendance (administrative record)
   b Verbal participation in the meeting (observational rating)
   c Perception of influence and power (questionnaire)
   d The degree to which decisions reached in comprehensive health planning were informed or uninformed decisions (observational rating)
   e Knowledge of the health planning agency (questionnaire)
2 Participant measures
   a Personal history (questionnaire measured age, education, socioeconomic status, race, etc.)
3 Internal social process measures
   a Group dynamics
      (1) Types of roles that evolved in the group (observational rating)
      (2) Cohesiveness—person's attraction to the group and group's acceptance of the person (questionnaire)
      (3) Importance of the group role (questionnaire)
      (4) The individual and groups' problem-solving ability (observational rating)
4 External social processes
   Beck attempted to control external social processes by having all individuals in the experimental period participate in the same decision-making group in the same building where behavioral and other direct measures could be made. All participants entered and terminated the experiment on the same dates.

---

pants, and internal social processes. External social processes were equated across the two models by meeting under the same external conditions (Table 7-2). As can be seen from Table 7-2 a variety of measures were used employing several different methods (e.g., archival, questionnaire, and observation). In addition, the personal history of the participants and the models' specific internal social process variables were assessed (e.g., knowledge of health planning) as well as more general variables (e.g., verbal participation in meetings).

Jobs for the Elderly

Gray (1980) created a job club for older workers and retirees and contrasted its effects with those of referral to a state agency charged with responding to unemployment. Table 7-3 shows Gray's measure of the characteristics of incoming participants in his study. The "Premeasure Questionnaire" was completed at intake through an interview process. Essentially, the form outlined in Table 7-3 provided a structure for an interview in which the background information was collected. Gray's measure includes some typical demographic information likely to be found in any participant questionnaire (e.g., age) and some program-specific information (e.g., to what extent is your current income adequate for your needs?).

Table 7-4 lists all the measures used by Gray. Outcome measures were collected through follow-up interviews, and job placement was verified through checking with the appropriate sources (employers, etc.). Assessment of internal social processes included variables which were specific to the environment in question (job search network as well as more general processes such as group cohesiveness). Table 7-4 also shows Gray's attempt to achieve external social situational equivalence.

Poor Readers

Tucker (1974) created two learning situations for a sample which consisted of both black and white students. One was a standard English situation which was contrasted and compared with the associative bridging or bilingual technique of teaching English. To compare the models and racial groups in demographic characteristics, Tucker obtained a personal history on all participants (Table 7-6). Table 7-5 presents a paper-and-pencil questionnaire used by Tucker to assess self-concept. While there are a large number of self-concept measures available, Tucker found it necessary to develop his own due to the inappropriateness of existing measures for his student sample. The self-concept questionnaire was given to students in group settings.

All measures of outcomes are listed in Table 7-6. Reading comprehension was measured by using an available and widely used standard scale, the Gates-MacGinitie test (1969). This allowed Tucker to compare the results of his experiment directly with those of other investigators. The other major focus of the study involved the attitudes of the young people. Measures were developed

TABLE 7-3

OLDER-WORKER RETIREE EMPLOYMENT SERVICE PROJECT PREMEASURE

Interview Date _____
Interviewer _____
Respondent's Name _____
Address _____

Condition: 1. Job Club _____
2. Information and Referral _____
Wave: 1. Premeasure _____

PREMEASURE QUESTIONNAIRE

Q 1	CHECK FROM OBSERVATION Sex	Male ---------------------------------1 Female-------------------------------2
Q 2	CHECK FROM OBSERVATION Race	White ---------------------------------1 Black ----------------------------------2 Spanish------------------------------3 Asian ----------------------------------4 Other (specify) --------------------5

Q 3   Who lives in the household with you?
Do you . . . (READ LIST: CIRCLE ALL THAT APPLY)

	Y	N
Live alone	-1	2
Live with spouse	-1	2
Live with others	-1	2

Q 4   (UNLESS RESPONDENT LIVES ALONE, ASK:)
How many people live in this household?
(COUNT RESPONDENT)

_____
(No. in household)

Q 5   What was the last grade you completed in school?

_____
(Actual grade)

Q 6   What is your occupation? If you are now retired, please tell me your previous occupation (PROBE TO GET EXACT OCCUPATION)

_____
(Occupation)

Q 7   What is your marital status now?

Married ----------------------------1
Divorced----------------------------2
Separated-------------------------3
Widowed ---------------------------4
Never married--------------------5

Q 7a   How long have you been

_____
(No. of years)

_____
(response from Q 7)

We need to know some information about your . . .

Spouse—if married
Ex-spouse—if separated/
               divorced
Deceased spouse—if widowed

Q 8   What was the last grade s/he completed in school?

_____
(Actual grade)

Q 8a   What is/was her/his occupation?
(PROBE TO GET EXACT OCCUPATION)

_____
(Occupation)

TABLE 7-3 (*Continued*)

Q *9*   How many living sons and daughters do you have? (Include adopted and stepchildren) (RECORD ACTUAL NUMBER)

_____

Q 10   Do you rent or own the place you live in now?

Rent --------------------------------- 1
Own --------------------------------- 2
Other --------------------------------- 3

INTERVIEWER: IF RESPONDENT IS UNABLE TO READ, ASK FOR HIS TOTAL INCOME WITHOUT USING CARD AND CHECK APPROPRIATE CATEGORY. FOR ALL OTHER RESPONDENTS, *HAND THEM CARD* AND ASK:

Q 11   What was your total household income over the last 12 months before taxes? We don't need to know the exact amount, just tell me the letter next to the appropriate amount.

A. Under $1,000
B. $1,000–1,999
C. 2,000–2,999
D. 3,000–3,999
E. 4,000–4,999
F. 5,000–5,999
G. 6,000–7,999
H. 8,000–9,999
I. 10,000–14,999
J. 15,000–19,999
K. 20,000–29,999
L. 30,000 and over
Don't know ---------------------- 13
Refused to answer-------------- 14

Q *11a* Do you receive any of this income from the following sources? (READ LIST)

	Y	N
Social Security ----------------	1	2
Disability benefits ------------	1	2
Pension -------------------------	1	2
Alimony -------------------------	1	2

Q *12*   Which of the following statements best describes how you would evaluate your present household income? (HAND CARD) You can refer to this card as I read the statements. Which one comes closest to your opinion?

My income is more than adequate to meet my needs ---- 1
My income is adequate to meet my needs--------------------------2
My income is somewhat inadequate to meet my needs-- 3
My income is terribly inadequate to meet my needs ----------------- 4

I'd like to ask you some questions about your employment history now.

Q *13*   Try to remember the job you held for the longest period of time. How many years did you hold that job?

_____
(No. of years)

Q *14*   Why did you leave your last full-time job? (DON'T READ LIST. CIRCLE ANSWER GIVEN BY RESP.)

Retired (if yes, ask Q 14a, if no check correct response)
Quit --------------------------- _____
Was fired -------------------- _____
Was laid-off ----------------- _____
Never worked before------ _____
Other _____ -------- _____
Don't know/no answer---- _____

Q *14a* When you retired did you do so voluntarily or were you forced to retire by your boss or because of company rules?

1. Voluntarily
2. Forced

TABLE 7-4
GRAY'S MEASURES

1 Outcome measures (structured interview)
  a Job placement
  b Current employment status (verified by other sources)
  c Income
  d Job satisfaction
  e Knowledge about job seeking
  f Job search activity
  g Program description
  h Attendance
2 Participant characteristics
  a Premeasure (personal) questionnaire (Table 7.3)
  b Job expectations (questionnaire)
  c Life satisfaction (questionnaire)
  d Optimism (questionnaire)
3 Internal social processes
  a Job search network (questionnaire)
  b Cohesiveness measured by sociometric choice (sociometric questionnaire)
4 External social processes
  Gray attempted to control external social processes by starting each program at the same time, having all subjects participate in an aging program operated by a local agency located in a particular sociogeographic area in a midwestern city.

to assess attitudes toward self, parents, teachers, and school. Although internal social processes were equated by experimental planning and external measures by having both programs in the same school (Table 7-6), Tucker was unable to include any further assessment of internal and external social processes due to resource constraints. This can often affect the amount and type of measurement which the community experimenter is able to undertake. As a general rule, it is a good idea to have some priority ranking of the areas of measurement to be considered. In Tucker's case getting an accurate measure of program outcome was of primary importance.

Energy Depletion

Leedom (1980) created a task-oriented approach to energy education and compared it to a group which was given only information and to a control group.

Leedom obtained a personal history of each participant so that she could check upon the sample equivalence gained through the random-sampling procedures (Table 7-8). A behavioral questionnaire inquiring about energy conservation activities is presented in Table 7-7.

Her home energy conservation survey was a structured paper-and-pencil measure with specific items and closed responses. It focused on the frequency of occurrence of conservation behaviors which could be performed by the

TABLE 7-5
TUCKER'S SELF-CONCEPT MEASURE:
Self-Concept of Ability Scale

In each of the following questions circle the number in front of the statement which best answers each question for you.

1 How do you rate yourself in scholastic ability compared with other students your age in high school?

1 I am among the poorest	**4** I am above average
2 I am below average	**5** I am the best
3 I am average	

2 What kind of grades do you think you are capable of getting in high school?

1 Mostly Fs	**4** Mostly Bs
2 Mostly Ds	**5** Mostly As
3 Mostly Cs	

3 For those high school courses you are interested in, how do you feel you will place?

1 Among the poorest	**4** Above average
2 Probably below average	**5** Among the best
3 About average	

4 Where do you think you would rank in a high school graduating class?

1 Among the poorest	**4** Above average
2 Below average	**5** Among the best
3 Average	

5 How do you rate yourself in scholastic ability as compared to those who have elected not to go beyond junior high school?

1 I am the poorest	**4** I am above average
2 I am below average	**5** I am the best
3 I am average	

6 Do you think you have the ability to attend a college?

1 No	**4** Yes, probably
2 Probably not	**5** Yes, definitely
3 Not sure either way	

respondents (high school students) and their family members. These questionnaires were administered in the classroom in a group setting.

Table 7-8 lists other measures used by Leedom to assess the outcomes and internal social processes. Leedom also controlled the external social processes by using schools in the same geographic area (Table 7-8). Leedom used several methods of measurement. In addition to the ones she created, she used the youth energy survey (Table 7-7), which was an established standard attitude

TABLE 7-6
TUCKER'S MEASURES

1 Outcome measures
  a Reading comprehension (Gates-MacGinitie Standard Test)
    (1) Speed and accuracy
    (2) Vocabulary
    (3) Comprehension
  b Attitudes (questionnaire)
    (1) Attitude toward self
    (2) Attitude toward parents
    (3) Attitude toward teachers
    (4) Attitude toward school system
2 Participant characteristics
  a Personal history
3 Internal and external social process measures
  No internal social processes were measured in Tucker's experiment. Regular behavioral
  checks of experimental group's integrity were made, but these checks were not used for
  assessment purposes. External social processes were held constant by convening
  experimental groups at different times of the day in the same room with the same teacher.
  Both programs began and ended on the same dates.

questionnaire available at the time she was planning this study (Stevens and Kushler, 1979). Hence, her measurement included a mix of already established measures and newly developed measures.

Smoking and Health

Coelho (1983) compared two different types of smoking cessation programs. A core element of one of the experimental models was behavioral expectations relevant to smoking behavior among participants. The measure presented in Table 7-9 was used to assess expectations about stopping smoking. Since there were no good-quality expectancy measures of smoking cessation available, Coelho designed the measure in Table 7-9. It was hoped that expectations would be a good predictor of smoking cessation behavior. This measure was given to participants as they entered the program and, therefore, prior to their assignment to the experimental models.

Table 7-10 includes other measurement procedures used by Coelho. Measures of outcomes, participant characteristics, internal social processes, and external social processes were completed. Participant information was used to compare random samples for sample equivalence and to relate participant information to outcomes. A variety of existing and new measures were used by Coelho to assess the operation of the three models of smoking cessation intervention. For example, the physiological indicant of carbon monoxide level required the use of a commercially available piece of equipment. This measure had demonstrated reasonable reliability and validity properties in

TABLE 7-7
HOME ENERGY CONSERVATION SURVEY

This is a survey of the kinds of actions you or members of your family have taken *during the past month* to conserve energy in your home. We are interested in separate ratings for you and for other family members. (In the case of sisters and/or brothers, give a combined rating if more than one individual is involved.)

Use the following scale:
    0 = not at all
    1 = once
    2 = twice
    3 = three times or more

Example: If you had carpooled twice during the past month, your father five times, your mother not at all, your sister once and your brother once, you would answer the following question:

Ridden to a social or recreational event in a car with two or more other people.

Yourself	Father	Mother	Sisters/ Brothers		Yourself	Father	Mother	Sisters/ Brothers
2	5	0	2					

LIGHTING

		Yourself	Father	Mother	Sisters/ Brothers
1	Turned off a light in a room which was discovered unoccupied	___	___	___	___
2	Turned off incandescent lights when leaving a room for 3 minutes or more	___	___	___	___
3	Turned off fluorescent lamps when leaving a room for 15 minutes	___	___	___	___
4	Switched to bulbs of lower wattage in halls, stairways, and other areas of general illumination	___	___	___	___
5	Check to see if light fixtures were clean	___	___	___	___
6	Switched to fluorescent lighting or to one large bulb in an area where a lot of light was needed	___	___	___	___
7	Switched from incandescent lighting to fluorescent in any other area	___	___	___	___

This measure also included sets of similar items covering *Appliances, Hot Water, Kitchen, Space Heating,* and *Insulation.*

other studies. Outcomes also included a questionnaire of smoking behavior. Finally, assessment of the perceptions of others (family members) concerning the participants' smoking were included.

Diversion of Juvenile Offenders

The research on juvenile offenders provided an opportunity to gain a detailed understanding of the ongoing social and intervention processes in the lives of

TABLE 7-8
LEEDOM'S MEASURES

1 Outcome measures
  a Youth Energy Survey (attitude scale)
  b Consumption records from power companies and fuel oil and propane dealers
    (administrative record)
2 Participant measures
  a Personal history (questionnaire measuring age, parents' socioeconomic background, etc.)
3 Internal social process measures
  a Home energy conservation survey (behavioral checklist)
  b Group involvement (essay questionnaire)
  c Workshop evaluation (perceptual scale)
4 External social processes
  Leedom attempted to equate external social processes by sampling students from schools
  located in the same geographical and socioeconomic area. The models were opened and
  closed on the same dates.

TABLE 7-9
EXPECTATIONS ABOUT PROGRESS IN STOPPING SMOKING

Please complete the following items, indicating your expectations based on what you know
about your group leader and the Stop Smoking Program.

1 I think this program will help me to stop smoking.

1	2	3	4	5	6
Strongly Agree	Moderately Agree	Slightly Agree	Slightly Disagree	Moderately Disagree	Strongly Disagree

2 I think this program is likely to help others to stop smoking.

1	2	3	4	5	6
Strongly Agree	Moderately Agree	Slightly Agree	Slightly Disagree	Moderately Disagree	Strongly Disagree

3 At the end of this program I expect I will:

_____1 Still be smoking at the same level as I am now.

_____2 Be smoking at a reduced rate, but will not quit.

_____3 Be a nonsmoker.

4 Six months after this program ends I expect I will:

_____1 Still be smoking at the same level as I am now.

_____2 Be smoking at a reduced rate, but will not quit.

_____3 Be a nonsmoker.

Name: _____ Date: _____

TABLE 7-10
COELHO'S MEASURES

1 Outcomes
   a Weekly measurement of a participant's carboxyhemoglobin levels (physiological measure)
   b A questionnaire given at the end of the program intended to evaluate the amount of smoking the participant currently does and her or his evaluation of the program (questionnaire)
   c Each week persons were given a number of tasks to complete. Coelho created a form to ascertain whether they had completed all of them. This involved such diverse tasks as daily cigarette counts to reading various articles about stopping smoking (questionnaire)
   d Persons' smoking behavior in particular situations (behavioral report)
   e Follow-up smoking questionnaire (questionnaire)
   f Absenteeism (administrative records)
   g Dropout rate (administrative records)
2 Participant characteristics
   a Historical information with an emphasis on health and past smoking behavior (questionnaire)
   b Participants' attitudes toward their own lifestyle (questionnaire)
   c Personality characteristics (questionnaire)
      (1) Locus of control
      (2) Social adaptability
      (3) Emotional control
      (4) Expectancy scale
3 Internal social processes
   a Group processes—group cohesiveness (sociometric questionnaire)
   b Smoking behavior in session (behavioral report)
   c Attitudes toward other participants (questionnaire)
4 External social processes
   Coelho controlled external processes by holding all meetings in the same room and building at different times. Models were opened and closed on the same dates.

the youths. This information was intended to provide a basis for comparison of treatment conditions. First, information was gathered to assess specific intervention activities (With what parties? At what time?, etc.). Second, information was gathered to provide a "picture" of the youth's daily activities—the kinds of activities in which delinquent youths participated in school, with family, with peers, etc. Twelve similar "life domain" areas were measured in this manner.

The use of these intervention process measures presents a situation commonly faced by the field researcher. Given the previously uncharted nature of this research agenda, it was necessary to develop the interview techniques in an exploratory fashion. For this reason, the first group of youths involved in the research served as a sample for measurement development. Interviewers were trained in open-ended interviewing techniques, practice interviews were completed, and tentative outlines for interviews were developed. Two strategies were followed in developing the interview schedules, which became the life domain and intervention interview schedules. First, all interviewers kept shorthand notes of the content of the first interviews. Immediate debriefing sessions with the senior staff member of the project were conducted upon completion of each interview. All interviews were audiotaped. Following completion of the first thirty-six interviews, all tapes were monitored to generate important items from interviews with referred youths, their parents, and nominated peers. After such lists were generated, items were screened with the audiotapes to assess their ratability, reliability, and scale properties. Subsequently, items were established using five-point behaviorally anchored scales.

From that point on the derived life domain and the intervention interview schedules were administered to referred youths, their parents, a nominated best friend, and a volunteer in the case of experimental youth. Following the generation of these initial items a rational and empirical approach to scaling was used. Thus, items which showed a constant similar pattern of response were discarded (i.e., items which all youths answered in the same way could provide little descriptive information). Table 7-11 presents the final eleven domains of measurement with *one* selected question presented as an example.

TABLE 7-11
INTERVENTION SCALES

---

1 *Amount of time.* Frequency and amount of contact, e.g., "How much time does the volunteer spend working on the case?"

2 *Positive involvement.* The extent to which the youth and the assigned volunteer get along and the lack of problems involved in the intervention process, e.g., "To what extent does the youth like the volunteer?"

3 *Parental involvement.* The extent to which parent(s) are included in the intervention and the extent of a relationship built up between the parent(s) and the volunteer, e.g., "How often does the volunteer talk with the parent(s)?"

4 *School intervention: Youth focus.* Extent of the intervention focusing on school behavior of the youth, e.g., "To what extent is the volunteer trying to get the youth to go to school more?"

5 *School intervention: System focus.* Extent of the intervention focusing on bringing improvement to the school environment by focusing on school staff, e.g., "To what extent is the volunteer working on curriculum changes?"

6 *Job-seeking activities.* Extent to which the intervention focused on getting the youth employment, e.g., "How much has the volunteer instructed the youth in job seeking?"

7 *Family intervention: Youth focus.* Extent to which the intervention focused upon changing the youth within the family context, e.g., "How often does the volunteer talk to the youth about home?"

8 *Family intervention: Parent focus.* Extent to which the intervention focused upon changing the parents' behavior in the family, e.g., "To what extent is the home intervention focused on improving the parent's household's rules?"

9 *Recreational activity.* Amount of recreation involved in the time spent with youth by volunteer, e.g., "How often do the volunteer and youth do athletic activities together?"

10 *Peer involvement.* Extent to which friends of the youth are involved in the intervention, e.g., "How often do the youth's friends spend time with the volunteer and youth?"

11 *Legal system intervention.* Extent to which the volunteer became involved in the juvenile justice system for the youth, e.g., "Has volunteer assisted in negotiating a court disposition?"

TABLE 7-12
DIVERSION MEASURES

1 Outcome measures
  a Arrests (archival)
  b Petitions to court (archival)
  c School performance (archival)
  d Delinquent behavior (interview)
  e Reported positive change (interview)
2 Participant characteristics
  a Personal history (interview)
3 Internal social processes
  a Intervention scales (interview)
  b Volunteer attitudes (questionnaire)
  c Intervention activities (log books)
  d Volunteer training performance (interview)
  e Group process (audiotape)
4 External social processes
  a Life domain scales (interview)
  b Court system decision making (archival and questionnaire)
  c All models operated in same geographic area
  d All models opened and closed on the same dates

As a result of this process, the eleven scales represented measures of sound psychometric quality which originated conceptually from the participants' perceptions of major life events and interventions.

Table 7-12 lists all the measures used in the investigation of the diversion program for juvenile offenders. Major social outcomes were measured through both archival and self-report sources (i.e., both self-report interview information and archival records were used). Participant characteristics were assessed by a demographic interview. Internal social processes were assessed using multiple techniques which included interviews, open-ended diary-like log books, audiotapes, and structured questionnaires. External social process assessment focused on events specific to individual adolescent delinquent youths (life domain scales) and the functioning of the juvenile justice system (court decision making).

The Lodge Society

The lodge society also used a multitude of measurement procedures to evaluate outcomes, participant characteristics, internal social processes, and external social processes. Table 7-13 presents a simple attitude scale measuring satisfaction with life in the lodge society.

Table 7-14 lists all the measures used to examine the lodge society. In order to examine outcomes specifically, measures of recidivism, improved employment, and personal enhancement were assessed through questionnaires completed by the participants and individuals who knew them well. These data

TABLE 7-13
LODGE RESIDENTS' SATISFACTION SCALE

Name _____ Date _____

All of the statements listed below are opinions about the community dormitory (Veterans Lodge or 49ers Janitorial Service). The statements listed below do not have any correct answers. Therefore, respond to every question even though it constitutes a "guess." Please complete the following form by checking the *one* alternative which you think most appropriate.

1 The small group is performing as hired employees in the dormitory setting

____Much better than similar patients from the same ward not living in the dorm
____Slightly better
____About the same
____Slightly worse
____Considerably worse

2 As for being responsible for planning meals and other domestic activities of the dormitory, I believe this group is

____A good deal better than similar patients from the same ward
____Slightly better
____About the same
____Slightly worse
____Considerably worse

3 The help that group members give their fellows while living in the dormitory is

____Almost always well done and realistic
____Sometimes well done and realistic
____About as frequently well done and realistic as poorly done and unrealistic
____Sometimes poorly done and unrealistic
____Almost always poorly done and unrealistic

4 So far as members being able to handle bookkeeping tasks, planning work activities, completing work, and receiving payment and the like it is my belief that they are able to handle these responsibilities

____Almost always very adequately
____Sometimes adequately
____Neither adequately nor inadequately
____Sometimes inadequately
____Almost always inadequately

5 Most members participating in the community dormitory are doing so

____Very willingly
____Somewhat willingly
____Indifferently
____Somewhat against their wishes
____Strongly opposed

6 I consider the establishing of community living situations for ex-patients

____Extremely worthwhile
____Somewhat worthwhile
____Neither worthwhile nor useless
____A waste of time and effort
____Completely useless

7 When everything is said and done, I believe this approach will make

____A considerable contribution to the mental health movement

142

TABLE 7-13 (*Continued*)

_____Quite a contribution
_____Some contribution
_____A little contribution
_____No contribution

8 The entire program of moving patients into the community as trained groups has affected me

_____Very positively
_____Somewhat positively
_____Neither positively nor negatively
_____Somewhat negatively
_____Very negatively

TABLE 7-14
LODGE ASSESSMENT DEVICES

1 Outcomes
  a Patient follow-up adjustment (questionnaire)
  b Patient evaluation of his own adjustment (questionnaire)
  c Evaluation of lodge by members (interviews)
  d Examination of "failure cases" (interviews)
2 Participant characteristics
  a Personal history (questionnaire)
3 Internal social processes
  a Expectancies about future of the lodge (questionnaire)
  b Group interaction (sociometric ratings)
  c Role clarity (behavioral ratings)
  d Acceptance by the group (behavioral ratings)
  e Attraction to the group (behavioral ratings)
  f Satisfaction (behavioral ratings)
  g Critical events (research journal)
  h Job inspection (work ratings)
  i Evaluation of job training (questionnaire)
  j Visitors' (log)
  k Member departure (log)
  l Medication (administrative records)
  m Tools and equipment (checklist)
  n Group decision process (audio recording)
  o Fiscal process (accounting books)
4 External social processes
  a Attitudes of relatives toward members (questionnaire)
  b Consumer evaluation of janitorial and gardening (questionnaire)
  c Neighbors' evaluation of lodge members (questionnaire)
  d Evaluation of lodge by significant individuals (interviews)
  e The lodge and comparative community programs were operated in the same geographical area.
  f The programs were begun and terminated on the same dates.

were collected every 90 days for 40 months. Participant background information was collected through a personal history questionnaire. The expectancies of the patients and their motivation for wanting admission to the lodge were assessed with questionnaires.

The internal social processes were assessed every 90 days with a variety of instruments, including scales of sociometric choice, role clarity, group acceptance, group attraction, and group satisfaction, which were designed to assess the group processes operative in the lodge society. Given the importance of group work projects, measures were established to assess group performance on each job, the value of job training, the number and types of jobs obtained, and checklists for the work tools and equipment. An examination of the administration of the lodge was kept through the use of a daily report, visitors' log, members' log, and medication log. Economic aspects of the operation were maintained through bookkeeping records. Groups meetings, executive committee meetings, and quarterly evaluation meetings were audiotaped to assess the decision-making process.

The lodge and its community control model were operated in the same general geographic location and opened and closed on the same dates. Since the lodge was embedded in a neighborhood setting, questionnaires and interviews were conducted with neighbors and interacting organizations to measure external social processes. These measures focused on attitudes toward the lodge, its work performance, interpersonal relationship with neighbors, and perceptions of significant others. In addition, the lodge society was closely linked with a particular hospital as the referral source for new members. The patients came from a hospital program designed to train each member in group functioning. The actual performance of the hospital group training program was monitored through group process measurement of leadership, decision making, work performance, and personal improvement within the hospital setting. Hospital administrative records also indicated each member's personal and clinical history as well as medication requirements.

The Role of Measurement in Community Experiments

This chapter has provided a general discussion of the measurement techniques and procedures used in community experiments. It has included a description of the general characteristics of measurement devices, the alternative types of scaling procedures available, measurement quality, and the alternative modes of measurement. The centrality of measurement in social experimentation cannot be overemphasized. No study is any better than the quality of the measures employed. The quality and acceptability of the measurement procedures will affect the likelihood that the study will produce important and significant results by controlling extraneous sources of error which can cloud results (Hays, 1981; Medler, Schneider, and Schneider, 1981). Further, the reliability and validity of the measures will affect the credibility of the study's findings in the eyes of potential consumers of the research. The ultimate utility of the findings rests, to some extent, upon the credibility that the research instruments have with the scientific community, the policy-making community, and the participant community.

The interactive nature of community research measurement also needs to be emphasized. While many standard instruments may be used and their formats maintained throughout the course of an investigation, "measurement tinkering and adjustment" is a major aspect of any community research measurement effort. This is due to the uniqueness and changing nature of many community research situations. Investigators need to be constantly sensitive to the quality of the information resulting from measurement procedures. Measures which "don't make sense" or "don't quite work in the situation" will need adjustment and refinement. In addition, it will be necessary for the community experimenter to verify the reliability and validity of measures employed in each particular community research situation. Given the particularistic nature of most community experiments, the community investigator is not safe in assuming that the adequate quality of measures developed in other settings with other populations is applicable to a new research setting until checked.

The measurement of social models will undoubtedly be affected by and affect the research design and the implementation of the innovation. What is reasonable and feasible within the operation of the social model will dictate what types of measurement are possible. Similarly, the demand for certain types of information requires that social models be operated according to a schedule which specifically requires collection of the necessary data. As has been stressed throughout this volume, the conduct of community experiments is a sequential problem-solving process, and measurement issues are one of the very important steps in this process.

CHAPTER 8

ACTIVATING AND ADMINISTERING THE RESEARCH MODEL

The first seven chapters have described community research activities which primarily involve conceptual and planning tasks. The premise underlying these activities is that the planned experiment, complete with innovative social model(s), research design, and measurement instruments, could be carried out under actual field conditions. Since it is necessary for the investigator to have all aspects of the experiment clearly in mind before it is implemented, an activation plan involving personnel, research space, administration, training, and the like needs to be created. Even though this chapter occupies a relatively small part of this book, the space allotted should not lead the reader to feel that these administrative issues are any less important than the research issues presented in other chapters.

This chapter addresses five issues that are essential to activating and administering social models in the context of a field experiment. Each of the five areas discussed here is as important as any aspect of the field research. Without careful and successful implementation, the best-laid plans will be for naught. Examples are presented to illustrate the issues as they have occurred in field research settings. Since the five areas cover considerable information, rather than presenting seven examples of each, as has been done in the preceding chapters, one example will be presented to highlight each issue.

In earlier chapters, issues of design, sampling, and measurement have been addressed but an actual experimental plan has not been presented. An experimental plan provides a time schedule for the procedures that will occur over the course of the experiment, and will be described first since it provides a generic outline of the remaining steps in implementation. Each of the subsequent steps will then be described in sequence.

EXPERIMENTAL PLAN

Creating an experimental plan entails listing the activities that must occur from the time the plan is created until the experiment is completed. Thus, steps for obtaining agreements to carry out the experiment, securing funding, creating a research team, activating and monitoring the models, collecting data, and analyzing data have to be placed on a time schedule with target dates for completion. In addition, the research team members responsible for each of the activities must be listed. This includes designating individuals responsible for such activities as piloting research measures, establishing the new model(s) in the community setting, and ensuring the proper operation of the experimental aspects of the program, including obtaining research data in a timely fashion. An important step in this process is the specification of "responsible persons" and "due dates" for all major research activities. An experimental plan is necessary for other reasons as well. It serves as the subject of discussion for persons whose administrative cooperation is necessary before research can begin. The plan for the entire research, including sampling procedures, design, timing, and the like must be presented to those who will be asked to cooperate in carrying out the project.

An example of Beck's (1973) experimental plan is presented in Table 8-1. Each of the tasks included in the plan was assigned to a member of the research team. Since Beck's research team was small (including only three people), she did not specify task assignments in the actual plan. Beck's experimental plan is typical in a number of ways. It includes tasks relevant to training group initiation (program operation), testing assessment devices (measurement), assigning volunteers to models (sampling and experimental design), and monitoring program functioning (implementation). Each of these tasks is specified, along with a relative due date. Dates are a very important aspect of the plan. The purpose of setting a date to begin program initiation focuses attention on the starting date and instigates planning to meet that deadline. Once a starting date has been determined, research activities can be assigned calendar dates. Dates give the research team a sense of the importance of the research events and their sequence relative to program initiation, action, and termination.

Another important ingredient of experimental plans is the need to maintain flexibility within the plan. The experimental plan will provide the focus for coordinating and sequencing activities. However, the "final experimental plan" is never finished until the study is completed. Additions to the plan may need to be made as the study proceeds. For example, some agency or group which was not known to the investigator initially may ultimately turn out to be essential to the operation of the model, and its cooperation would thus have to be worked into the experimental plan. Similarly, external events may suddenly occur that preclude completion of a task on the specified date. If uncontrollable

TABLE 8.1
BECK'S EXPERIMENTAL PLAN

Experimental phase	Time scale	Research activity
Pre-experimental activity ↑	Minus 18 months	Obtain research grant
	Minus 8 months	Assemble research team
	Minus 6 months	Trial of survey device under model field conditions Modification and perfection of survey device
	Minus 5.5 months	Administer pre-experimental survey to all agency members Recruit volunteers for training program Conduct preliminary analysis of pre-experimental data
↓	Minus 3.5 months	Recruit additional volunteers Assign volunteers to training and comparison groups Notify volunteers of respective assignments Trial test of meeting interaction device under model field conditions
Initiate models	0 months	Initiate Experimental Phase I
↑	Plus 2 months	Assessment of Phase I progress within training group Initiate Phase II
	Plus 4 months	Assessment of Phase II progress within training group
Experimental activity	Plus 6 months	Assessment of Phase III progress within training group Terminate experimental period
	Plus 7 months	Administer postexperimental survey of volunteers
↓	Plus 9 months	Administer postexperimental survey to all agency members
Close models ↓	Plus 12 months	Collect attendance data for postexperimental period
Post-experimental activity ↑		Begin postexperimental data analysis Begin planning phase for next experiment
↓	Plus 16 months	End write-up and publication of experiment

Source: Fairweather, G. W., Tornatzky, L. G., *Experimental Methods for Social Policy Research*. New York: Pergamon Press, 1977, p. 253

events occur that require alterations in the experimental plan, adaptation of the remaining schedule of activities will have to be made. Having the experimental plan will focus attention on the remaining research events and their sequence, which should allow the needed flexibility for emergency planning.

ADMINISTRATIVE AGREEMENTS

One of the core components of the community research process is the establishment of administrative agreements with individuals, groups, or organizations important to the implementation of the social models and their evaluation. The types of issues which could be included in administrative agreements are virtually endless. As a rule, major areas of cooperation needed from existing agencies, groups, or individuals should be included in administrative agreements. In this section, five major areas which are commonly the topic of administrative agreements will be described. Examples of the issues covered in each will be highlighted.

Organizational Location of the Social Model

A major decision in implementing community experiments is the location of the social model. A common aspect of the location decision is whether or not the social model will be conducted within a functioning agency or organization in the community. When this occurs it is necessary to make a detailed administrative agreement with an existing organization covering all the aspects of program and research operation. Tucker's (1974) poor readers' study was carried out within the school buildings where Tucker was a school counselor. Gray (1980) was able to implant his innovative job club in an existing agency for the aging.

On the other hand, it may be decided that the type of innovation requires the establishment of a separate organization. The lodge model (Fairweather, 1969) required creation of a new community setting since the lodge did not fit well into any existing organizational structure; therefore, it was necessary to make arrangements *outside* the mainstream of current agencies' operations. With the lodge society it was necessary to provide housing, medical care, food, job training, and other living and working facilities for a group of individuals who needed to own and operate their own business.

This demonstrates that the type of innovation may largely determine where it fits in the community. If it does not fit into any existing agency or program, it is then necessary to create a support base for the program in the community itself. Similarly, Davidson et al.'s (1983) diversion model required placement outside the juvenile justice system. Inherent in the program design was the notion of keeping youthful offenders outside the jurisdiction of the juvenile court, which is the central idea of diversion. As such, the volunteer diversion model had to be placed outside the existing youth-serving agencies to ensure that diversion occurred.

All of the aforementioned involved finding a location where the innovation can be implemented. Implantation in an existing organization has the advantage that many of the necessary accoutrements for the project are already present. These may include research facilities, some research employees, governmental licenses when necessary, fiscal capability, and so on. The difficulties are that the agency may be hostile to a new program, particularly a research project, believing that it may in some way suggest that organization programs are inadequate. If a new model is implanted in an existing agency it should be done on a small scale (e.g., one or two wards in a mental hospital, a few cells in a prison, a small building in a residential area, etc.) for political and logistic reasons. In addition, the unobtrusiveness of a small program provides a less visible situation for model implementation and, hence, less opportunity for external forces to control or destroy it.

When the innovative program does not have a supporting agency and begins independently in the community, numerous administrative agreements usually have to be reached with existing community organizations for the model to survive. For example, agreements may have to be made with unions, rehabilitation agencies, housing authorities, and so on. This is particularly true when the innovation departs significantly from contemporary organizational practices. In such cases, completing the research outside of traditional organizations is the only option open to the innovative researcher.

The agreements concerning the organizational and physical location of the social model must be accomplished prior to actual initiation of the program. Such issues as physical location, organizational relationships to host agencies, and organizational relationships to referral sources all need to be settled prior to social model initiation. Severy, Houlden, and Wilmoth (1982) have explored a number of techniques to determine the receptivity of the selected environment to the innovation. This helps prevent early failure when the model is implemented. Even with these precautions, however, unanticipated issues related to program organizational location will sometimes not become evident until after social model operation has actually begun. This may require altering initial agreements or drawing up of new agreements. For example, 6 months after the initiation of the volunteer diversion project mentioned throughout this volume, it became obvious that an administrative agreement would have to be negotiated with the schools. While it was assumed that local school districts would welcome the involvement of volunteers with delinquent youths, such was not the case in actual practice. The specific relationship of the diversion project to the local school district became the subject of a rather extensive negotiation process well into program operation.

Funding

Agreements for the physical and organizational location of the innovative model are only part of the support required for model operation. A second agreement that is necessary is arranging for funding. This requires presenting a proposal to those agencies or groups that might have research funds for a particular problem or to organizations that would permit and themselves support research in their own organization. During the course of the past 30 years, the senior author has participated in a large number of funding agreements, varying from organizations such as the National Science Foundation, the National Institutes of Health, the National Institute of Mental Health, state agencies (e.g., for energy, maternal health care, mental health), and other public agencies (e.g., schools, city commissions, planning departments, etc.), as well as private industries (such as those devoted to energy conservation, organizational functioning, and employee relations). All the aforementioned have funded innovative experiments within their organizations or supported experimentation in groups over which they had monetary or administrative control.

It has also been the authors' experience that many researchers who started out needing a particular amount of financing found that these needs could not be met. It is, therefore, necessary for field researchers to have in mind at least two ends of the financial continuum when they begin negotiating for funds. The upper limit represents the *maximum amount* of money the experimenter would need if all other aspects of the research were to be carried out under ideal conditions. The second figure is the *minimum amount* of funding below which the researcher could not go if there was to be a serious attempt to carry out the project.

Two additional issues should be kept in mind once the investigator has determined maximum and minimum funding limits. First, some social innovation research endeavors may not actually take large amounts of new funds. Within the supporting groups or agency the redirection of existing fiscal resources may cover the additional expenses needed to create a new social model and assess its efficacy. Similarly, many social models which arise in community experimentation may be less expensive than the program they are designed to replace. Second, the investigator needs to be absolutely certain about the fiscal support level below which the investigation is impossible. There will be a definitive level (although it may not involve new money) of support necessary to carry out a basic investigation which will produce interpretable outcomes. For example, removing all costs for interviewers and record data collectors from a budget may render the particular experiment useless. Careful negotiation of all support issues is indispensible to innovative field research.

Research Concerns

The preceding sections have provided a discussion of agreements about location and funding. Agreements about the research process itself are equally important. There is probably no single area of research concern that is as misunderstood and more controversial than the notions of *random assignment* and/or *random sampling.* Since random assignment and sampling are an essential aspect of an experimental design, specification of these procedures within administrative agreements is essential. Failure to include specification of exactly how random assignment and sampling are to be accomplished is illustrated by the following experience of the second author. In establishing random assignment procedures for the first year of the volunteer diversion project, it was agreed that upon referral of a delinquent youth the juvenile officer of a local police department would make the assignment to the experimental model. A set of blind envelopes were prepared by the research team. These envelopes were to be used by the officer to make a random assignment of each youth to the new social model (volunteer diversion) or its alternative. Inside the envelopes were slips of paper indicating group assignment. These slips had been randomly drawn by the research staff. Following the first thirty referrals, the second author was meeting with the police lieutenant to review project operation when the following conversation took place:

Police Lt.: "Do you people ever want these extra opened envelopes and forms back?"

Davidson: "What envelopes are those?"

Police Lt.: "You know, the ones you gave us to inform the kids whether or not to go to the diversion program."

Davidson: "How is it that you have extras? I thought you only opened one for each youth. Tell me how it is you use them?"

Police Lt.: "Well, when we think a kid would be right for diversion, we fill out the forms you gave us for referral. Then we open an envelope like you told us. If it's a kid we really want to get into the diversion project and the slip in the envelope says 'project' then we tell them to call the number you gave us. If the slip says "release," we just open another envelope or envelopes until we find one which says 'project.' So here are the extra envelopes."

The remainder of this conversation will not be repeated here. However, it should be obvious that failure to specify completely the random assignment procedure *and* provide an immediate check on compliance resulted in the biased assignment of the first thirty youths. They were necessarily discarded as participants in the research effort.

Similar concerns apply to other aspects of administrative agreements concerning research issues. The importance of including specification of measurement procedures cannot be overemphasized. Articulation of the schedule, individual responsibility, and location of measurement are critically important. Also at issue is access to needed data. If the investigation calls for access to administrative records it is crucial that permission about the conditions under which access is to be provided be negotiated prior to implementation of the models. Leedom's (1980) research, mentioned in earlier chapters, required the collection of actual energy use data as an outcome of the energy conservation education model she employed. Lengthy negotiations were required before local utility companies were willing to provide information concerning actual energy use in the experimental and control households.

Given the complexity and number of these issues, it often becomes necessary for the researcher to explain details of the experiment. This should include its purpose, experimental design, and measuring instruments. In such cases, the experimentalist becomes a teacher and an advocate for community experimentation simultaneously. Whether or not researchers can find an appropriate location, gain funding, and establish research arrangements is often more dependent upon the knowledge and persuasiveness of the investigator than it is upon the value of the experiment itself.

Human Subjects Issues

Human subjects issues have been at the forefront of social, natural, and medical sciences over the last decade. A good deal has been written concerning participation of human beings in research and most professional groups have established standards for such procedures (McReynolds, 1981; American Psychological Association, 1984). In addition, many governmental agencies (at this juncture, all federal agencies) have very specific guidelines which govern the participation of human beings in research. This represents one important point in field research where the humanitarian values and the scientific needs of the researchers become intertwined. The ethical researcher, as detailed in Chapter 2, considers the protection of each participant's civil and personal rights above all else in the experiment and, therefore, never knowingly violates these constitutionally guaranteed rights. When considering human subjects issues, all potential effects upon participants must be considered and examined carefully. Only after an examination of all issues has been made and resolved positively should people be asked to volunteer for participation in any social model.

While it is well beyond the scope of this volume to cover all the specific requirements of major funding agencies and professional associations concerning human subjects' participation in research, a number of summary principles can be presented. In addition, an example of a voluntary participation agreement will be presented to give the reader an idea of the types of agreements required.

At the center of most human subjects issues is the requirement of informed voluntary participation. This general principle means that in all community research the participants must make a knowledgeable voluntary decision to participate. This usually means that they must be informed about what the research will involve, the voluntary nature of the research, and that they have the right to withdraw at any time during research. While informed consent was an extremely controversial issue at one time, the controversy has essentially disappeared and it is now a routine procedure that voluntary participation in any research is required. Acceptance of this principle is cause for some caution on the part of community researchers, since ensuring informed voluntary participation will usually involve the investigator in advocating the rights of participants in many circumstances, even when the population of interest is part of a nonvoluntary social system (e.g., prisons, hospitals, schools, etc.).

A second general question that often arises in human subject review concerns the relationship between potential benefits and risks to the problem population. The investigator will often be asked to give a prior assessment of a theoretical risk/benefit ratio when conducting the investigation. Individuals who participate in a new social model will always do so at some risk. However, the risk of new social model participation must be weighed against the risk associated with the status quo. Such risks must be balanced against the potential benefit to the participants as well as the potential for societal benefit from implementation of the new model. It is for this reason that the only models worthy of implementation and evaluation from a humanitarian perspective (see Chapter 2) are those that the researchers believe would improve the quality of life of the recipients. It is at this point in research planning where the need for a humanitarian perspective becomes paramount. No potential participants should be asked to become research subjects in any social model that will not theoretically improve their life's benefits.

It must also be recognized here that the traditional manner in which society handles a problem (the control) is still the best way to solve the problem so far as society is concerned *until* a more beneficial program has been empirically demonstrated. From a societal perspective, the traditional program is the most beneficial until scientists accumulate evidence that they have a better program. For this reason, the traditional control constitutes the most beneficial program available in a society *until* research is completed and experimental evidence suggests that the newly created program is more beneficial. Only at this temporal point (and after several replicates) is the innovative program considered to be empirically (not theoretically) more beneficial than the traditional control program. The process of disseminating the new program begins at this time and not before. The community researcher can anticipate discussing potential benefits of the new model with institutional groups responsible for reviewing human subjects procedures. Funding sources, human service organizations, and many large research-oriented institutions (e.g., university and private research institutes) have review procedures which safeguard the rights and well-being of human subjects.

Table 8-2 presents the voluntary participation agreement used by Gray (1980) in his employment research with elderly individuals. This agreement includes a typical written explanation of the project in both its service and research aspects. The schedule of assessment is outlined, the random basis for program participation is described, and the voluntary nature of participation is detailed. The form also includes space for signature by the researcher and participant.

The Necessity of Written Agreements

During the final stages of negotiating administrative agreements, it will be necessary for the investigator to present a written agreement to the agency(ies),

TABLE 8.2
OLDER WORKER-RETIREE EMPLOYMENT SERVICE CONSENT FORM

Name of Client

I have agreed to participate in a job finding program, the Older Worker-Retiree Employment Service which I understand to be part of a research project conducted by Denis Gray under the supervision of William Davidson, Ph.D. I also understand that I will receive $3 for each of the three interviews in which I will cooperate. I am aware that the materials and program are of an experimental nature and that I may withdraw from participation at any time. While the results of the study will be made available to me, I understand that there are no assurances that this program will provide specific results in the form of a placement. I agree that the information which I provide through this program will be available for use in evaluating the project and subsequent published reports, with the understanding and assurance that my personal identity and the information about me will remain confidential.

Signature

Witnessed   Date

---

organization(s), group(s), and critical individual(s) in the community that will be involved in the research. The need for a written document cannot be over-emphasized. It must be signed by the investigator and the others involved. While strictly speaking this is typically not a legal document, the written nature of the agreement(s), including critical signatures, enhances the chances that the agreements will be honored. Such agreements not only set forth what organizations and agencies agree to provide—research necessities such as space, access to staff, clients, customers, etc.—but they also stress what the researcher agrees to do for the organizations and agencies. For example, the researcher usually agrees to give the organization research information as soon as it becomes available so that the cooperative organization can use it in upgrading its own programs, to keep the administration informed of any difficulties that might emerge that could reflect upon the organization, and so on.

In Chapter 4, the need for the researcher to understand the problem population and the conditions under which the problems occur was stressed. It further was pointed out that persons interested in a particular problem population ought to spend considerable time working in the daily routine of organizations that deal with these problems as well as experiencing the problem itself as much as possible from the social position of those who will later become research participants. The knowledge gained from these participative experiences is of inestimable value when it comes to obtaining agreements, particularly if the organizations are those with whom the person has been working.

Obtaining research agreements may be difficult and time-consuming. Such agreements usually hinge upon the persuasiveness of the field researchers. Persuading others to support an experiment can be viewed as "selling" scientific methods rather than a single model. This is an important distinction because the well-trained scientist usually believes that scientific results are the best evidence for justifying a social program.

It is, therefore, usually basic for scientists to persuade others to use consensually valid scientific methods rather than using social programs whose benefits are not established at the time an experiment begins. Thus the scienctist is advocating the use of scientific methods to evaluate programs, *not* a particular program itself.

Agreements are the pivotal point upon which the future of any longitudinal experiment will hinge. It is probably fair to say that more community experiments have been stopped prematurely due to faulty negotiations and agreements or lack of them than have been lost due to faulty experimental design and research procedures.

An administrative agreement should cover the following content areas (Fairweather & Tornatzky, 1977):

1 An understanding that the research budget is to be expended in the manner and for the purposes intended in the research proposal;
2 An understanding giving the researchers authority to select and randomly assign persons to the conditions presented in the experimental plan;
3 An agreement to support the experiment when it receives complaints about social treatment, funding, or staffing;
4 Agreements concerning the sharing and/or assignment of personnel, funds, and/or space;
5 An understanding not to interfere with the model in the proposed experimental plan;
6 An agreement not to violate the integrity of the research design or to participate in procedures designed to curtail a full-time research effort;
7 An agreement not to seek either inflammatory or self-serving publicity.

In turn, the experimenters could agree to:

1 Not exceed the dimensions of the agreed-upon experimental program in size, type, or duration;
2 Not violate any of the existing institutional norms except those agreed upon by all parties as an inherent part of the research;
3 Provide those services proposed in the research proposal;
4 Give periodic progress reports, as appropriate, to all cooperating parties;
5 Not change any of the agreed-upon procedures without specific permission from cooperating units; and upon emergence of any unforeseen difficulties involving other cooperating units, the experimenters will request a meeting to discuss these problems.

Establishing these reciprocities between administrators and the research team is essential, not only to clairify the obligations of each but also to provide a mechanism for continuing communication between the participating parties, each of whom should be interested in finding solutions to the social problems which are their joint responsibility (pp. 136–137).

Point 2 in this list is especially important because the value for the researcher of the random-sampling procedures goes beyond their value from a scientific perspective. Random-sampling procedures are probably the most difficult procedures to arrange since most administrators do not understand the scientific basis of sampling. Accordingly, such procedures often require extensive negotiations. This results in a greater knowledge of scientific procedures on the administrators' part and an increased knowledge of administrators' and participants' problems from the researcher's point of view. Thus, random-sampling negotiations give the researcher an excellent diagnostic instrument with which to evaluate the interest that administrators have in the proposed research project. Since it is not uncommon for administrators to seek publicity and to try to obtain additional funds for their organization, it is not uncommon for them to be willing to say verbally that they will support a research project, but when faced with the specifics of random sampling, sometimes they will lose their original interest, espeically if it is simply a reflection of a drive for money and political power. For the experimenter, however, this is not a loss. Under these conditions negotiation for random-sampling procedures has identified an individual whose group or organization is probably not interested in pursuing a scientific study and who therefore cannot or will not assume the responsibilities inherent in such an investigation. It is far better for the researcher to know this early so that he or she can then decide if, under these conditions, the experiment should remain in this locale or whether it would be better to seek another location. Thus, the random-sampling procedure serves several purposes. It improves the scientific merit of the research; it provides an evaluation tool for the researcher to understand the motivation of the administrators; and it helps educate each party in the folkways and mores of the organizations with which they will be working if the research is supported.

An example of an administrative agreement can be found in Table 8-3, which presents the administrative agreements obtained by Coelho (1983) in his stop-smoking experiment.

RESEARCH TEAM

Armed with signed agreements about the research project and funding, it is now necessary for the researcher to begin the process of organizing a research team. Typically, the research team involves persons whose ordinary jobs are in the field setting—mental health workers, judges, community workers of various types, industrial workers and executives, and so on. There are also the field researchers, and persons expert in various areas of community organization and process who need to be consulted from time to time. Let us take a look at the persons who might be needed in a project as workers on the research itself and as consultants to the project.

Those who work daily in agencies and organizations that interact with the public often view researchers with suspicion. They frequently believe (and sometimes correctly) that experimenters simply enter the scene, gather data,

TABLE 8.3
COELHO'S ADMINISTRATIVE AGREEMENT

The following is a statement of cooperation between Richard J. Coelho, and the Program Coordinator of the American Lung Association of Michigan. This research is being conducted to investigate different models of smoking cessation and their effect on the abstinence behavior of participants in each model.

The following responsibilities of each are:

On the part of the program coordinator of the American Lung Association

1 Allow Mr. Richard J. Coelho to conduct a study of the two smoking cessation models as outlined in the document entitled "A Proposed Investigation of the Effectiveness of Three Package Stop-Smoking Programs."
2 Agrees to assist Mr. Coelho in the implementation of the study through the training of a community volunteer in the operation of the current smoking cessation clinic entitled "FREEDOM FROM SMOKING."
3 Allow Mr. Coelho access to posters, pamphlets, and any other educational materials needed in the facilitation of the FREEDOM FROM SMOKING clinic.

On the part of Richard J. Coelho

1 Agrees to assume full responsibility for the design, implementation, analysis, and publication of the study as outlined in the above-mentioned document.
2 Agrees to follow approved university procedures for ensuring the confidentiality of information from participants in the study.
3 Agrees to make available all reports on research as they become available.
4 Agrees to use the information collected from this research to meet doctoral dissertation requirements.

Richard J. Coelho	Coordinator, American Lung Association

and leave, while they go on working forever with the problem population and receive no help from the researchers at all. If field research is to prosper, both as a scientific and humanitarian activity, this feeling must be replaced with one based upon a positive view of research and the degree to which it can help the organization improve its programs.

It is for this reason that the director of the research team should attempt to create both a service and research role for all persons in the project, with the possible exception of consultants, so that all individuals will be involved in both service activities and research. This can be achieved by assigning particular tasks to individuals that are beyond their typical role. For example, a nurse may be given the role of collecting drug data and writing a section in a publication dealing with some aspect of drugs; a community administrator may, if he or she is willing, help research efforts by collecting administrative records and also writing a section in a publication about this aspect of the research, and so on.

The important point is that involving people in the project from its conception to its termination is the best possible way to gain their support. This should help ensure that all aspects of the research project are carried out properly. In this way, a commitment is made to the project as a whole and not to the individual's professional group such as psychologists, social workers, and so on. It is this research group's cohesiveness that permits attainment of the research group's goals and is, therefore, the central organizing principle around which excellent research teams operate. It is most important to differentiate this group cohesiveness and group goal attainment from an individual scientist's own goals, which can permeate scientific activity and often result in individual reward, while the group itself receives little or no benefit.

Another quality of a good research team concerns the use of consultants. In contemporary society it is almost inconceivable that persons could create small-scale innovations and implant them in organizations or the community without legal advice. It is, therefore, necessary to seek legal counsel, particularly if the implantation is not in a specific organization where a legal staff is available. While this may sound like a difficult hurdle to overcome, in reality there are many lawyers willing and able to serve on such research teams with little if any remuneration. It is also often necessary to have medical, business, and other professionals as consultants for the research project. This is particularly important if the product of the program is one that could be conceived of as a product competing with other groups or organizations in the community. For example, it may be necessary to achieve agreements with unions and businesses in the community if one wishes to engage in a similar activity.

Other consultants necessary to the research project are those having specific scientific knowledge that can be used to help define the problem, create the research design, or aid in instrument construction, data collection, and data analysis. Social and natural scientists with specific knowledge about a particular problem are essential consultants. For example, if socioeconomic indicators are extremely important aspects of a particular problem—unemployment for example—economists, sociologists, and political scientists whose areas of concern are local and national employment should be consulted because they might suggest some crucial aspects of this research problem and its parameters that are unknown to the experimenters and that should be explored and measured.

To gain a clear understanding of the composition of a field research team, it is instructive to examine in some detail the research team established to create and evaluate the lodge society (Fairweather, 1969). Table 8-4 lists those involved in the research and their primary institutional affiliation. As the reader can see from the first row in the table there were three organizations involved in carrying out this research: (1) the mental hospital, from which patients came into the community setting; (2) the university, responsible for establishing the lodge society in the community and for its relationship with the rest of society; and (3) finally, the lodge society participants, who established and worked for their own nonprofit corporation. Since there were three entities involved it should be clear to the reader that much cooperation was necessary between the three organizations, exemplified in the list shown in Table 8-4 of persons working for the various organizations.

TABLE 8.4
PERSONNEL PARTICIPATING IN THE HOSPITAL-COMMUNITY STUDY WITH THEIR
PRIMARY INSTITUTIONAL AFFILIATION

Hospital		University		Nonprofit rehabilitation corporation
Service	Research	Consultants	Research	Service
One psychiatrist One social worker Two nurses Four nursing assistants	One chief social innovative experimenter (principal investigator) One experimental assistant	Legal Accounting Insurance Statistical Computer Medical Janitorial	One chief social innovative experimenter (principal investigator) Two social innovative experimenters Three experimental assistants	Board of directors

The reader will notice that the chief social innovative experimenter—the leader of the research group—had a position in both the university and the hospital, making him a person who could work with personnel from both groups. Others held membership in only one group. For example, the psychiatrist, social worker, nurses, and nursing assistants worked for the hospital setting for their training as group members, as well as for other aspects of hospital treatment such as proper drug dosage and the like. The research team included people from both the hospital and the university who were responsible for the day-to-day operation of the lodge and for obtaining and analyzing all the data from the experiment.

Consultants are also shown in Table 8-4. Among them were a lawyer, an accountant, and an insurance executive, who all were responsible for consulting with the lodge society members about their integration into the broader community. For example, if legal problems emerged in the relationship of the nonprofit corporation with a union or another work organization, the lawyer was active in finding a solution to that problem. The accountant helped the lodge society members keep accurate books, and the insurance executive made certain they were covered with proper insurance, both in their society and their work situation. In addition, a medical consultant took care of their medical needs and a janitorial consultant helped the society's members learn and expand their knowledge of the janitorial business. Statistical and computer consultants aided in the design of the experiment and analyses of research data. The nonprofit corporation was the organization which sponsored the lodge society members as workers and gave them adequate coverage under worker's compensation laws and the like.

It should be clear from this brief discussion of the research team member-ship and their roles that continuing communication and interaction was nec-essary throughout the experiment to carry out both the organization's function of a self-governing, autonomous society and, at the same time, provide the adequate professional coverage and research evaluation necessary during the course of the experiment.

No experiment of any consequence can be carried out in the community without the help of a large number of people. These people need to be orga-nized into a research team with a group goal of initiating and carrying out the research project. Acceptance of the group goal and adherence to the procedures necessary for completion of the project are an essential part of the field experimentation.

ACTIVATING AND MONITORING THE MODELS

If the research team has been organized, roles detailed, and all administrative agreements executed, the time has come for model activation. Whether the small-scale model is implanted in an agency, organization, or the community, the researcher and the participants must now begin to play their roles in the program itself. This might be a small-scale operation such as in a schoolroom (Tucker, 1974), or a major community undertaking, such as the development of a small society as illustrated by the lodge research (Fairweather et al., 1969). Nonetheless, the starting date arrives and all the research activities and pro-cesses begin at once. There will be, as most readers can probably surmise, an early period for making minor adjustments and fine-tuning research and service operations. This is particularly true at the outset because most of the involved persons and organizations will be entering this particular situation for the first time. At this point the team moves from verbal planning to action.

While any number of idiosyncratic issues will arise as one moves from plans for the social experiment to its actual operation, four sets of issues occur with enough frequency to warrant comment here. Each of these seems inherent in the process of social innovation and group development. The field experi-menter is advised to anticipate such issues and turn them into a research advantage whenever possible.

First, turmoil can emerge, generated by the conflict of two issues: (1) partic-ipant and staff ownership of the innovative social model, and (2) consistency of the model's operation with regard to its original design. While it is impor-tant for staff and/or participant morale to feel "ownership" of the program, it is equally important that experimental constancy is maintained. To accom-plish these twin goals simultaneously it will be necessary for the research leader to reinforce continuously the norms of goal equivalence through discussion involving staff members. In this way a constant awareness and commitment to both goals (personal involvement and experimental constancy) can be achieved.

A second tension which community researchers may face following innovation activation can result if an effective innovation has been created. When a new program is clearly successful, a negative perception of existing agencies or groups dealing with the same problem may develop. For example, when juvenile offenders were diverted successfully from the court in the voluntary diversion project, the sphere of influence of the juvenile court was threatened (Seidman, 1983). Since one of the measures used to determine the funding level of juvenile courts is caseload (number of clients), successfully diverting juvenile offenders who did not return to the court effectively reduced the caseload, and hence the organization's financial base was threatened. Thus, the very individuals and organizations upon whom the innovation depended for administrative support were jeopardized by the success of their own supported research program. Such research consequences should be anticipated when possible and action taken so that the threatened organization or individual can receive compensatory rewards for their cooperation (Saul, 1982).

A third issue which might arise during the activation phase occurs when the roles for the innovative social models require that staff engage in what they may see as professional norm-violating behavior. Many professional groups have worked long and hard to establish acceptable modes of professional behavior which can have a powerful influence on the personal comfort the staff has in activating innovative social programs. While there are numerous examples from the social models presented in this volume, the lodge society (Fairweather, 1969) seems most illustrative. It will be recalled that a core component of the lodge society was a membership-owned janitorial service. This business used various equipment, including a truck for personnel and equipment transportation. During initial phases of lodge operation, it was necessary for the staff to drive the truck until appropriate licenses were obtained for the members. The psychologist who was responsible for work site operation initially strenuously resisted putting on work clothes and driving the truck to work sites since he did "not receive a Ph.D. in order to drive a truck." Yet, without a researcher to help organize and measure such activities, the innovation's implementation and evaluation would not have been possible. Being clear with all team members about what their roles may involve is the best preventive medicine for such issues. However, even with adequate planning, the types of situations which come up in operating community experiments will inevitably involve the need for creative solutions to such situations.

A final common issue which can arise concerns staff morale. Most of the content areas in which the community researcher will work will involve highly intransigent social issues. If this were not true, there would be little interest in developing innovative approaches. The reality of this situation is that even the most successful of innovations will not completely solve the problem in question. In short, some of the patients will return to the hospital, some of the youths will be rearrested, people will continue to smoke, some families will increase their energy use, etc. This situation, combined with the idealism of most individuals attracted to community experimental work, can produce research team disillusionment and dissatisfaction. While there is no expectation that this issue can ever be totally eliminated in community work, its impact can be minimized by involving all individuals in multiple roles, allowing for role flexibility, enhancing group cohesiveness, continuously reviewing the probabalistic nature of experimental work, and accepting the fact that no treatment cures everyone.

Each of these issues, and a host of others which may arise in any given community research, should make it clear that some of the original research plans may go awry. It is especially important, therefore, that communication between administrators and researchers be conscientiously carried out from the beginning to the end of each experiment. This longitudinal process of continuous communication also helps to eliminate early (hopefully, before actual research is underway) those individuals who have little, if any, commitment to problem solution. Continous communication is absolutely essential for harmoniously completing longitudinal field experimentation and is the interpersonal foundation upon which social models can be created, implanted, activated, and evaluated for the length of time required to complete the field experiment.

An example of what can happen to an agreement during the course of an experiment, even after lengthy and thorough negotiations, can be found in the research of Ives (1974) with drug offenders. He had received a signed support document from organizational administrators, permitting the random assignment of drug addicts to an innovative program and to a traditional drug program. Once the research had started, it became clear that the administrators were far more supportive of the traditional than the innovation program because they had developed it. In the early phases of the study, the innovative program began demonstrating some very positive results. Soon the administrators decided that they could no longer support the innovative program and canceled the prior agreement for the random assignment of drug addicts. Needless to say, the experimental project was lost and the outcomes of the innovation constrasted with the traditional program never obtained.

A major review of the project after its premature termination indicated that the administrators had, from the beginning, been more interested in gaining publicity for their program than they were in evaluating its processes and outcomes. It appeared clear that their long-term commitment to program evaluation and improvement was not the same as that of the researchers and that this value difference was the basis for early termination of the program. Extended and more in-depth discussion in the negotiating phase prior to the experiment might have illuminated this conflict. If the conflict had been clearly perceived by all parties and constantly discussed, its resolution might have been possible.

This experience highlights one of the most difficult problems in longitudinal field experiments. It is not only gaining access to the problem population and establishing random-sampling agreements but making certain that the flow of participants under the agreed-upon sampling procedures is carried out for the duration of the project. Any organization that wants to destroy an experiment can do it no more effectively than preventing the flow of participants into the models. Random assignment of participants, therefore, often becomes the focal point for the emergence of conflict when strained interpersonal relationships emerge.

It is during the longitudinal time span of the field experiment that the research team must make certain that the research innovation and the comparative model(s) are carried out as planned and that the integrity of the models is maintained. For example, if the program has group decision making as a key ingredient, it is important that all decisions be made in a group manner, even though it might be necessary to change where a meeting is held, the timing of a meeting, etc. It is important to understand that for the research to produce interpretable findings, the underlying social models' operating procedures must be maintained and carried out according to the theoretical principles upon which they are based.

The continuity and consistency of experimental models must be ascertained over time by systematic *monitoring*. To accomplish adequate monitoring appropriate procedures are arranged so that the models are evaluated periodically to find out if they are proceeding according to their basic design. Since the models can change over time, it is necessary to monitor the models continuously to make certain that experimental conditions are being met.

To take one example, in carrying out research in the juvenile delinquency diversion, Davidson et al. (1982) used four methods to monitor condition integrity. The diversion project involved assigning volunteers to adolescent youths one-on-one, and the volunteers' data could, therefore, be used to monitor the research. The first monitoring method used resulted from the volunteers' weekly written reports of case goals, weekly activities, reports of significant events, and plans for the following week. These data emanating from the volunteers' intervention with their assigned youths were matched with the experimental activities spelled out for them in the design. The social processes of the models could thus be monitored weekly. Second, volunteers, youths, and their parents were interviewed at 6-week intervals. These data provided an overall assessment of model compliance. Third, all supervision sessions were audiotaped. These tapes were recordings of weekly staff meetings held to review model integrity. Finally, during the training phase, volunteers were tested weekly to determine their mastery of the experimental procedure they were to employ. Unless adequate mastery of the innovative model processes was demonstrated, the volunteer was not assigned to the research program.

As monitoring occurs, it is also necessary to continue data collection, which is typically made at various points throughout the course of the experiment. Since most field experiments are time-trend designs as shown in Chapter 6, the data as collected should be stored in the appropriate place and, if possible, put on computer cards and tapes so that when the study has finally ended progress can be quickly made toward complete data analysis.

TERMINATING THE ACTION PHASE

According to the experimental plan, there will come a time when the model will need to be terminated. If one or more model(s) have been demonstrated to be more beneficial than the other models, it is the investigator's responsibility to attempt to continue that particular model's existence and, indeed, its broader adoption. Even though the experimental phase must end, it is important from a humanitarian perspective that any model(s) shown to improve the life benefits of the participants compared to the traditional model be continued. It is toward this end that the research team now devotes it energies. The possibility of the agency in which the innovation is implanted taking over the program as one of its own offerings can be tried. If the program is in the community perhaps other arrangements for its continuation can be made.

It must also be recognized here that no planning should begin until the outcomes of the program are known. *Only* programs that have shown significantly improved benefits to the problem population should be continued. If significantly improved benefit is shown, the researchers should combine scientific information with action and in this way use their research findings to help establish the program on a permanent basis. If it is impossible to continue the beneficial model, the experimental program will need to be closed down and arrangements made for all the participants to receive the best placement possible. At the particular moment in history when the study is completed, careful program closing may be the only option available. Nonetheless, it is the field experimenters' obligation to ensure that the beneficial model's advocacy not end with only a publication of the research results. Such publications, while scientifically appropriate, do not usually result in beneficial innovation adoption (Fairweather, 1974). For this reason, the research teams' humanitarian obligation is to continue an attempt to disseminate the beneficial model, a subject that is addressed in Chapter 11. First, however, the next chapter will present the basis for evaluating the quality of the innovative model research to ascertain model effectiveness.

CHAPTER **9**

EVALUATING THE INNOVATIVE SOCIAL MODEL

At this juncture, the research team has now carried out the entire investigation, during which time a large number of observations, interviews, behavioral measurements, process measures, administrative records, and outcomes have accumulated. All this information was detailed in the original research plan. It is now necessary to evaluate the information carefully and attempt to make inferences about the validity of the new models in terms of both their outcomes and processes. To some this would be considered a monumental task; however, in the life of a field experimentalist, this is simply another phase in successfully completing the field research which was planned and carried out in the preceding weeks, months, or years.

From a scientific perspective, it is important to recognize that the entire research project has been carried out so that this phase of the research project can be completed. Without an accurate comparison of different models and an understanding of the processes which produced their outcomes, all the preceding work and planning will have been wasted. For this reason, the researchers have spent a considerable amount of time making certain that their collected data were valid and reliable and also accurately measured those aspects of the program considered to be most important.

As with many chapters in this book, this chapter may be viewed as an outline of evaluative techniques since a detailed presentation of them is far beyond the scope of this book. Nevertheless, the importance of this chapter should not be overlooked. It attempts to give the interested reader some understanding of the manner in which different evaluative and statistical techniques, whose actual computations can be found in a wide variety of books, are used.

The purpose of this chapter, therefore, is *not* to give the reader precise and detailed computational tools, but rather to furnish an overview of the different types of methods and how they can be collectively used to answer the questions asked at the beginning of the research. Only a few selected techniques will be given in this chapter, but Chapter 10 will examine the analyses used in the seven experiments that have been presented as examples throughout this book.

NARRATIVE-DESCRIPTIVE TECHNIQUES

Like most scientific research, the development and assessment of social models have a history of their own. Planning the experiment, making the research agreements, and administering the program all have occurred over a period of time which has very likely included periods of both developmental difficulties and smooth operation throughout the life of the experiment. Thus, periods with little difficulty and ease in following the research plan are often followed by periods of difficulty and critical incidents which could affect the research project, which are themselves followed by periods of little difficulty, and so on. Unlike the rather cursory presentation of research that often occurs in scientific journals, it is absolutely essential that the reader understand the developmental history of the social models being evaluated. It is for this reason that a narrative-descriptive account is so meaningful in portraying information that describes accurately and clearly the interpersonal processes and organizational and personal interactions that occur during a field experiment. It is also important to present information that shows the effective involvement of the participants, staff, and other persons. Field research does not occur in a vacuum and, for this reason, likes and dislikes, positive and negative attitudes, and feelings of elation and despondence are present during the course of any major experiment in a field setting. Information that presents the feelings and attitudes of others in carrying out the processes of the social models is essential to understanding the research results. It is for these reasons that narrative-descriptive accounts of the research are so essential in field experimentation. The understanding of interpersonal processes that can be transmitted by narrative descriptions is found in an example from the lodge society evaluation (Fairweather et al., 1969):

> Mr. March, who was again working overtime in the office to keep things ship-shape, made a really extraordinary speech to me. It was mainly about the issues of personal freedom and the difficulty of having to judge other persons under difficult circumstances. He was speaking specifically about the case of Mr. Ring, saying how much he regretted the fact that Mr. Ring had done what he had done. How much he regretted the eventuality now open about Mr. Ring—that he would have to leave the lodge. And how much he regretted this, especially because he saw the value of the lodge to people like Mr. Ring and knew very well that he had very slim chances outside of the lodge. But still, how complicated this was by the fact that all the other men at the lodge had to be protected also and that it was more important to save the lodge as an institution for the benefit of the greater number of men than it was to risk it

being harmed by keeping Mr. Ring. It was a speech, I think, that was full of awareness of the difficulties of making decisions like this on a very high intellectual level.
It seemed to confirm the extent to which Mr. March has become a very capable
holder of the job of business manager (p. 92).

It is probably true that accounts like these are just as important to the understanding of social processes as the statistical analyses and graphical presentations to which our attention now turns.

GRAPHICAL PRESENTATION

While narrative-descriptive accounts of field experiments may be viewed as an
historical presentation of the individuals and the social processes that brought
about the models' outcomes, we might call graphical information the geometry
of model analyses. Longitudinal studies over time can often be best compared
by looking at different kinds of graphs and exploring the curves which present
research information. Thus, two models, A and B, can be graphed over time
on variables which might show similarities or differences or, for that matter,
might actually show a widening of the differences that existed from initiation
to termination of the models. All forms of outcomes over time can be graphed
and can show rather clearly the comparisons of the experimental models on
the particular data selected.

There are different types of graphs that are helpful. Time-trend graphs can
elaborate outcome differences quite clearly. Figure 9-1 presents a time-trend
comparison of group discussion on the small-group ward and the traditional

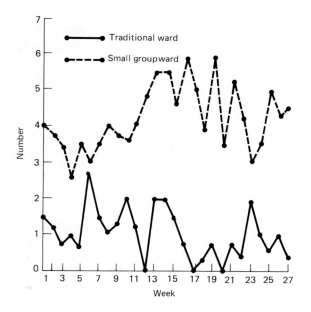

FIGURE 9-1
Mean number of topics with eight
or more discussants for each
treatment program. (*Source:
Fairweather, G. W., and
Tornatzky, L. G.,* Experimental
Methods for Social Policy
Research. *New York: Pergamon
Press, 1977, p. 282.*)

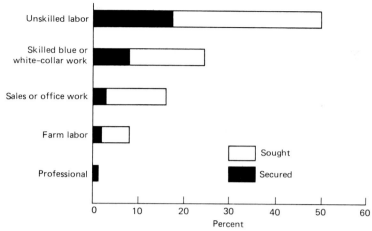

FIGURE 9-2
Type of work sought and secured. (*Source: Fairweather, G. W., et al.,*
Community Life for the Mentally Ill. *Chicago: Aldine, 1969, p. 230.*)

ward. It shows that the frequency of group (eight or more people) discussion is much higher on the small-group ward (operated by patient groups), contrasted with the traditional ward (operated by mental health professionals), and that it continues over time. Whether these differences are significant or not (might have occurred by chance alone) will await a statistical analysis but it is easy to see from this particular graph that it is a useful technique for presenting information.

Another type of graph, the bar graph, is often used for a quick assessment of research data. Figure 9-2 shows the type of employment sought and secured by patients discharged from a mental hospital.

It is important to recognize that eventually information from the research will be shared with administrators, service people, and other researchers. It is for this reason that narrative-descriptive accounts and graphs are so important. Persons without an extensive background in statistical methods can understand and perceive the differences that exist through descriptions and graphs.

STATISTICAL TECHNIQUES

A critical step in the analytic process involves the use of statistical techniques. They provide an objective standard against which observed relationships can be assessed. Statistical techniques might be considered analogous to legal "standard rules of evidence," used in making court decisions. From this perspective, statistics are the scientists' "standard rules of evidence," the evidence accepted by other scientists as valid indicators of the success or failure of models. There are essentially two types of statistical techniques that we will be concerned about in analyzing the data from field experiments. They may be classified under two general titles: *comparative* and *associative*. Let us now explore these two types of statistics and see how they can be helpful to field experimentalists.

Comparative Techniques

At the outset of the research, it is essential to state the research goals as specific hypotheses or research questions in the planning phase of the experiment, i.e., leadership model *A* will yield more beneficial outcomes than leadership of model *B;* or will the different leadership styles in models *A* and *B* yield different outcomes? Whether formal research hypotheses stated as propositions or simply research questions are used depends on the state of knowledge in the particular problem area where an investigation is being carried. Problem areas rich in scientific tradition and theoretical knowledge allow the proposal of formal hypotheses. On the other hand, many problem areas encountered by the community scientist do not have the scientific or conceptual history which permits the statement of formal hypotheses. In such a case, research is established to answer specific questions such as "Does the new model yield significantly more beneficial outcomes than the traditional model?" Whether the researchers are testing hypotheses or attempting to answer research questions, however, the prior specification of the variables to be examined, the types of analyses to be performed, and the expected results are essential ingredients of the research process.

In order to test hypotheses and examine research questions for a model comparison experiment, appropriate comparative statistical techniques must be selected. In general, this involves selecting techniques appropriate for testing the research hypotheses or answering the research questions with the collected data. When the data collected from the models take the form of bell-shaped curves (normal distribution), such as the distribution shown in Figure 9-3, parametric statistical techniques are the comparative techniques usually used. When data collected from models do not take the form of bell-shaped curves, such as the distributions shown in Figure 9-4, nonparametric statistics are the evaluative techniques of choice.

FIGURE 9-3
Two score distributions with different means. (*Source: Fairweather, G. W., and Tornatzky, L. G., Experimental Methods for Social Policy Research. New York: Pergamon Press, 1977, p. 286.*)

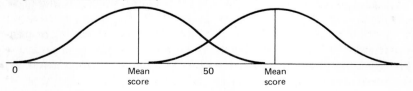

| 0 | Mean score | 50 | Mean score |

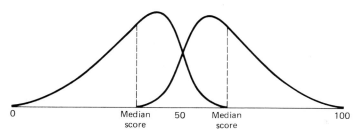

FIGURE 9-4
Two score distributions with different medians. (*Source: Fairweather,*
G. W., and Tornatzky, L. G., Experimental Methods for Social Policy
Research. *New York: Pergamon Press, 1977, p. 286.*)

Both parametric and nonparametric statistical methods compare distributions of data collected from the two or more models that are or have been in
operation. In the case of parametric statistics the most common comparison is
the central tendency of the distributions, which is called the *mean*. It is a simple arithmetic average of all scores in the model (see Figure 9-3). Nonparametric statistics usually compare another measure of central tendency called
the *median* (see Figure 9-4).

Thus, parametric statistical techniques are typically used with "normally"
distributed data, and nonparametric techniques with distributions that are not
"normal." Parametric techniques are usually thought to be more powerful and
sensitive, and there are more of them to choose from, but they require stricter
assumptions about the characteristics of the data being analyzed, including
several beyond that of "normal" distributions. These include the assumptions
that interval or ratio scales have been used, that the variances are homogeneous (equivalent) in all models compared, that research observations have
been made independently, and that scale scores are additive. Nonparametric
statistics, while not as powerful, require fewer assumptions about the characteristics of the data employed. Generally, nonparametric techniques do not
require assumptions about the distributions of the data, their variances, or the
types of scales employed. But, independent observations are also required.

Nonparametric Techniques

The remainder of this section will provide a selected menu of available nonparametric techniques to be used with the types of research designs described
in Chapter 6. Again, the reader is reminded that this section is not intended to
be an exhaustive review of inferential statistics; rather, it is intended as a selec-
tive overview. For a more detailed and comprehensive understanding of nonparametric statistics the reader is encouraged to pursue the subject in a text
such as Hollander and Wolfe (1973), Conover (1980), or Edgington (1969)
which are designed to cover this subject matter adequately.

1 Simple Design—Comparing Two Models with One or More Levels   The nonparametric techniques comparing two models can be divided into those that use matched participants and those that do not. Three common techniques for comparing two models when participants are matched are the *sign test,* the *Wilcoxon signed rank test,* and the *Walsh test.* While there are others, these three procedures are the most common for comparing two models when matching has been included.

The sign test is most commonly used when each of the matched pairs, one of which has participated in each of the two models, can be directly compared as having more of or less of a selected variable than its matched pair. There is no consideration of the size of the difference between the two members of the pair, only the directionality of the difference. If it is further possible to assign a value to the difference, the Wilcoxon rank sign test is used. To take an example, the difference in energy units used by matched households could be ranked and the difference in ranks between a conservation training model and a traditional (control) model compared. While both of these procedures are useful, they are unfortunately not very powerful. If the data allow one to go a step further (i.e., compare the matched pairs, rank the pairs, *and* assign a magnitude of difference between the pairs) a more powerful technique—the Walsh test—can be employed. The Walsh test requires the distributions to be symmetrical, not necessarily normal, before it can be appropriately applied.

But comparing two models without having matched pairs also is a frequent occurrence. While the advantages of preexperimental matching are many, it is not always possible to match participants, particularly under the usual research circumstances where the entire subject pool is not available at one time. A variety of statistical procedures can be used in this situation to compare the models, depending on the size of the sample and the characteristics of the distribution of the data collected. The most common concern is the manner in which the outcome data are classified.

When outcome data fall into two categories (e.g., success or failure, employed or unemployed), the *chi-square test* and its concomitant corrected versions for small cell sizes are the most commonly used techniques (Yates, 1949). Provided certain minimum criteria for expected cell sizes can be met, the chi-square test can further be used when the number of outcome categories goes beyond two categories (e.g., improved, no change, worse).

Another commonly used technique is the *median test.* This technique requires no assumptions about the distribution of the data, but allows a comparison of the number of participants who are above or below the median value on the outcome scales.

If the outcome data are of an ordinal nature—that is, a relative position can be assigned and the relative position has meaning—the *Mann-Whitney test* can be used with matched pairs. Data that fall on an ordinal scale can also be compared using the Wilcoxon rank sum test for unpaired comparisons. In this case, the scores for all conditions are ranked and then summed ranks of the two conditions are compared.

2 Complex Design—More than Two Models with One or More Levels The discussion of statistical techniques for more than two models again can be divided into those that involve matched participants and those that do not. When the outcome data result in nominal or ordinal scales, nonparametric methods must be employed. If the outcome data are nominal, the *Cochran Q test* can be employed. If outcome data are ordinal, the *Friedman test* is useful. Assuming there are three different intervention models and a traditional (control) model and the sample is divided into units of four participants each (one in each model), each matched group of four is ranked from one to four (lowest to highest outcome scores). The Friedman test uses these ranks to compare the models.

Without matched participants, the median test and chi-square tests mentioned above can be used with designs expanded beyond two models. If, however, outcome data are continuous (not necessarily normal) and the measurement is an ordinal scale, the *Kruskal-Wallis test* can be used to compare the outcomes of more than two models. In the Kruskal and Wallis test, all participants are ranked from the highest to the lowest outcome scores and then the conditions are compared for all the ranks of the participants. This test examines the probability that the models have different distributions of ranks.

Parametric Techniques

When outcome data meet the assumptions of parametric techniques, these are the preferred statistical procedures to use. If the data are normally distributed, have homogeneous variances, and interval or ratio scales, parametric techniques should be employed. Historically, there have been intense debates as to the conditions under which parametric tests or nonparametric tests are to be employed (Moses, 1952; Siegel, 1956, pp. 18–34; Edwards, 1960, pp. 111–114).

In general, except with extremely large sample sizes, it is best to require outcome data to meet the scalar, distributional, and variance properties required before proceeding to use parametric techniques. While the nonparametric techniques reviewed in the preceding section are of great use to the field researcher, parametric tests allow more sensitive comparisons of the differences between experimental models, there are more of them, and they are applicable to time-trend designs.

In general, parametric statistical techniques are concerned with testing for the significance of differences between the means of the outcome scores for the different models.

1 Simple Design—Two Models with One or More Levels Whether or not the participants in the two models are matched pairs, the most common statistical test employed for comparing two models is the *t test*. Basically, the *t* test involves a comparison of the differences between model outcome means as a ratio of the overall variability in the data observed. There are different computational formulas for preexperimental matched and unmatched samples. In cases with two or more levels the appropriate statistic is the *F* ratio.

2 Complex Design—More than Two Models with One or More Levels   The most common statistical techniques for comparing more than two models are a series of methods known as *analyses of variance*. These methods are used to compare the outcome means of each model by examining the distributions of outcome scores in each condition.

Simple analysis of variance is used to compare three or more models. This is also referred to as a one-way analysis of variance. When designs using different levels are used, those that involve additional independent variables besides the models such as organizational level or time, *complex* analyses of variance are employed. In these instances, the analysis indicates the extent to which there are statistically significant differences between the models and also whether significant differences occur among other levels of participant variables such as age. Taking energy conservation as an example, the experimentalist might wonder if differences in all models occur more frequently in one age group (i.e., 20–30, 30–40, etc.) than another.

A specific type of complex analysis of variance, the factorial design, has been found to be an especially useful design in field experiments. This design is used when the models and a second independent variable can be ordered so thay they represent points along a continuum. For example, the researcher might be considering three skills training programs identical in content but located in situations representing increasing degrees of social autonomy. In this instance, for example, parolees might be randomly assigned to an employment skills program in the prison where they remained institutionalized 24 hours per day, in a work release setting where they returned to the prison at night, and in an alternative independent living facility in the community. In addition, a critical question may be the extent to which individuals with different lengths of institutionalization might be successful in the three different skills program locations. Hence, inmates with short-, medium-, and long-term institutionalization could be proportionally randomly assigned to each program. The impact of the three points on these two continua (length of incarceration and degree of program independence) could then be evaluated. In a case like this, the interaction between program independence and length of incarceration is of equal interest with the effects of program independence and previous institutionalization viewed separately.

3 Simple and Complex Designs at Multiple Time Points   Many of the social experiments in this volume involve the tracking of an outcome or social process over time. Such data are most often analyzed using the analysis of variance with repeated measures. In this instance, the time dimension is treated as an independent variable in the analysis of variance. While the longitudinal nature of the repeated measure design makes such analyses extremely powerful from both a statistical and conceptual standpoint, a major difficulty is often encountered which limits the widespread use of the repeated measures analysis of variance. Given multiple measures over time of the same participants, the statistical procedures currently available require complete data at all time points for each participant. In naturalistic settings, this requirement often cannot be met because of loss of participants from data analysis. The participant's score may be missing for assessment point(s) simply because he or she has left the program or cannot be located for follow-up information. For example, in following recipients of job placement over the course of 2 years, interviews may be prescribed every 2 months for the 2 years. Let us assume that at each time period, 90 percent of the subjects are successfully found and interviewed. Even so, this could result in a 40 percent subject loss for the total experiment. Careful planning for such eventualities and "fall-back" analytic methods need to be anticipated by the community experimenter when time-trend analyses are used.

More complex analyses of variance can be employed, but are seldom of major value in the field research setting. As the number of factors and number of levels of each factor increase, the complexity of the research project increases rapidly. Typically, only two dimensions are examined at a time and usually with no more than four levels each. Thus, complex designs are rarely used in community experimentation; in fact, the complex design can sometimes obscure salient results in field settings.

Table 9-1 summarizes methods available to the experimentalist and described in this section, and also describes situations in which each is commonly employed. As repeatedly emphasized throughout this chapter, the cursory summary presented here is not a presentation of all the statistical methods found in many excellent texts or courses in inferential statistics. The interested reader is referred to Fallid and Brown (1983), Hays (1981), Keppel (1982), or Wood (1981) for a complete explanation and computational examples of many of the techniques covered here. In addition, our discussion has assumed that the reader would have already taken a course in elementary statistics. If this is not the case, such training and exposure is recommended to anyone before using any of these procedures in the field research setting.

ASSOCIATIVE TECHNIQUES

An equally important step in the analytic process of understanding social innovations comes from examining the internal and external social process variables and their relationships to outcomes. Extremely complex analyses of variance designs are rarely used in longitudinal social model comparative experiments since the number of models an experimenter can field at one time is limited. Thus, examination of the social processes relationships to outcomes is usually accomplished by associative techniques (Davidson et al., 1981). These analyses are completed whether or not there have been findings of sta-

176

TABLE 9.1
A SUMMARY OF NONPARAMETRIC AND PARAMETRIC STATISTICAL TESTS APPLICABLE TO SOCIAL INNOVATIVE EXPERIMENTS

Experimental design	Nonparametric statistics — Scale			Parametric statistics — Scale
	Nominal	Ordinal	Interval	Interval or ratio
Two models with matched participants		Sign Wilcoxon signed rank	Walsh	t
Two models without matched participants	Fisher exact probability Chi square	Median Mann-Whitney Kolmogorov-Smirnov Wald-Wolfowitz Wilcoxon rank sum		t
More than two models with matched participants	Cochran Q	Friedman		One score per participant: Analyses of variance Simple type Multiple classification Factorial design Latin square design Randomized block design
More than two models without matched participants	Chi square	Median Kruskal-Wallis		Two scores per participant: Analysis of covariance Repeated scores per participant: Analysis of variance Trend analysis

Source: Fairweather, G. W., and Tornatzky, L. G., *Experimental Methods for Social Policy Research*. New York: Pergamon Press, 1977, p. 296.

tistical significance between models using the comparative techniques described earlier.

Typically, there are a number of variables collected in longitudinal social experiments. In other sections of this volume, these variables have been labeled as "participant" and "internal and external social processes" (Tables 3-2 and 3-3). In examining participant characteristics and the social processes reflected in these measures, there are many associative techniques that can be used. All such techniques try to define the extent to which there is a demonstrated relationship among individuals, processes, and outcomes. In the longitudinal social experiment, the investigator is also interested in such relationships as they occur within and across time periods. Thus, relationships among participants, social processes, and outcomes of the social models being examined are of crucial interest. For example, the researcher may want to determine whether there are different relationships between the personalitites of the participants and one or more social variables in one social model as compared to another. Or the experimentalist may wish to explore whether these different relationships are related to outcome differences produced by the models. Such examinations are critical in gaining an understanding of the social dynamics of the different social models.

This section will briefly describe associative techniques commonly used in field research. The level of sophistication and the depth of coverage is intended to mirror the preceding section on comparative techniques. Hence, the interested researcher is again referred to appropriate texts for further technical description and computational skill (Ferguson, 1981; Hays, 1981; Edwards, 1984).

Correlations

Methods used to examine associative relationships are generically referred to as *correlations*. In general, correlations express the degree of relationship between two or more variables. The value of a correlation coefficient ranges from $+1.00$ to -1.00. A correlation coefficient of $+1.00$ indicates that there is perfect positive association between two variables. Thus, as the score on one variable goes up, the score on the other correlative variable also goes up, and as the score for the first goes down, the score for the second also goes down. On the other hand, a -1.00 correlation coefficient means that there is perfect negative correspondence between two variables. As the score for one variable goes up, the score on the other goes down.

To further clarify the meaning of correlation coefficients, Figures 9-5 and 9-6 are presented. Using the correlation coefficient for ranks (rho), Figure 9-5 presents a graph of data showing a $+1.00$ correlation coefficient. The reader will note that when $x = 1$, $y = 1$; when $x = 2$, $y = 2$; and so on. This shows a perfect agreement between the two measures displayed on the vertical and horizontal axes. A perfect negative correlation (-1.00) is displayed in Figure 9-6. This graph shows that when $x = 1$, $y = 10$; when $x = 2$, $y = 9$; and so

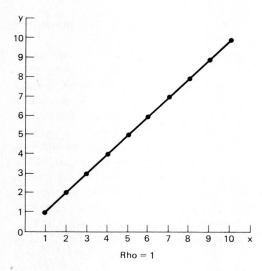

FIGURE 9-5
Regression line placed through the points
(*x, y*) for a rank correlation of +1.
(*Source: Fairweather, G. W., and
Tornatzky, L. G.,* Experimental Methods
for Social Policy Research. *New York:
Pergamon Press, 1977, p. 282.*)

on. This relationship of two variables, *x* and *y*, shows a perfect negative or inverse relationship. Namely, the highest score on the horizontal axis corresponds to the lowest score on the vertical axis.

The line drawn between the data points in the two figures is commonly referred to as the *regression line.* The slope of the line also geometrically expresses the direction of the relationship. Positive relationships have regression lines represented by a positive slope. Negative relationships have regression lines with negative slopes.

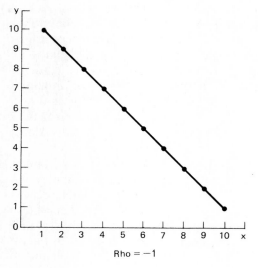

FIGURE 9-6
Regression line placed through the points
(*x, y*) for a rank correlation of −1.
(*Source: Fairweather, G. W., and
Tornatzky, L. G.,* Experimental Methods
for Social Policy Research. *New York:
Pergamon Press, 1977, p. 282.*)

There is a critical issue that continuously arises about the logical inferences possible from associative techniques. Regardless of the strength of the relationship observed, even when $r = +1.00$ or -1.00, a causal relationship between the variables *cannot* be directly inferred. Suppose a researcher found a perfect positive correlation between hat size and reading speed. It seems highly unlikely that a large hat size would cause improved reading speed or vice versa. However, a third variable, age, is highly correlated with both and would likely be a good candidate for a causal inference. Since in the aforementioned example correlation age is not measured or considered, its possible causative effect could be overlooked. Thus, it cannot be inferred from a correlational analysis that one variable causes the other or vice versa.

It should also be pointed out that the two examples given in Figures 9-5 and 9-6 are the ideal case. In the real world it is rare, if indeed it occurs at all, that two distributions of data are in perfect agreement. There is more typically some "spread" around a "best fit" regression line. Figure 9-7 represents a much more realistic view of field research data. The regression line in this case is the "best fit" line. The criterion most often used for the "best fit" line is that it is the line which reduces the squared deviations (the squares of the distances of each point from the line) to a minimum. This is commonly called the *least squares criterion.*

There are many aspects of correlations important to understand. Listed below are several central principles about correlations and their use:

1 A correlation is represented by a straight line which minimizes the sum of the squares of the plotted distributions of two variables (except for *eta,* see **5f** below).

FIGURE 9-7
Regression line and plot of points (x, y) for a positive correlation. (*Source: Fairweather, G. W., and Tornatzky, L. G.,* Experimental Methods for Social Policy Research. *New York: Pergamon Press, 1977, p. 282.*)

2 The data for computing correlation coefficients must be at least ordinal-scale data. Specific correlation techniques are used depending on the scale or type of data employed.

3 Correlations express the degree of association between variables and say nothing about causation.

4 The statistical symbol for the correlation coefficient is r. The strength of the association is usually expressed as r^2 and referred to as the percent of the variance of one variable accounted for by the other.

5 Depending on the type of scale used, the following specific correlation coefficients can be computed:

   a If truly dichotomous data are used, the phi coefficient can be computed.

   b If dichotomous data representing an underlying continuous variable are used, the tetrachoric correlation should be computed.

   c If categorical data are employed, the contingency, C, should be computed.

   d If the relationship between a continuous and dichotomous variable is being examined, the point biserial correlation is computed if the dichotomous variable is truly discrete, and the biserial correlation is used if it is assumed to be continuous.

   e If the relationship between ranked data is examined, the rank correlation, rho, can be computed as shown in Figures 9-2 and 9-3.

   f If the relationship is *not* a straight line, the correlation ratio, eta, can be computed.

   g The most common correlation coefficient, the Pearson product moment correlation, is used when examining relationships with interval or ratio data.

Usually, the community experimenter needs to examine the relationship between more than two variables at once. Several sophisticated techniques are very useful here. The simplest, the partial correlation, allows the experimenter to examine the relationship of two variables while holding a third variable constant. For example, one can examine the relationship between school performance and socioeconomic status while holding age constant. In a sense, this procedure discounts the effect that age may have had on the size of the correlation.

There are additional types of analyses commonly employed by the community researcher in examining the interrelationship among many variables. First, one may be interested in reducing the number of measures to a workable few dimensions. The general types of procedures for this reduction are called *factor* or *cluster analyses* (Tryon & Bailey, 1966; Gorsuch, 1974). Each of these procedures allows the researcher to examine the relationships among a large number of variables by reducing them to a few clearly defined dimensions, thus increasing the ease of data analysis and conceptual understanding of the data.

Another problem facing the community researcher involves examining the relationship between one variable and several other variables. For example, if one had four group process variables—leadership, cohesiveness, group composition, and type of membership—and was interested in their joint relation-

TABLE 9.2
ASSOCIATIVE TECHNIQUES AND THEIR USE

Use	Technique
Relationship of one variable with another variable	Phi coefficient Biserial correlation Point biserial correlation Tetrachoric correlation Rank correlation (rho) Pearson product moment correlation Contingency coefficient (c) Eta (n)
Relationships among many variables	Principal components analysis Factor analysis Cluster analysis (V type) Path analysis
Relationship of one variable with many variables	Principal components analysis Path analysis Cluster analysis (preset)
Relationship of many variables with one variable	Multiple regression Cluster analysis (pre set)
Relationships of many variables with many variables	Canonical correlation Cluster analysis (intercorrelation among cluster definers)

ship to a single outcome such as group performance, associative procedures which can be employed for this type of analysis include multiple regression, discriminant function analysis, or cluster analysis using the outcome as a preset variable (Klecka, 1980; Pedhazur, 1982).

Another method attempts to explain phenomena through multivariate associative techniques. It is called *path analysis* (Wright, 1960; Duncan, 1966). Here the researcher specifies a set of hypothesized relationships between variables, translates these hypotheses into a set of structural equations, and analyzes the equations. In these analyses, the researcher selects minimum levels of significance and tests whether the hypothesized relationships meet these levels. For those that do, a "path diagram" is presented to depict graphically how the variables are related.

Finally, the researcher may be interested in the joint relationship between two sets of variables, for example, examining the relationship between multiple process variables and multiple outcome variables. Procedures such as *canonical correlations* are useful here. They allow an examination of the internal structure of the two sets of variables and then an examination of their interrelationship. Table 9-2 presents a summary of the correlative techniques commonly used by community experimentalists.

In this chapter we have presented an overview of the major analytic methods used in comparing models and understanding their social processes. It should be clear by now that the social innovator-experimenter should use whatever comparative techniques are necessary to permit the most accurate inferences possible from the data generated by the experiment. As for comparing the social models, observations resulting in narrative descriptions, graphs, and statistical techniques are the most important methods. But comparative techniques do not stand alone in providing the experimenter tools for examining the processes and effects of social models. Examination of the relationships between and among participant variables and internal and external social process variables provides experimentalists with an understanding of how participant characteristics and social processes are related to each other and to outcomes.

In any single study, it is common that many comparative approaches are used. These techniques, in combination with associative techniques, provide the bases for interpreting the results of social experiments. How graphical presentations, narrative discussions, and comparative and associative statistical procedures are used depends to some extent upon the intended audience and its background knowledge. Usually, narrative descriptions and easily interpreted graphs are used to add depth to the presentation of the statistical results.

Many of the data analytical problems faced in the field experiment will be beyond the immediate knowledge of the community researcher. For this reason, statistical consultation will be needed in planning and evaluating most field experiments. This is even more true nowadays with the increasingly common use of high-speed computers and advances in multivariate analysis. While it remains the responsibility of the community researcher to make ultimate decisions about appropriate statistical techniques, it is often necessary to use a statistical consultant to elaborate the options available.

Research planning needs further emphasis at this point. Early planning for testing research hypotheses and answering research questions by use of statistical analyses is essential. While it may sound easy to complete successfully the comparative statistical procedures described here, having information and data stored in such a fashion that they can be easily used by computerized statistical packages requires considerable planning. Even though all the comparative procedures and associative techniques described here are available in computerized packages such as SPSS (Statistical Package for the Social Science; Nie et al., 1981), BIOMED (Biomedical Computer Programs, Dixon & Brown, 1979), SAS (Institute Statistical Analyses System, Helwig & Council, 1979), and the like, making early plans for the procedures that will be most useful should be an integral part of research planning. Part of the planning should involve the designation of analytic alternatives so that if the collected data do not meet the mathematical assumptions for the analytic technique of first choice, an appropriate second choice will be available. Such alternatives are necessary for adequately testing the research hypotheses or answering research questions. Seeking statistical and computer consultation before the first datum is collected is a wise and prudent rule that should be followed in any field research.

CHAPTER 10

MAKING INFERENCES ABOUT INNOVATIVE SOCIAL MODELS FROM THEIR EVALUATIONS

After the analyses have been completed using a variety of comparative and associative procedures, it is necessary to begin making inferences from the findings. While in this book we have separated these two stages—(1) comparative and associative analyses and (2) drawing inferences—in actuality they are interrelated. The process of drawing inferences usually involves completing analyses which provide preliminary answers to stated hypotheses or research questions; making preliminary inferences; returning to the data for additional analyses, resulting in further verification *or* in questioning the preliminary conclusions reached; and checking on unexpected findings which may have occurred to see how they fit into the preliminary inferences.

Throughout this process it should be pointed out that statistical tests and standard levels of statistical significance are only *one* source of information to be used. It must be remembered that finding a statistical significance only indicates that the observed differences or relationships are unlikely to have occurred by chance. Thus, statistical significance provides no guarantee that the results are meaningful in either a social, theoretical, or practical sense. The basic logical issue is: What are the observed significant differences or relationships due to? For this reason a note of caution is injected here. Many social scientists in recent years have placed a high value on statistical significance without considering whether or not the mathematically derived numbers represented in a statistical test of significance are either logically or socially significant. To decide whether statistical and social significance are themselves related requires a basic understanding not only of research methods but of the social problem itself. It is for this reason that personal observations and experiences with the social problem to be evaluated have received such emphasis in this book. Simply finding that two social models yield significantly different statistical results without a concomitant knowledge of the problem itself from workaday observations can lead to erroneous conclusions made from the collected data.

Without minimizing its importance, therefore, it must be understood that statistical significance is only one step in the logical process of understanding social models and their effects. As mentioned above, it is too often the only criterion used in drawing conclusions. An adequate understanding of the problem at the day-to-day level as well as issues of planning, implementation, and control is necessary to make the logical leap from statistical significance to social significance. Let us now attempt to understand this process of integrating personal and problem knowledge with research results.

Aiming at Inferences

In drawing inferences from social model experiments, the community researcher is usually concerned with the question of whether or not the new social model is more beneficial than the traditional model. Typically, a statistical one-sided hypothesis or research question is employed. Since it is clearly the goal of social innovation to improve the life benefits of the participants, the generic hypothesis in all social innovative experiments is that the innovative model(s) will produce significant improvement in the participants' lives contrasted with the traditional model. In comparing the outcomes of the social innovation with the traditional approach, the first question therefore is "Do the differences observed reach statistical significance in favor of the new model *and* are the differences meaningful to the policy makers and the participant groups?" This hypothesis may be formally stated in the following manner: The innovative model will improve the life benefits of the participants contrasted with the traditional model. Such a hypothesis is called a one-sided hypothesis because the equivalence or failure of the innovative model means that the model has *not* significantly improved the life benefits of the participants, and hence, is not an acceptable new model to be disseminated (why create a new model if the old one does as well?).

Such one-sided hypotheses and their tests of statistical significance can be illustrated through the test described earlier. In the simplest case the community researcher would have two group means, one for the innovative social model and one for the traditional approach. The community researcher is interested in testing the hypothesis that the average score (mean) of the innovative participants is significantly greater than the mean of the traditional (control) participants where higher scores are considered to be more adaptive. The statement of this generic hypothesis in statistical terms is presented in the descriptive material found in Figure 10-1. After calculating a *t* test comparing the means for both models, an assessment of the probability level of the *t* value can be ascertained. Figure 10-1 shows that the value of the *t* statistic must fall

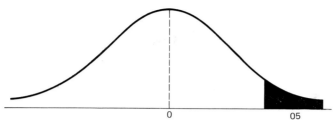

FIGURE 10-1
The one-sided hypothesis—the social change experimentalists'
one-tailed test of significance for the statistical hypothesis that the
mean of the experimental model (m_em) $\leq$ the mean of the control
(m_c) against the alternative $m_em > m_c$. If the computed t falls in the
shaded area, the statistical hypothesis $m_em \leq m_c$ can be rejected.
(Source: Fairweather, G. W., and Tornatzky, L. G., Experimental
Methods for Social Policy Research. *New York: Pergamon Press,
1977, p. 346.)*

within the shaded area. Such a t value indicates that there are only five chances
or less in 100 that the differences between the two model means obtained could
have occurred by chance. When a t value of this magnitude is found, the community experimenter has reasonable statistical grounds (.05 level or less) for
concluding that the innovative social model is more effective than the traditional model.

Assuming that such a t value is found, it still must be carefully integrated
with the other information emerging from the study before significant model
benefits can be inferred. Since statistical significance alone is not sufficient for
determining the efficacy of a new social model or to gain an understanding of
its operational processes, the finding of significant outcome must be integrated
with other findings from the defining characteristics of the sample and the
internal and external social processes that may have been responsible for generating the differences. To accomplish this it is necessary to examine the relationships between participant characteristics, outcomes, and internal and
external social processes thought to be components that might account for the
innovation's outcomes. This additional information may help to pinpoint
causal connections among participants, processes, and outcomes. Only after
this has been accomplished can the social significance of the findings be
addressed.

Another issue which must be considered in drawing inferences about the
benefits of an experimental model is its generalizability. Assuming the validity
of the findings as outlined above, the question now becomes: "To what extent
is there reason to believe that the observed benefits of the innovative social
model would occur if the model were replicated in other geographical areas so
that it could be more useful to society?" This second area of inference is very
complex and requires that the community researcher examine a number of
dimensions that exist before drawing conclusions. Since it is doubtful that any

single community research can be generalized to all settings, persons, and times, there are three types of information that have been considered in the sampling procedures and the research design that must now be reviewed again. This review takes the form of answering three questions:

1 Is the sample used in the study still representative of the problem population in general?

2 Are the social contexts in which the model operated, including internal and external social and organizational relationships, representative of those which will be encountered elsewhere?

3 Is the social outcome criterion used representative now (weeks or months later) of the social outcomes commonly used in today's social practice?

In considering the representativeness of the sample, a number of participant characteristics should be considered. Obviously, the demographic characteristics of the individuals, groups, or organizations to which one wishes to generalize should be similar. For example, if the experimenters created an alternative educational model for junior high students, the original innovative model should be tried with junior high students and thus should be restricted to them. Even so, one would also be concerned with the demographic comparability of the sample youths and other youths who might use the program. Comparisons of the original sample with current national or local samples can often provide an estimate of comparability.

Another characteristic which must be considered is the manner in which participants entered the program. If the program involved only volunteers, a motivational component might be involved so that generalizations should be restricted to volunteers.

Additionally, the community researcher should examine the extent to which different types of participants are successful in the new social model. To accomplish this goal at this point in the inferential process, the researcher needs to explore the participant successes and failures (Morrell, 1979; Whitaker & Severy, 1984). Even though a statistically significant benefit may be demonstrated in favor of the social innovation, undoubtedly some failures have occurred. Let us assume for sake of example that 90 percent of the failures were in a particular classification such as students who were educational underachievers. Let us assume that an examination of the participant data showed that 90 percent of the failures have not completed high school. Further examination of social model functioning might show that the skills necessary for task accomplishment include skills learned in high school. Such information sheds light on the limits of successful model outcome attainment with respect to the problem population. For this reason an examination of program failures is important.

Consideration of the representativeness of the social context requires similar logical scrutiny. Examining the formal and informal characteristics of the contemporary social context is critical in determining the permissible generalizations. Such dimensions as organizational size and structure, community social climate, and geographic location are only a few. Using the example presented above, if the innovative alternative classroom for junior high school students was found to improve academic achievement significantly when operated in a neighborhood community center, one would not want to generalize to other geographical settings in which the alternative classroom could be operated such as a traditional junior high school until a replicate had been field-tested.

The situational specificity of social outcomes must also be considered in determining the generalizability of findings. Most social outcome criteria come from archival measures, self-reports, reports from significant others, and so on. Differences in these sources can cause problems in generalizing from one model to another, i.e., one city's crime rate to another, and the like. This problem is not insurmountable but requires an understanding of exactly how social outcome criteria are measured, the local meaning of different archival outcome measures, and a knowledge of the interrelationships among the criteria collected under different circumstances.

Each of the issues set forth here indicates the risk of attempting to generalize on the basis of a single study or the single trial of a social innovation. It shows, for example, why longitudinal experiments with repeated measures are essential for valid inferences. While longitudinal experiments improve the accuracy of inferences they cannot replace the need for replication and continued monitoring of the efficacy of replicates. In short, the scientific investigation of the validity of social models should not stop even after the original longitudinal prototype has been experimentally examined.

EXAMPLES OF INFERENCES MADE FROM EVALUATING THE MODELS

The remainder of this chapter will be devoted to presenting evaluation examples and demonstrating how to make inferences from them. Evaluations of the seven social models which have been used throughout this volume are presented along with the researcher's inferences. Space does not permit presenting the entire results of each of the researchers reported here. Instead, critical analyses have been selected to represent a range of comparative and associative approaches to evaluation.

Citizen Participation in Health Planning

It will be recalled that Beck (1973) was interested in increasing the participation of health service consumers in health planning activities. For a memory refresher of Beck's experiment the reader is referred to its discussion in Chapters 5 through 8. She created a social participation training model in an attempt to increase consumer participation and compare its processes and effectiveness to traditional methods of involving consumers in health planning.

The most important issue for Beck at the outset was to find out if there would be differences in consumer participation in health planning meetings that could be produced by training consumers in autonomous group decision making (innovative model), when compared with the usual practice of simply inviting volunteer citizens to attend these health planning meetings and represent health consumers (traditional control model). A particularly salient issue in this regard was the need to increase the verbal participation of consumers in the planning meetings since Beck had observed that when consumers did attend planning sessions they seldom participated in the discussions and usually left all major decisions to health professionals. Hence, her first goal was to produce increased levels of consumer verbal interactions by training consumers separately in decision making in a supportive group situation with the hope that the small-group behavior learned there would transfer to the actual health planning meetings.

Consequently, Beck began training a group of consumer volunteers who comprised the participants in the autonomous group experimental model. The results of their group training showed increased verbal participation, role clarity, cohesiveness, and improving group problem-solving ability as evidence that the preexperimental training period had created an autonomous problem-solving group. A graph showing increased member participation is shown in Figure 10-2 and is described by Beck in the following way:

Verbal Participation

Figure 10-2 presents the average speaker frequency during group meeting discussions by phase of social participation group development. It shows the changes over time that occurred in the average number of comments made by participatory group

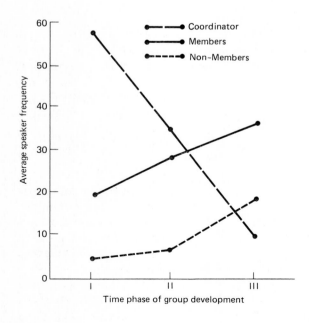

FIGURE 10-2
Average speaker frequency by phase of participatory group development. [*Source: Beck (1973), p. 69.*]

members, non-members guests, or the coordinator. If a cohesive participatory group were formed, it would be anticipated that there would be a sharp decrease in conversation by the coordinator as time progressed and a corresponding increase by the members. The results displayed in the figure confirm this effect rather dramatically . . . (Beck, 1973, p. 68).

Having evidence of autonomous group development, she now computed a series of outcomes analyses, comparing the behaviors and perceptions of the trained autonomous group members and their untrained control in the actual planning sessions. In an especially important first comparison, she analyzed the health planning knowledge possessed by the consumer support group participants and contrasted their knowledge with the untrained consumers. The results are presented in Table 10-1. It shows that in all five areas of knowledge, significantly greater knowledge (as shown in the higher mean scores) was achieved by the consumer support model.

Table 10-1 also shows that these mean differences were unlikely to have occurred by chance—four of the five knowledge areas were significant at the .05 level and one at the .01 probability level. Beck also showed that the attendance of persons belonging to both groups (consumer training and traditional control) differed significantly during the follow-up period with more consumer training group personnel attending the health planning meetings after formal measurement of the meetings had been discontinued. In addition, other analyses showed that the trained consumer group had significantly different perceptions contrasted with the untrained control. They perceived themselves as having more influence and power in the health planning sessions than the control members. This is highlighted in an abstract of a presentation made by a consumer-trained group member at one of the planning meetings (narrative-descriptive technique). The participant made the following statement:

If the agency truly wants consumers who are ready to be involved in the planning activities of such a program and not always critics on the fringe, then it must give

TABLE 10.1
COMPARISON OF INNOVATIVE CONSUMER TRAINING MODEL AND
TRADITIONAL MODEL ON POSTEXPERIMENTAL KNOWLEDGE

	Test of Significance	Model Means	
Knowledge area of comparison	t test	Consumer support	Traditional
General information	S .05	2.25	1.87
Staff names	S .01	2.40	1.55
Committee names	S .05	1.78	1.32
Chairperson names	S .05	2.40	1.58
Work program items	S .05	1.41	1.01

S .05 = significant at $p < .05$
S .01 = significant at $p < .01$

staff support to consumers. This staff support, time, money, and most important interest commitment to the importance of the role of the consumers has to come tonight or it will not be in the budget or the work program for 1973–74. Therefore, the Consumer Support Group recommends that this Board take two steps: (1) fulfill the commitment to the Consumer Support Group project in staff time or free the money for the Consumer Support Group to hire its own staff this summer; (2) hire staff in behalf of the consumers on a permanent basis (p. 93).

Beck used a wide variety of evaluative techniques (observations, narrative descriptions, graphs, parametric and nonparametric techniques) to compare and contrast the decision-making processes of the social model where participants were trained in social interaction and decision making contrasted with a model using a typical untrained volunteer approach. The participants from both these models interacted in health planning meetings with health providers. From these analyses, her own observations, and background medical knowledge Beck made the following inferences:

The ultimate objective of the training program (model) was to increase effective participation of the group members in health planning decision-making. This was quantified by their participation in formal and informal decision-making activities of the agency. Results demonstrated *a significant increase in participation in the informal communication network* during the six month experimental period. *Increased formal participation* of the original and small group participants however, *was apparently a delayed effect not being statistically significant until the post experimental period.* . . .

In sum, the results demonstrated that a viable alternative does exist to doing nothing about the problems of consumer participation. . . . The results demonstrated that an autonomous small group training program can transmit information to its members and reinforce the legitimacy of their participation in agency decision-making. Most importantly they demonstrated that partcipation in this program resulted in greater, more effective participation in agency decision-making activities (pp. 102–103).

Jobs for the Elderly

In order to provide more meaningful roles for older people, many of whom were retirees, Gray (1980) established a job club and contrasted it with a traditional employment job referral program. His main concern was with the lack of a social and employment role for the aging population. His experimental plan involving a description of the job club and its traditional control can be found in Chapters 5 through 8. As outcomes for the job club Gray contrasted those who participated in it with the traditional employment service at 4-week periods during the course of the experiment. As Table 10-2 shows, he found significant differences in favor of the job club in higher placement rates, higher continued employment rates, more income, and more hours worked when the two models were compared. The significant differences in placement, employment, income, and hours worked also increased over time on all measures. One example of this increase over time is shown in the employment area presented in Figure 10-3.

TABLE 10.2
A COMPARISON OF EMPLOYMENT FOR THE JOB CLUB MODEL AND THE TRADITIONAL MODEL

Area of comparison	Probability level for tests of significance (analysis of variance and chi-square)	Means or percentages	
		Job club innovative model	Traditional model
Placement rate	S .001	87%	26%
Continuous employment	S .001	58%	16
Income (4-week period)	S .02	$147.91	$11.95
Hours worked (4-week period)	S .01	32.69	9.67

S .01 = significant at p < .01
S .001 = significant at p < .001

Gray also compared a number of process measures to understand more clearly the basis for the treatment success. He found that those who attended the job club meetings had significantly more knowledge about searching for jobs than the traditional model participants and that they also created a job search network significantly more frequently than the traditional participants.

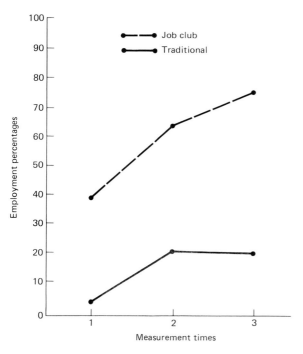

FIGURE 10-3
Percent employment of job club and traditional models at the three measurement times.

He also found significant differences associated with the two models on a scale of their satisfaction with life—job club participants were more satisfied. No significant differences were obtained by contrasting the job club with the traditional program on personal optimism and other personality measures. From all his research data Gray made the following inferences:

> These results indicate that meaningful increases in the employment rates of older job seekers can be achieved by careful implementation of a job club program tailored to the needs of this group. However, the relatively low status of many of the obtained placements should serve as a signal that real progress in this area will only come about through systems level changes in the economy and the workplace (p. 3).

Poor Readers

Tucker (1974) designed an associative language bridging "learning model" which he compared with the traditional "standard English" classroom learning model for reading improvement. The goal of the innovative model was to use the childrens' black dialect as a basis for learning (bridging to standard English) which should, therefore, improve the child's reading performance. Tucker also focused the research on the potential effectiveness that the new model might have for white as well as black students (see Chapters 5 through 8). Tucker employed this research strategy to examine the models' effects on reading performance and related attitudes.

To evaluate the effectiveness of the innovative bilingual associative bridging model as contrasted with the traditional standard English reading model, Tucker compared a number of academic achievements by the experimental participants of the two models. The first comparison concerned improvements in vocabulary, and as Table 10-3 shows, highly significant differences were obtained in favor of the innovative learning model (higher mean gain scores). No differences due to race were found. Comprehensive tests were also given

TABLE 10.3
POOR READERS' OUTCOMES

	Test of significance	Mean gain score	
Area of comparison	Analysis of variance	Innovative model (bilingual)	Traditional model (standard English)
Reading performance			
Vocabulary	S .001	12.10	1.64
Comprehension	S .001	11.76	3.27
Attitudes			
Attitudes toward teachers	S .01	4.95	1.00

S .01 = significant at $p < .01$
S .001 = significant at $p < .001$

after the reading was completed. Table 10-3 again shows highly significant gains by the associative bridging learning model participants contrasted with the traditional standard English participants (higher mean gain scores). Tucker also compared attitude change toward parents, school, teachers, and self. Table 10-3 shows that the only significant attitude difference obtained was attitudes toward teachers. The participant means show mean attitude gains scores of 4.95 for the innovative model and only 1.00 for the traditional model. Thus, while three of four attitudes did not change significantly (school, parents, self) in the two models—attitudes toward teachers did—they improved significantly more in the innovative model. Again, no significant differences for white as contrasted with black students occurred.

The measurements presented in Table 10-3 were derived from pre- and posttest score differences. However, Tucker also assessed the process of learning over time. At the end of each week a comprehensive test was given concerning the material that had been read during the week. Graphs of both black and white students in the innovative model and standard English models are shown in Figure 10-4. A test of significance showed a close resemblance to the graph with no significant differences associated with race but very clear significant differences ($F = 47.30$, $p < 0.001$) associated with the experimental models and for time ($F = 18.02$, $p < 0.001$). The graph also shows that the highest scores for both black and white students were earned by the associative bridging innovative model participants.

FIGURE 10-4
Means of the four groups at the ten measurement times. [*Source: Tucker (1974), p. 47.*]

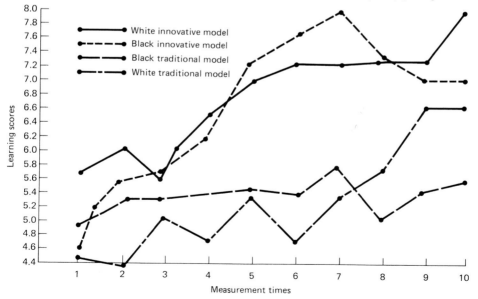

In completing his analyses, Tucker computed correlations of the performance and attitude scores and found that the performance scores clustered
together as one group of highly associated measures. A second group of measures—attitude scales—formed a more loosely knit yet interrelated cluster.

After examining all the results, Tucker made the following inferences:

> The main findings of this study show associative bridging significantly improves the
> performance of all students—black and white alike. This is an especially important
> finding because many researchers, both black and white, have promoted the position
> that it is difficult for both racial groups to achieve at the same rate and level by using
> the same material. Thus, the effect of this experimental (model) was profound in the
> area of performance—it has a great impact upon reading for all participants.
>
> There also was a significant time effect in the learning situation . . . (although most
> attitudes did not change, attitudes toward teachers did). Even so the research infor-
> mation indicates that the effects of associative bridging improved learning for the
> entire experimental period of ten weeks . . . persons can improve their performance
> while not changing their attitudes or change their attitudes while not affecting their
> performance. . . . It appears, therefore, that an educational system that concentrates
> on only one aspect does so at the expense of the other (pp. 53–54).

Energy Depletion

Leedom (1980) was concerned with the attitudes and behaviors about energy
conservation children learned in high school. She was, however, uncertain
about the type of educational program that would bring about improvement.
Accordingly, Leedom developed different training models for children in
energy conservation awareness and behavior (see Chapters 5 through 8). She
conducted an experiment comparing an information workshop model, a task-
oriented model, and a typical school participation model (control).

In order to compare the three different approaches in changing attitudes and
behaviors about energy consumption, Leedom created a scale measuring attitude change about energy consumption as well as a behavioral scale which
directly measured energy usage. The attitude scale contained eight subscales.
Their analyses showed that five of eight conservation attitude areas reached
statistical significance. Table 10-4 shows the five areas and their mean scores.
An examination of the means in Table 10-4 shows that in all five attitude areas
the task-oriented model achieved the highest mean scores followed by the
information model and finally the control model.

The significant F tests and the means in Table 10-4 show rather convinc-
ingly that the task-oriented approach to changing attitudes about energy consumption is probably a significantly more productive approach than either a
traditional workshop or regular classroom lectures.

However, Leedom was also interested in changes in consumption behavior.
To measure accurately changes in energy consumption behaviors, she measured both electricity use (exclusive of heat) and fuel use for space heating
(excluding electricity). Analyses of variance for these two uses—electricity and

TABLE 10.4
COMPARISON OF TASK-ORIENTED, INFORMATION, AND CONTROL MODELS
ON ATTITUDES ABOUT ENERGY CONSERVATION

Area of comparison	Test of significance	Means		
Energy conservation attitude	Analyses of variance	Task-oriented model	informational-only model	Control model
Willingness to sacrifice	S .001‡	4.1204	3.7300	3.6290
Willingness to take specific actions	S .001‡	3.8148	3.5200	3.2304
Home-related activities	S .001‡	4.0074	3.8640	3.4839
Government involvement	S .01†	4.3056	4.0300	3.9839
Its importance	S .05*	4.2963	4.0729	3.9758

*Significant at .05 level
†Significant at .01 level
‡Significant at .001 level

195

heating—showed no significant differences between the experimental models in either electricity use or fuel consumption.

Leedom also conducted a home energy conservation survey of family members of the students involved in the three experimental models. Two general behavioral measures resulted from this survey. They were: (1) the variety of conservation tasks performed in the home, and (2) the total number of times all conservation tasks were performed. Analyses of variance showed no significant differences resulted from the conservation activity of the families in the different experimental models. From these results and her own observations Leedom made the following general inference:

> The present study suggests that a task-oriented approach to energy education is the most effective means of changing or imparting to high school students the appropriate attitudes concerning energy conservation. Further, the present study also suggests that a passive, information dissemination approach to energy education may be totally ineffective as a vehicle for changing energy conservation attitudes. Finally, and perhaps more importantly, these results do not provide any evidence that changes in energy conservation attitudes result in corresponding changes in behavior (pp. 78–79).

Smoking and Health

Coelho (1983) compared an innovative stop-smoking program model with the American Lung Association's stop-smoking model and a traditional control model in which the participants continued their normative ways of attempting to stop smoking. A description of the study can be found in Chapters 5 through 8. The central issues addressed in Coelho's experiment concerned (1) the efficacy of the treatment models in stopping smoking behavior, (2) relationship of personality characteristics to reduction of cigarette consumption, (3) relationship of sex difference to cessation of cigarette smoking, and (4) whether or not the group dynamics of the different programs were related to consumption reduction.

Coelho used several different outcomes because of the disagreement among researchers about which measure was the most important. The three outcome measures recommended were (1) the number of cigarettes smoked per day, (2) the percent of the baseline (amount of prior smoking), and (3) abstinence rates. All measures were taken at four time periods: (1) before the experiment started, (2) at the end of the experiment, (3) 1-month follow-up, and (4) 3-months follow-up.

Table 10-5 revealed that all three outcome measures showed a significant cessation of cigarette smoking in favor of the innovative cigarette smoking program model. Table 10-5 also shows that these cessation outcomes were ranked from best to worst in the following order: (1) innovative model, (2) American Lung Association model, and (3) traditional model. Coelho also found in his repeated measure analyses of variance that significant differences occurred over time for all three outcomes. As one illustration, the significant consump-

TABLE 10.5
COMPARISON OF CIGARETTE CONSUMPTION ON THREE OUTCOME MEASURES

Area of comparison	Tests of significance	Model		
	Analysis of variance	Innovative	American Lung Association	Traditional (control)
			Means	
Cigarettes consumed per day	S .001†	13.84	18.95	27.61
			Percentages	
Percentage of baseline smoking	S .001†	28%	47%	83%
Abstinence at end of treatment	S .05*	62%	30%	18%

*significant at .05 level
†significant at .001 level

tion reduction over time in cigarettes consumed per day is shown in Figure 10-5. The graph does, however, raise an issue about the long-term effects of all the programs since once the program terminates the cigarettes consumed per day begin to increase.

In addition, Coelho found no significant differential effects in consumption reduction when he compared men and women participants. Personality test scores as revealed in locus of control test scores were unrelated to cigarette smoking, as was age. But social support and program satisfaction were associated with low cigarette consumption. The relationships of these measures with smoking cessation behavior are seen in the correlations of Coelho's cluster data presented in Table 10-6.

The analysis of the results along with other observations and experiences gained by Coelho before and during this smoking cessation experiment led him to make the following inferences:

> The innovative model appears to be more effective in curtailing cigarette consumption for both men and women than either the American Lung Association model or depending on the person to stop smoking on their own (traditional model). In addition, the innovative model was more effective in helping persons reduce consumption levels at all assessment periods. Satisfaction with treatment and social support

FIGURE 10-5
Cigarettes consumed per day for three models by time period.
[*Source: Coelho (1983), p. 77.*]

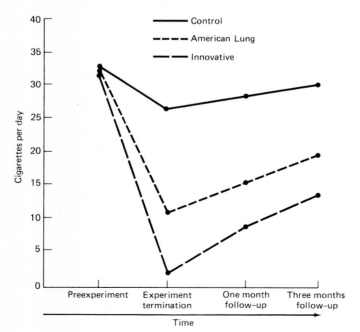

TABLE 10.6
CORRELATIONS OF CLUSTERS WITH SMOKING CESSATION BEHAVIOR

Clusters	Correlations with smoking cessation behavior
1 Program satisfaction	.42
2 Social support	.26
3 Age-related factors	.02
4 Personality test 1: Chance locus of control	.06
5 Personality test 2: Internal health locus of control	−.02
6 Personality test 3: Powerful others external locus of control	.04

appears to be associated with the cessation of smoking behavior. But the one- and three-month follow-up shows a gradual increase of smoking behavior after the programs stopped and thus suggests that improved treatment models should be found before broader adoption occurs (p. 57).

Juvenile Delinquency

The research on developing volunteer-based diversion programs for juvenile offenders focused on the extent to which specific diversion program models were more effective than juvenile court processing (control model) in preventing criminal recidivism. Answering this question called for multiple assessment of youths who had received services from several alternative volunteer-based diversion programs.

The research on juvenile offenders required the development of six experimental models. Each of these models was then compared on a variety of self-reports and archival measures. The reader is referred to Chapters 5 through 8 for the detailed description of each of the experimental models.

In order to draw accurate inferences about the relative efficacy of diversion models for juvenile offenders, four types of analyses were completed. First, it was necessary to examine the equivalence of sample participants so that later comparisons of outcome differences, if found, could be attributed to the experimental models rather than to sample differences. While this research involved randomly assigning youths to the models, it was still possible for the samples to be different. Hence, the first analyses included a comparison of youths in the six different models on selected demographic information—criminal history, past school performance, previous self-report of delinquency, and life activity variables. No significant differences were found. These analyses, therefore, indicated sample equivalence of the six experimental models.

A second type of analysis was completed to evaluate the theoretical and field congruence of the five experimental models. A very important issue in drawing inferences concerning a model's impact on outcomes concerns the extent to which the experimental models are theoretically and operationally the same during their actual field operation. This is especially important in this experiment since the degree to which the models were carried out in the field in a manner consistent with their design depended upon the activity of trained volunteers. A series of three interviews with participants (youths, parents, and volunteers) were developed. A summary of the results of these interview measures is presented in Table 10-7. The essential conclusion from Table 10-7 is that the operation of the five experimental models adhered to their conceptual design with one exception—the court model, which shows only 38 percent agreement with the design. Accordingly, further analyses of outcomes will have to be interpreted carefully for the court model with an emphasis upon actual field operations and not the theoretical paradigm. The other four models showed 100 percent behavioral adherence to the planned model. To take one example, it was intended that the action model represent broadband intervention which was focused on environmental contingencies and opportunities. Table 10-7 indicates that this happened.

Another example shows the operational congruence of the relationship and family models, which were intended to be relatively narrow interventions and

TABLE 10.7
MODEL INTEGRITY FROM PROCESS INTERVIEWS

	Model*				
Process variables	Action	Relationship	Attention placebo	Family	Court
Parental involvement	+	+	+	+	+
Family intervention: Family focus	+	+	+	+	−
Family intervention: Youth focus	+	+	+	+	−
School intervention: System focus	+	+	+	+	+
School intervention: Youth focus	+	+	+	+	+
Job-seeking activity Peer involvement Recreational activities	No Distinctions Made—None Found				
	+	+	+	+	−
Legal system intervention	+	+	+	+	−
% of model compliance	100%	100%	100%	100%	38%

*An operational definition of each model can be found in chapters 5 through 8.
+ = level of activity consistent with model design
− = level of activity inconsistent with model design.

only in the family area. The relationship model participants were also primarily involved in only recreational activities. Table 10-7 confirms the field validity of these models. In summary, it was concluded that the five experimental models were in fact different and also consistent with their conceptual base, except for the court model. This general theoretical and practical congruence (four out of five models) allowed a clearer interpretation of the outcome results, which will follow.

The third set of analyses involved an examination of intermediate outcome (life circumstances affected by the intervention). This was necessary to understand the differential outcome effects of the models and the relationship between these outcomes and the social change outcome (recidivism). Table 10-8 shows the models' comparison on major life events in the home, school, employment, peers, legal system, and positive change in activities. As can be seen from Table 10-8 there were no significant differential effects in either employment or reported positive change. However, significant differences did occur in positive home involvement, positive school involvement, activities with peers, legal system involvement, police recidivism rates, and court recidivism rates. The action model produced high levels of school involvement and low levels of home involvement, involvement with peers, and reentry through the legal system. The relationship model produced high levels of involvement in home and school and relatively low levels of involvement with peers and the legal system. The attention model produced low levels of involvement in the home and school and low levels of involvement with peers and the legal system. The family model produced high levels of involvement in the home and low levels of involvement in the school, with peers, and in the legal system. The court model produced high levels of involvement in home and low levels of involvement in school and with peers. Somewhat unexpectedly, the court model also produced high levels of reentry into the legal system. Finally, the control model produced low levels of involvement in home and school and high levels of involvement with peers and the legal system.

These results shed light on the differential impact of these six experimental models. It appeared that the first four experimental models resulted in low levels of legal system involvement. All the first four experimental models were successful in keeping youths out of the juvenile system. On the other hand, it was hoped that the different experimental models would also produce high levels of involvement in home and school. It appeared that each of the four experimental models was successful in producing these effects to some extent. It was also hoped that the experimental models would produce alternatives to peer group involvement, resulting in lower levels of peer group activity. All experimental models were successful in doing this while the control model appeared to increase this involvement.

The final set of analyses was undertaken to examine the social change outcomes. This was done through the self-report of delinquency and court petition and arrests. The second section of Table 10-8 presents a summary of these results. All four diversion models produced significantly lower levels of police

TABLE 10.8
SUMMARY OF YOUTH OUTCOME ANALYSES

			Models				
Life event outcomes	Action	Relationship	Attention	Family	Court	Control	Tests of significance
Positive involvement in the home	Low*	High	Low	High	High	Low	S .05†
Positive school involvement	High	High	Low	Low	Low	Low	S .05†
Employment-seeking activities	—	—	—	—	—	—	NS
Activities with peers	Low	Low	Low	Low	Low	High	S .05†
Legal system involvement	Low	Low	Low	Low	High	High	S .05†
Positive change in home, school, and free time activities	—	—	—	—	—	—	NS
Social change outcomes			Percentages				
Court recidivism rate	.39‡	.33	.52	.46	.67	.62	S .05†
Police recidivism rate	.55	.42	.48	.67	.83	.67	S .05†
Self-reported delinquency	—	—	—	—	—	—	NS

*"High" groups displayed significantly more of the activity and were not significantly different from other "high groups." "Low" groups displayed significantly less of the activity and were not significantly different from other "low groups."
†Significant at .05 level.
NS nonsignificant
‡Numbers are actual recidivism rates.

arrests, and the action, relationship, and family models produced significantly lower levels of court petitions. These results indicate the superiority of volunteer-based diversion models when contrasted with usual court processing. There were no differential effects in self-reported delinquency.

In making inferences about the alternative models for diverting juvenile offenders, four major conclusions seemed justified by the data, field experiences, and statistical analyses. The first was that the experimental models probably involved equivalent participants. The second was that the models were generally operationally different and consistent with their conceptual base. Each of these two conclusions was essential for allowing accurate inferences concerning observed intermediate and social change outcomes. In life event outcomes, three high-intensity experimental models (action, relationship, and family model) were equally effective in producing positive social role involvement and minimizing involvement with the juvenile justice system. The attention model was also successful in minimizing legal system penetration but did not appear to yield positive effects in social role involvement. The court model did have positive social role effects but also failed to minimize penetration into the juvenile justice system. Finally, the control model (court treatment as usual) failed to produce positive social role involvement and increased juvenile justice system penetration. It further increased the level of peer involvement. These intermediate outcomes were mirrored in the social change outcomes. In essence, the three high-intensity treatment models were equally effective in reducing further delinquency. Overall, the alternative diversion models were successful in reducing the penetration of youths into the juvenile justice system and further reducing their subsequent recidivism.

Chronic Mental Illness

The lodge society was established in an attempt to reduce recidivism for chronic mental patients and to provide them with a meaningful role in the community for which employment was considered an essential feature. The lodge society was compared with traditional programs in the community which served as the comparative model in this experiment. Because of the 5-year nature of this experiment and the vast accumulation of data, the dynamics of experimental inferences need to be explained in some detail.

To understand the analyses and inferences that were made from them, it is necessary to follow sequentially a number of analyses and their related inferences. First, it is necessary to examine the equivalence of the model samples obtained by matching on the variables of age, diagnosis, and length of hospitalization, and then randomly assigning the matches to the models. Table 10-9 shows that so far as empirical comparisons are concerned (no demographic category reached statistical significance), sample equivalence was obtained through these matching and random-assignment procedures. Since it seems reasonably clear that the samples were as equivalent as the experimenters could hope to make them by random draw, the first inference in comparing

TABLE 10.9

COMPARISON OF LODGE AND NONLODGE GROUPS ON DEMOGRAPHIC CHARACTERISTICS

Area of measurement	Volunteer lodge group	Volunteer nonlodge group	Tests of significance
Median Age	41	43	NS*
Race, %:			
White	81	80	NS
Other	19	20	
Military Service, %:			
Service-connected pension	41	54	
No service-connected pension	59	46	
Military service, 0–122 weeks	49	49	NS
Military service, 123 weeks and over	51	51	
Military ran, buck private	28	29	
Military rank, PFC or higher	72	71	
Neuropsychiatric Hospitalization:			
Median age at first hospitalization	27	29	
Median number prior hospitalizations	2	2	NS
Median weeks prior hospitalizations	233	262	
Type of Hospital Admission, %:			
Voluntary	44	46	NS
Commitment	54	54	
Parents' Marital Status, %:			
Married and living	12	18	NS
Other	88	82	
Brought up by, %:			
Both parents	42	55	NS
Other	56	54	
Days since Last Contact with Relatives, %:			
0–89 days	64	64	NS
90 days and over	36	36	
Employment:			
Social classification of last job, %:			
Lower middle class and upper lower class	21	29	NS
Lower lower class	79	71	
Median number of jobs held in last 10 years	2	2	NS
Median Highest Grade Completed	11	12	NS
Drinking behavior, %:			
Heavy drinkers	35	26	
Social drinkers	39	48	NS
Nondrinkers	26	26	
Police Arrests, %:			
One or more	59	57	NS
None	41	43	
Marital Status, %:			
Single and never married	64	54	NS
Other	36	46	
Current Monthly Income while Hospitalized, %:			
0–$101	53	47	NS
$102 and over	47	53	

* Nonsignificant

Source: Fairweather, G. W., et al., *Community Life for the Mentally Ill.* Chicago: Aldine, 1969, p. 205.

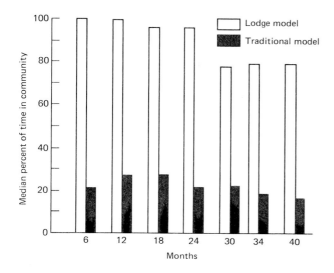

FIGURE 10-6
Comparison of lodge and control models on time in the community for 40 months of follow-up. *(Source: Fairweather, G. W., et al., Community Life for the Mentally Ill. Chicago: Aldine, 1969, p. 205.)*

the models is that if significant outcome differences should later occur, these differences probably cannot be attributable to participant differences in the two models.

Having logically disposed of the problem of sample equivalence we can now proceed to look at the testing of the major social change hypotheses about recidivism reduction and community employment. Figure 10-6 shows a graph of 40 months of follow-up in the lodge society as contrasted with the participants in the traditional model. These differences at the different time periods on the graph reach statistical significance varying from the .001 level to the .05 level. Since at every time period the lodge members spend more time in the community, it appears that the society has yielded significant improvement in the recidivism rate contrasted with traditional community treatments. But what about the employment rate? Figure 10-7 shows the differences are even more dramatic here. These differences were also significant at the .001 or .01 level at each time period (6 to 40 months). It seems clear, therefore, that a second inference can be made from this study—the lodge society significantly increased the time spent in the community and the number of hours employed contrasted with traditional community programs.

But at what cost are these differences obtained? Figure 10-8 shows that the lodge society cost only one-third the amount of hospitalization at its beginning and finally the lodge became self-supporting so that no expenditure of funds was needed. Indeed, the participants eventually became tax-paying citizens. The third inference, therefore, is that the lodge society costs less money than traditional programs. But this experiment was also designed to compare the less chronic with more chronic patients. The comparable categories were neurotics, short-term psychotics, and long-term psychotics. Differences between

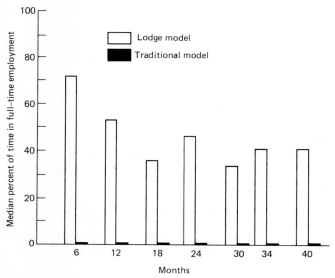

FIGURE 10-7
Comparison of lodge and control models on employment for 40 months of follow-up. *(Source: Fairweather, G. W., et al.,* Community Life for the Mentally Ill. *Chicago: Aldine, 1969, p. 206.)*

the diagnostic groups were significant for traditional treatment programs with the most chronic patients having the highest recidivism and lowest employment rates. No significant differences were obtained between the most and least chronic patients for the lodge society in recidivism or employment. Thus, the differences between the most and least chronic patients virtually disappeared in the lodge society. From this information we can infer that the lodge society was just as successful with the most chronic patients as it was with the least chronic patients, whereas in the traditional model failure continues at a higher rate with the most chronic patients.

Other analyses showed very little difference in the two models concerning participant satisfaction with living in the community, social interaction, leisure activities, and physical activity level. A note of caution needs to be injected here in terms of the interpretation of these data since scores on all scales measuring satisfaction were extremely high for participants in both models. Interview data suggest that this occurred because the participants in both models were happy to be out of the hospital. Being in the community itself, therefore, was such an attraction to individuals, whether they were in the traditional or lodge model, that differences in satisfaction disappeared as they did in other social process areas because all scores were so high.

In addition to these statistical analyses a wide variety of other information was collected, all pointing in the direction of the benefits of the lodge society.

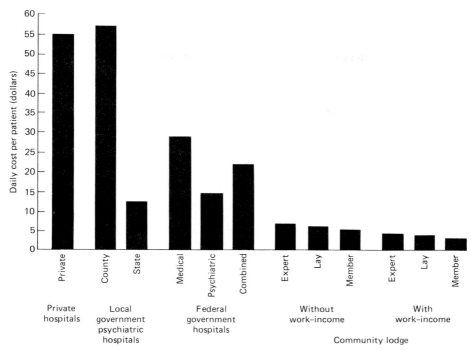

FIGURE 10-8
Mean daily cost per person for alternative treatment settings in California Bay Area, 1964–66. *(Source: Fairweather, G. W., et al.,* Community Life for the Mentally Ill. *Chicago: Aldine, 1969, p. 212.)*

A great deal of data on the internal social processes of the lodge society was not comparable with the traditional program since task groups rarely spontaneously occurred in traditional programs. Many of the instruments on social process showed high group cohesiveness, adequate leadership, and high morale in the lodge society. An example illustrates some of the interpersonal aspects of the society which are not obtainable from looking at the statistical analyses. It was recorded in an experimenter's research log. In this particular instance the lodge society experimentalist had just entered the society for his first evaluation. About this first visit the research log states:

> The difference in the atmosphere between this place and the hospital is very striking for someone who steps into it cold and with no preparation, as I have done. It really has the feeling of a going business, with none of the "marking time" mood of the hospital. In trying to analyze why it produces this impression, I've decided that at least one reason is that the lodge is far more subject to contingencies set by the outside community than is the hospital. The simple fact of sending groups of men to do productive work in the community for wages has generated a whole series of behaviors which are in contrast to those in the hospital. Because the men at the lodge are

engaging in a whole series of activities which are necessary to operate in the community as a business, there is a general atmosphere of purposefulness. The men are engaged in meaningful tasks in the sense they are tasks which will produce a money reward in the society at large. This activity, plus the general absence of "busy work" or "work as therapy" . . . generates the atmosphere I have described (Fairweather et al., 1969, p. 70).

Other information from the analyses of external processes showed a strong positive relationship was established between the lodge society and the local neighborhood. Interviews revealed that the neighbors perceived the lodge society members as responsible workers who were an asset to the community. These perceptions were the same as those held by other businesses and community organizations. From this information the experimenters inferred that when a full citzenship role is achieved by former mental patients, the relationships among individuals are more likely to be that of social equals where each accords the other the rights and obligations of citizenship. In such a case, negative feelings and reactions against the mentally ill tend to disappear.

Summarizing the separate inferences just mentioned, the experimenters inferred that the lodge society yielded a number of advantages that makes it a more beneficial treatment than the traditional programs to which mental patients are usually assigned in the community. First, it reduces recidivism and increases employment which helps establish the individual as a citizen in the community. Second, the cost is significantly lower and, in fact, finally reaches a point where society is getting money in return from the members through taxes on their work income. Finally, and probably most important, the reaction of others to former mental patients who are given lodge societal membership is positive, which in turn affects the perceptions of members about themselves.

We have presented in this chapter a picture of evaluation results and the logical inferences that can be made from them. We have tried to illustrate the dynamic process of inference based upon statistical data and daily experience in attempting to solve a problem which leads the experimentalist to draw socially realistic conclusions about model benefits. Once having sufficient evidence to satisfy the experimentalist and other members of the research team, the beneficial model then needs to be placed in operation in other locations. It is toward the pursuit of that dissemination process that the next chapter has been written.

CHAPTER 11

DISSEMINATING
BENEFICIAL INNOVATIONS

Once an innovative model has been evaluated as being more beneficial than a traditional model, it becomes part of the scientists' social responsibility to make the innovation available to society. Assuming that the criteria of careful scientific scrutiny outlined in the preceding chapters have been employed, the next logical step in the change process involves innovation dissemination. This chapter will address the "why and how" of disseminating social programs that have been evaluated and found to be beneficial. What will be covered here is planned, purposive, and active methods of dissemination which can occur within a scientific context.

The topic of dissemination is a broad one indeed. Havelock (1979), Rogers (1983), Downs and Mohr (1976), and Tornatzky et al. (1984) have written extensively about it. This chapter will address the process of dissemination within the theoretical context of planned social change which has been outlined throughout his volume.

THE GENERIC PROCESS OF DISSEMINATION

The beneficial new model must be promoted through a number of social processes so that the innovation can be spread throughout a society. These processes are collectively called *dissemination* and are usually begun by an advocate or advocates who perceive the innovation as something desirable that might be used by the society and for which they can be the distribution "salespeople."

LaPiere (1965) believes that the advocate must perceive some personal reward in the process of being an advocate for a new social or technological innovation. The reward appears to be personalized for each advocate—some perceive immediate profit, some perceive fame, some perceive personal achievement, and some perceive service to others. Whether or not the perception of personal reward is basic to the importance attached to the innovation by all advocates, however, is unknown at this time. What is known is that without persons to advocate the use of the new innovation it is highly unlikely that the innovation will be adopted and used.

History is replete with examples of innovations that have never been adopted. Fairweather and Tornatzky (1977) have elsewhere given an example of this:

> The lack of systematic adoption of new innovations is not exclusively the province of the public sector. For example, in the American automobile industry one major innovation, the V-8 engine, was initially adopted by Chevrolet in 1919, discarded one year later, eventually picked up by the Ford Motor Company some 13 years later, but not fully adopted by the industry at large until 20 to 30 years following that. Another example that has clear relevance to the present environmental situation is an early version of the stratified charge automobile engine that was reasonably pollution free. Needless to say, that early low pollution engine has yet to be adopted by the major automobile manufacturers (Gunn, 1973).

Another example is provided by the National Aeronautical and Space Administration which was involved in a major dissemination effort concerning various innovations developed in the space program. The lack of interest of most organizations in adopting these new innovations was given in this summary:

> Of the 21,000 companies which NASA thought could use the inventions, 30 companies or 0.15% had adopted or seemed to have a good prognosis for adoption. Of the 3,100 companies from the preceding 21,000 which had agreed with NASA that the invention did sound relevant, 1% were in this adopted or likely to adopt group of 30, and of those 550 companies which on further investigation with NASA did not drop out of contact or say "No," only 5.5% ended in the final favorable group of 30 who had adopted or seemed to have a good prognosis for adoption (Wright, 1966).

Experiences such as these show very clearly that even when innovations are promoted, there is no guarantee of their adoption by societies' members. For without advocates, innovations rarely if ever spread throughout a society. To look more closely at the process of innovation advocacy it may be helpful to examine the adoption of innovations as they developed in agricultural research. Historically, agronomists developed new agricultural products such as hybrid seeds or new fertilizers to increase crop yield. But they soon realized that the discovery of such crop improvements did not itself lead to their use by farmers (the adopters). For this reason, a complex system of county agents located around a state and linked with the researchers was established to promote the dissemination of new products as they emerged. The county agents very often worked individually with farmers who might use these newly dicovered products. They found that the process of adopting a new product takes a considerable period of time.

A curve representing the development of interest by the individual adopter of an innovation was created by Havelock (1979) and is presented in Figure 11-1. He describes the individual adopter's personal involvement curve as similar to a learning curve:

> As is indicated in this figure, the initial slow rise represents a slight involvement as the individual (adopter) becomes aware of an innovation and begins to be interested in it. The greatest increase in involvement comes as the person actively seeks information about the innovation and begins to consider how the innovation could be applied to his own particular needs. Involvement continues to be great as he tries out the innovation and adapts it to suit his own circumstances. As the person becomes accustomed to the innovation, the rate of involvement decreases, and, finally, no further increase in involvement occurs once a decision is made either to adopt or to reject the innovation. If the innovation is accepted it becomes a routine part of the adopter's behavior; the "learning" has taken place (Havelock, R.G., 1979, Chap. 14, p. 7).

FIGURE 11-1
Involvement of an individual during the adoption process. *(Source: Havelock, R. G., Planning for Innovation Through Dissemination and Utilization of Knowledge. Ann Arbor, MI: The University of Michigan, CRUSK, 1979, pp. 10-16.)*

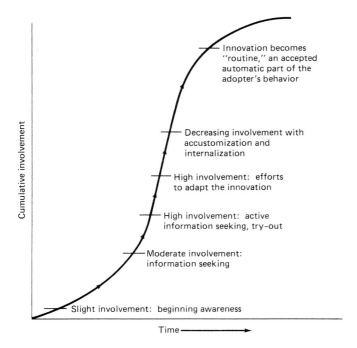

Figure 11-2 shows the generalized curve of adoption representing the adoption process as presented by Rogers (1983, p. 247). In this graph, Rogers shows that after the innovators themselves have created and adopted the model, other adopters range from those who adopt early, to the laggards who adopt late. The adopter's categories (early adopters—laggards) are divided into percentages of the adopting populations as represented in standard deviations. This curve shows that the initial adoption of the new product or program is a slow process that may take several weeks, months, or years. If the innovation is to be adopted widely, there is a period of more rapid adoption and finally what appears to be a fad effect occurs. That is, "everybody gets on the bandwagon." It is at this point that the innovation has been adopted widely and only a few laggards (nonadopters) remain.

To illustrate the adoption curve further (Figure 11-2), let us explore the adoption of a new drug among doctors in a midwest region which was studied by Coleman, Katz, and Menzel (1966). What the researchers found was that there was a period of little adoption after the drug was introduced. Then a more rapid rate of adoption occurred, and finally most of the physicians in that area were using the drug. The researchers also found that the most influential persons in drug adoption were other physicians who, in turn, notified their professional friends about the advantages of using the new drug. These researchers found that advertising was much less effective than interpersonal communication among physicians in promoting the adoption of this new medical innovation. Thus, the curve (Figure 11-2) was clearly represented in the spread of the use of a new drug. Curves like this have been found in areas as diverse as agriculture and mental health. It has also been found that the more complex the innovation, the less likely it will be to be adopted quickly so that the adoption curve takes place over several years rather than weeks or months (Fairweather et al., 1974). Even so, for a society to function well innovation dissemination should occur when society needs new solutions to its problems. It is

FIGURE 11-2
Adopter categorization on the basis of time of adoption. *(Source: Rogers, E. M., Diffusion of Innovations. New York: The Free Press of Glencoe, Inc., 1982.)*

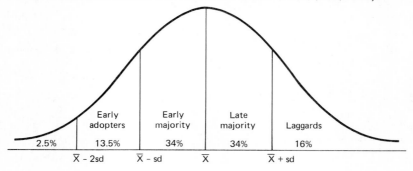

therefore necessary to try to harness these change processes so that orderly social change can occur as needed.

AN EXPERIMENTAL APPROACH TO DISSEMINATION

Even though the adoption processes and rates of dissemination have been studied for years, recent reviews of the dissemination literature (Fairweather & Tornatzky, 1977; Tornatzky et al., 1983) point out that there is a lack of scientific guidelines for action or principles of dissemation research. Scientific methods especially need to be used here because it is necessary to find out for each innovation what dissemination processes will spread its use throughout society. To accomplish this goal a systematic comparison of alternative approaches to the dissemination process of each new social model needs to be developed. Thus, it appears necessary for scientists not only to create valid innovations and to understand their salient processes, but also to advance from the art to the science of dissemination. To initiate this process it is important to provide a theoretical background with operational definitions of the dissemination process itself. To reach this goal the theory of human behavior holding that actions are a function of participant and internal and external social variables needs to be applied to the dissemination endeavor. The generic paradigm emanating from this theoretical position can be stated as follows: *The outcome of any implementation or dissemination effort is a function of the participant and social situational variables operative in the dissemination attempt.* Thus, the participant and social situational variables found in Tables 3-2 and 3-3 need to be examined for their contribution in each innovation dissemination. This can be done in an experimental context.

Outcomes

As with all the social experiments, there are many potential outcomes, particularly of dissemination studies. Even so, *the social change outcome criterion* of dissemination efforts can be considered to be the sheer number of beneficial models that have been adopted by individuals, groups, or organizations in the adopting population. As with the social change outcome criterion for social models, the social change outcome criterion for dissemination investigations is thus a relatively simple behavioral measure—number of adoptions. Beyond this outcome and hence quite aside from the number of adoptions is a second important outcome concerning the degree to which each new adoption yields similar outcomes to the prototype model.

Dissemination research therefore needs to address these two issues: (1) How many replicate models have become operative, and (2) to what extent do these replicate models produce the same outcomes as those observed in the successful original model?

To summarize, the social change outcome criterion in dissemination research is the number of adoptions; of equal concern and as primary is the assessment of the extent to which each replicate produces outcomes and processes similar to the prototype model.

Phases in the Dissemination Process

There are many definitions of the process of innovation dissemination, but the first step in the dissemination process, regardless of the definition used, involves determining what individuals, groups, or organizations should be the target of the dissemination effort. The *target population* may be individuals, groups, or organizations. While it is always necessary to inform individuals of the benefits of the new model, whether they represent only themselves or an organization, there are some innovations where the individual is the sole decision maker concerning innovation use. For example, the use of curricula materials in classrooms usually is the decision of the individual professor in most universities. Thus, the dissemination of a new reading curriculum would usually focus on professors as the target population.

On the other hand, many social innovations are targeted for groups or organizations because a total social system or subsystem is involved in their use. A new drug treatment program for drug abusers, for example, may be best implemented through drug treatment centers in a city, county, state, or around the nation. In some cases, it may be necessary to create new organizations to disseminate new effective social programs. Sometimes the very nature of a social innovation requires the establishment of new organizational support for its dissemination. For example, many of the operating principles of the lodge society (no live-in professionals, for example) are antithetical to the norms of most mental health organizations which usually emphasize live-in professional staff. Thus, it was often necessary to create new support organizations, usually nonprofit corporations, which could implement the lodge society, rather than depending upon existing mental health organizations (Fairweather et al., 1974).

Which type of target population is best for a given innovation is a topic about which the field knows very little, at least with acceptable scientific certainty. It is a domain in which extensive future research will be needed. Once one has an innovation that, in the judgment of the experimenter turned advocate needs to be disseminated, alternative target populations will need to be considered. However, whether individuals, groups, or organizations are targeted, previous theory and research indicate that a four-stage sequential process is usually involved when innovation dissemination results in societal adoption (Fairweather & Tornatzky, 1977). These four stages are: the approach, persuasion, activation, and diffusion. The roles of participant and internal and external social process variables need to be examined for each phase in order to evaluate how they affect the processes and outcomes of the approach, persuasion, activation, and diffusion phases. Figure 11-3 elaborates this paradigm.

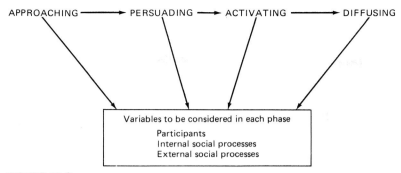

FIGURE 11-3
Variables affecting the four phases of the dissemination process.

The various phases of dissemination—approaching, persuading, activating, and diffusing—can be established as experimental investigations so that each and every phase is contingent upon what is learned in the preceding phase. For example, a small sample may be used to find out what method of approach is most effective and this approach can be used later for all succeeding individuals, groups, or organizations. Empirically establishing the most effective processes for each phase can be used in the four phases of the dissemination process. In short, the scientific methods which have been described in earlier chapters of this book can and should be applied to each of the four phases of innovation dissemination. Thus, in the social change process the community scientist role is best described as involving continuing cycles of innovation development research and dissemination research. To further clarify these issues the next section will place the dissemination processes in an experimental context.

The Approach Phase

The first step in the dissemination process involves approaching the potential target population. There are many specific methods of approaching individuals, groups, and organizations that could be used. Each specific option includes some variant of two general techniques: personal and indirect approaches. Personal approaches involve direct human contact between the advocate and the target population. Indirect approaches use other media for communication. Mixed approaches are often employed. Approaching individuals, for example, can be done through television or mass media, or through group approaches such as educational or professional meetings, workshops, mailings, or professional literature. Groups and organizations can be approached in similar ways.

A good deal of dissemination stops before it begins. Many initial approaches aimed at the target population never lead to subsequent persuasion attempts.

Professional and popular literature is replete with information about unsuccessful approaches to dissemination. In the typical scientific dissemination an article or book is written about the innovation. A high proportion of the potential adoption audience for these successful innovations may never read the article and hence will never hear of the innovation. To date, the scientific literature even lacks systematic knowledge about successful approach strategies. Such basic questions as the most appropriate modality of approach for a particular innovation and who should be approached have rarely been systematically examined, particularly in a comparative experimental context. But the procedures necessary for dissemination experiments seem simple enough if appropriately applied.

First, let us assume that the target population has been identified and that the dissemination strategies will, therefore, be aimed at a particular population of individuals, groups, or organizations. Earlier studies can be used as examples. Leedom (1980) would choose school districts through which she would implement conservation energy courses. On the other hand, Coelho (1983) would aim his stop-smoking campaign at smokers, who he would consider as the appropriate sampling unit to whom to disseminate the beneficial nonsmoking program. In disseminating the lodge society the target population was mental hospitals (Fairweather, Sanders, & Tornatzky, 1974). They were asked to create a lodge society in the community to which the hospital program could be linked.

The next step in the dissemination experiment is to design different types of approaches that have the potential of being meaningful to the selected target population. For example, if the target population is composed of persons who wish to quit smoking, an advertisement in a local newspaper may be sufficient. In fact, Coelho found this approach yielded a far greater number of volunteers than he could treat. On the other hand, in a study disseminating antibiotic medication, Coleman, Katz, and Menzel (1966) found that the best people to disseminate medical innovations were respected physicians in the medical community. Thus, the individuals who constitute the target population will, to some extent, determine or limit the types of approaches that will be useful. For example, one might try advertising in the newspaper, radio advertising, television presentations, letters, and so on in the nonsmoking experiment, to find out which technique would bring the greatest number of volunteers to a nonsmoking program. On the other hand, articles in various technical medical magazines by respected physicians might be the best approach with a medical innovation.

The need for an experiment to find out the best approach should be clear by now. Despite the "hunches" mentioned above, the only way to find the best approach to the target population is to compare the possible strategies that might appeal to that group. No amount of common sense or insight can provide a significantly valid way to approach members of the target population. For this reason, the first step is an experiment where a representative sample of the target population is assigned at random to different conditions of approach. In this way, different methods of approach are compared to find out which one(s) yield the greatest number of volunteers for the persuasion phase.

The Persuasion Phase

Once the best approach strategy has been ascertained experimentally, a similar investigation of the persuasion phase is needed. There seems to be general agreement in the literature that before an adoption decision is reached there is a process of information exchange, reflection, and consideration of the innovation by the prospective adopters (Fairweather & Tornatzky, 1977). The persuasion phase will bring the target population from a state of initial awareness accomplished in the approach phase to a *decision* about adopting the innovation (see Figure 11-1). But again, very little is known about the comparative efficacy of different persuasion techniques, particularly with different types of innovations. Therefore, the persuasion phase will also involve an experimental comparison of different types of persuasive techniques. Here the experimentalist asks such questions as: "Is information regarding innovation effectiveness more persuasive in convincing the target population to adopt than information about economic incentives, or are both necessary?"

Whether the target population is an individual, group, or organization, a variety of personal and indirect types of persuasion can be attempted. It is important to understand that different target populations may be interested in the same innovation for quite different reasons. For example, when an innovation is found that reduces energy consumption, some potential adopters will be interested in it because it will protect natural resources, others will see it as a means of reducing household energy expenditures, and still others will see it as a way of increasing profits. For this reason, the most critical aspect of the persuasion phase is the appropriate match between the target population, the style of persuasion, the content of the persuasive message, and the legitimacy of the advocate.

Once volunteers for further dissemination activities have been obtained from the approach phase, the persuasion phase begins. Again, the field experimentalist is faced with a decision about what techniques to use in an attempt to persuade the target population to actually adopt this particular innovation. There are, of course, a wide variety of types of persuasion. Some are written, such as pamphlets; some are visual, such as movies or television; some are action-oriented, such as active participation in a program; and so on. With a particular innovation and a particular target population the type of persuasion that is appropriate and most productive with the target group at that particular time is typically unknown. It is for this reason that a second experiment should be conducted for the persuasion phase of the dissemination effort. Accordingly, from those who volunteer to permit persuasion, members of the target population are randomly assigned to different conditions of persuasion to find out which condition of persuasion will yield the highest number of volunteers willing to activate the new model. For example, persons or organizations who have volunteered to be persuaded might be randomly assigned to viewing a film, reading biographical information, or visiting the actual project site.

Since the advocate is also of importance here, the effectiveness of different types of advocates—those with different personalities, different professional credentials, and so on—should also be explored. The completion of the persuasion phase should yield a number of volunteers who will go on to the activation phase with the added advantage to the experimentalist that the most effective type of persuasion, among those attempted, will be known.

The Activation Phase

Assuming some individuals, groups, or organizations have decided to adopt the innovation in question, it is then necessary to move from persuasion to actual model replication to activate the innovative model. However, program integrity makes activation a very difficult phase. It is necessary to reproduce exactly the original model with equivalent samples if similar outcomes are to be expected and their comparability to the original model results obtained. Accordingly, very specific information and guidance have to be given to the adopters for replication to occur. When a social innovation is activated by a new adopter, demonstrations may be necessary. Thus, if one is adopting an effective program for child abusers, a site visit to an ongoing program may be necessary so that the adopters can see and participate in the successful program. Such firsthand experience is sometimes necessary to achieve workaday operational similarity to the original innovation.

To obtain program identity with the experimental social program, ongoing monitoring of the replicate becomes a critical aspect of the activation phase. This is necessary for two reasons. First, the disseminator needs to provide the adopters feedback and consultation about their successes or failures in operating the new social model. Since many social innovations will require new practices and roles, ongoing feedback and support for such changes are typically required. Second, the disseminator will be interested in collecting data relevant to examining the success of the replicate. Success needs to be examined both in terms of the actual replication of the original innovative model's practices and procedures, and in terms of observed outcomes.

Following the experimental persuasion phase, some subset of the initial sample will make the decision to proceed with actual program implementation and thus will become actively involved in attempting program establishment and operation. This is yet another critical area for comparative experimentation. This third experiment (approach and persuasion experiments have already been done) needs to answer the general question of what ingredients lead to successful activation. More specifically, what types of activation lead to successful implementation of social models which are actual replicates of the prototype model.

From this sample of the target population who have now volunteered to activate the new program, a third experiment is formed. This experiment requires the random assignment of volunteers to different types of activation strategies. There are probably an almost infinite number of activation strategies, only a few of which can be mentioned here, but from them the reader should get a conceptual view of the basic ideas of activation. Activating a program by written information or by actual experience might be compared. In such a case, a written manual would be created for one experimental condition, whereas participation in an actual program would occur for another. These two types of activation strategies could then be evaluated and compared for their success. In comparing activation strategies assessment of both replicate program integrity and outcomes needs to be undertaken. Of primary concern is the extent to which different activation strategies replicate the original models' processes and outcomes. The experimenters need answers to such questions as: Do face-to-face interaction or written introduction modes of program activation produce social models that most closely replicate the innovative social model's processes and outcomes?

The Subsequent Diffusion Phase

The final step in the dissemination process includes subsequent diffusion after some of the target population has a model activated. This occurs when the original target population to which the innovation was disseminated becomes involved in spreading the innovation to other individuals, groups, and organizations. In this way innovations are disseminated to the larger society by the first wave of adopters. Diffusion is a process which historically has most often occurred without planned intervention. Once a social program becomes popular it can become a "fad program." Under such circumstances "everybody wants to have one." Our history is replete with the quick, unplanned spread of social programs with little thought given to program integrity through careful diffusion. The community researcher needs to be particularly sensitive to these circumstances and should examine closely the continued integrity and effectiveness of such diffused innovations. It is inevitable that today's innovative solutions will become tomorrow's traditional models and the process of building alternative innovations will begin anew.

The conditions under which new adoptions are diffused are essentially unknown except in a descriptive sense. This has occurred because many new social programs are simply diffused after some initial adoptions, and no research about the salient diffusion processes is carried out. To remedy this situation, there are two general questions which experimentation needs to address in the diffusion phase: (1) the issues of the conditions under which new adoptions can be maximized, and (2) the relationships between subsequent diffusion conditions, quality of activated replicates, and the social outcomes they produce.

Having created a number of adoptions of the new innovations in the community in the activation phase, it now becomes necessary to attempt to disseminate additional replicates from these existing new models. From a scientific perspective, here again an experiment is required. It is necessary for different types of diffusion strategies to be tried and compared. This can be done by randomly assigning successful replicate programs to different diffusion strategies. For example, we might assign half the new innovations at random to the dissemination strategy of meeting locally with similar organizations in an attempt to convince them to also adopt the new program. The other half of the sample might be sent information about the new program from a centralized office that would arrange a particular reward for persons or organizations that adopted the new program. The important point to grasp here is that, as in the other three phases (approach, persuasion, and activation) the diffusion phase can itself be subject to experimentation and can thus enhance our knowledge about the diffusion of a particular innovation as well as generating knowledge for future diffusion experiments.

Cyclical Nature of Dissemination Research

It is important to understand that even the most successful dissemination efforts will fail with some potential adopters. For this reason, the dissemination effort may involve further experimentation with these nonadopting individuals, groups, or organizations. The experimental disseminators may wish to recycle those persons or organizations who did not participate in the most effective conditions through these experimentally established productive dissemination conditions. Such a recycling process allows for replication of the most effective conditions with the nonadopters at each of the phases in the dissemination process.

Even these recycling strategies may leave individuals, groups, or organizations that do not adopt the innovation. Further experimentation with such difficult individuals, groups, or organizations may provide the potential for important findings about the social change process. It has often been observed that the social program landscape is littered with social institutions highly resistant to changing their programs in spite of their known questionable effectiveness. Unfortunately, we know very little, by scientific standards, about what influences such resistance to change. Thus, dissemination experiments have two purposes—the generation of knowledge about the dissemination processes *and* the spread of effective social models. It is extremely likely that the need for such experiments will increase in the future as new beneficial innovations become more prevalent.

The Logistics of Dissemination Experiments

So far this chapter has described the four phases of the dissemination process and the general application of the experimental method of each of them. But little has been said about actually carrying out such experiments in the field.

To gain an appreciation of the actual role the community experimenter plays in the dissemination process, we will select a hypothetical organization and describe the behaviors required for movement through the dissemination process. The role behaviors described here occur over and over again in dissemination effects in different fields such as mental health, education, and technology (Tornatzky et al., 1983). Thus, these person-organizational interactions represent general behavioral activities that are needed whenever and wherever experimental dissemination occurs.

The scientist-advocate's interpersonal and social activities during the four phases of the dissemination process involve a great deal of personal "give and take" and require time as well as personal involvement. Many hours of discussion, presentation of information, and attention to personal feelings and group processes occur while each phase is being completed. The involvement of the community experimentalist—the scientist-advocate in this role—is presented in Figure 11-4. It shows the scientist-advocate's role requirements with an organization in each phase of the dissemination process. As can be seen from Figure 11-3 the scientist-advocate's role changes with each new dissemination phase. The relationships between the scientist-advocate and the organization are indicated by reciprocal arrows.

In the approach phase, as shown by the arrows, the scientific innovator's task is to approach and find an individual within the organization who is dissatisfied with current practices and is interested in trying something new. Once this inside agent is located, the innovator explains the results of the experiment to her or him and he or she in turn conveys the information to the organization's members and attempts to locate a group of people within the organization who will be interested in further information about the innovation. The contact between the innovator and this newly developed group lays the groundwork for trying the persuasion tactics designed for the particular audience in this organization. Let us assume, for example, that the outside innovator working with the inside change agent agrees that the persuasion phase can be tried. Together with the inside change agent, the persuasion tactics begin by setting a date for the trial of the different persuasion tactics.

Once the persuasion tactics have been performed, the organization responds positively or negatively to program activation. A certain number of organizations will want to activate the innovation. When successful, the inside change agent has organized an adopting group within the organization who works with the scientist-advocate so that the replicate program can actually be started and operated.

By this time in the dissemination process the scientist-advocate and the organizational adopting group perceive themselves as a social unit. In the diffusion phase, therefore, a goal of this combined group becomes finding other individuals in the local community, state, or region who would be interested in the innovation and who themselves might establish a new program. Working together, this new advocacy group helps these newly discovered adopters activate the innovation. Once this network of adopters is operative, they take over the diffusion activities and the scientist-advocate returns to other research work but is available for diffusion consultation.

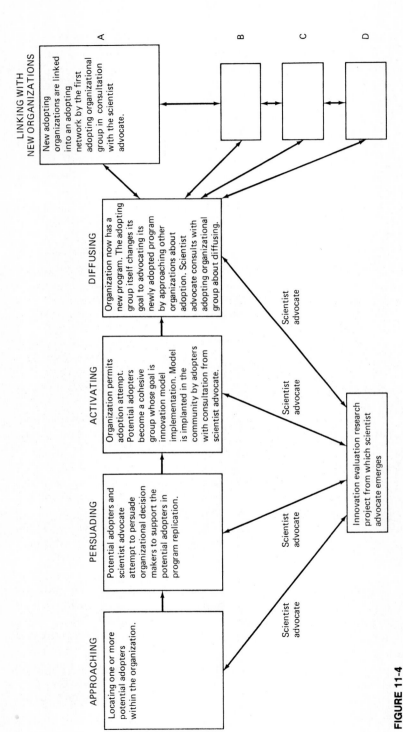

FIGURE 11-4
Organizational dissemination process.

In the discussion of the scientific evaluation of model-building experiments presented in Chapter 3, it was pointed out that all the participant and internal and external social processes need to be accounted for. A glance at Figure 11-3 shows this very clearly.

While the same experimental variables need to be accounted for in both dissemination and model comparison experiments, there are some very distinct operational differences. First, dissemination projects often cover a wide geographic area. If sufficient funds are available, the effort should be national in scope. Under such conditions, the researchers have to change their experimental procedures from those used in model development and comparison which usually takes place in one geographic area, to procedures usable with a much wider geographic audience. Accordingly, the research team has to do considerable traveling and has to serve as a linking agent with individuals or organizations in the large number of places where data have to be collected. Much of the research staff's time is spent in training local persons to carry out the research procedures in their organization's area and to prepare the data for the dissemination research staff. This geographic expansion creates the necessity of having a wide variety of administrative agreements with a large number of people who become research associates in the overall project, thus expanding the research staff dramatically.

The broad geographic area involved and the large number of people also require a great deal more supervision. The research staff has to make certain that the new model is implanted in the proper socioeconomic climate and, at the same time, that it is an exact replicate of the initial model. This is one of the most difficult aspects of dissemination research because local groups will often attempt to change the new model to fit into local conditions. Even though some slight modifications will and should occur, it is essential that the experimentalists, who are the only ones who have adequate knowledge of the functioning of the model at that historical moment, do not permit change that might endanger the outcome of the models. They must remember that the validity (problem-solving potential) of the model itself is the scientific evidence showing significantly improved benefits to the problem population. Each model must therefore be an exact replicate—or as exact as possible—of the initial model so that once it is implanted it will give the same results as the initial model.

One of the great fears of dissemination researchers is that models that are not exact replicates will become disseminated and that they will not give the same results as the prototype models, so that advantages found with the prototype will not appear in the newly adopted models. For this reason, the research staff who created and administered the prototype model must become involved, at least in the activation phase of the dissemination experiment, so that the new models are exact replicates of the prototype. If this occurs, the results have a high probability of being equally as beneficial as the original and, thus, each replicate that gives equivalent beneficial results improves the probability that the next model will give the same results. Accordingly, the dissemination process can be used as a process to explore further the probabilities of new models generating the equivalent benefits of the prototype, thus determining the model's generalizability.

A DISSEMINATION EXPERIMENT: THE LODGE SOCIETY

The lodge society national dissemination experiments covered a 10-year period. They represent the most complete dissemination experiment for which there is a scientific experimental record. For this reason, the first lodge dissemination experiment, taking 5 years, is presented here as the primary example of "how" and "why" such experiments are conducted.

Based on the effectiveness of the lodge society for chronic mental patients described in the last chapter, a national experiment was undertaken to advocate the use of the lodge program and to examine the relative efficacy of various tactics to be used in the different phases of the dissemination process. A 5-year experiment involved 255 mental hospitals as the target sample. This included all but eight mental hospitals in the United States. These eight were randomly discarded because they were not needed in the experimental design. The experiment addressed dissemination issues in three stages. The first stage included examining different techniques for approaching and persuading the various mental hospitals to proceed with adoption of the new lodge society. In this combined approach-persuasion phase, several different dimensions were investigated, as shown in Table 11-1. The figure also shows the number of hospitals in each cell. The first dimension shown at the top involved the professional social status of the personnel in a mental hospital. Previous studies had shown that the social status of mental health workers was ranked from highest to lowest by other professional persons in the order of superintendent, psychiatrist, psychologist, social worker, and nurses. Accordingly, the issue arose as a research question about whether or not approaching persons in different social status positions would yield different results. There was some indication from the literature that persons who were highest in the social status hierarchy were more likely to be those who would move an adoption along by obtaining an organizational consensus about its adoption (Fairweather, 1964, 1969, 1980).

A second dimension was action. A considerable amount of research information suggested that written material, workshops, and involvement in actual demonstrations might yield different results so far as persuading the participants to adopt was concerned. There are distinct differences between an actual demonstration, a written (brochure), or a verbal (workshop) approach. For a demonstration to occur a hospital had to commit an actual ward and staff in a mental hospital to be set aside for the demonstration; for the brochure condition an organization was only required to agree to permit brochures to be distributed to hospital personnel; and for a workshop the hospital had to agree that personnel could attend the workshop meetings. Thus, the demonstration

TABLE 11.1
APPROACH-PERSUASION PHASES OF THE EXPERIMENTAL DESIGN SHOWING THE SOCIAL STATUS, ACTION, URBAN-RURAL, AND STATE-FEDERAL RESEARCH CONDITIONS

	Social Status											
Action	**Supt.**		**Psychiatry**		**Psychology**		**Soc. work**		**Nursing**			**N**
Brochure												
State	8	7	8	7	8	7	8	7	8	7	75	85
Federal	1	1	1	1	1	1	1	1	1	1	10	
Workshop												
State	8	7	8	7	8	7	8	7	8	7	75	85
Federal	1	1	1	1	1	1	1	1	1	1	10	
Demon-stration												
State	8	7	8	7	8	7	8	7	8	7	75	85
Federal	1	1	1	1	1	1	1	1	1	1	10	
	urban	rural	urban	rural	urban	rural	urban	rural	urban	rural		
	51		51		51		51		51			255

Source: Fairweather, G. W., Sanders, D. H., and Tornatzky, L. G., *Creating Change in Mental Health Organizations.* New York: Pergamon Press, 1974, p. 77.

condition, in contrast to the workshop and brochure conditions, required that the hospital agree to give something tangible—to set aside a ward and staff for demonstration purposes.

There was also considerable question about whether or not hospitals located in urban areas would yield the same results as those in rural areas. Since the lodge society required that the participants operate their own business it was commonly believed that location in an urban community would offer better prospects for the business part of the program than hospitals located in rural communities. And, finally, there was a question about whether or not state hospitals would adopt the lodge society more quickly than federal hospitals. The argument here was that state hospitals were closer to the people and hence did not require persuading those in Washington. It was further argued that because of this geographic difference state hospitals were less bureaucratic and would, therefore, be able to more quickly implement the lodge society.

Table 11-1 shows how the approach phase was combined with the persuasion phase to answer these questions. The activating phase compared face-to-face consultation with written instructions in helping adopters start the operation of their lodge. The diffusion phase consisted of a study of how lodge societies were spread from the adopters to others. An overview of the four phases is shown in Figure 11-5.

The comparative analysis of the approaching and persuading phases showed that of the four experimental conditions (actions, social status of the contract, geographic locale, state-federal), only the action dimension yielded a significantly different number of persuaded hospitals. Neither the social status of the contact, whether the hospital was located in the city or the country, or whether state versus federal funding was used, affected movement toward adoption. As shown in Table 11-2 the advantage of action demonstrations and workshops contrasted with written material was highly significant. When workshops were contrasted with active demonstrations it was clear that hospital entry into the organization was much easier to accomplish when the original commitment was limited to permitting a workshop meeting for hospital staff. But as the process changed from discussion to action the hospital personnel also had to change from being an audience to making a firm commitment to change. As this change occurred (from observers to participants) the advantage of the active demonstration approach became more evident. If a hospital agreed to start a demonstration ward it was far more likely to agree to start a lodge than if it had had the "workshop show." Clearly, the commitment necessary to establish a demonstration project selectively eliminated many disinterested hospitals from the persuasion process while the workshop condition did not.

The activating phase of the dissemination process was the focus of a second

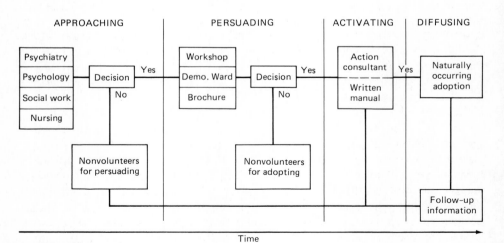

FIGURE 11-5
Phases of the lodge society dissemination research process showing the action occurring in the approaching, persuading, activating, and diffusing phases. *(Source: Fairweather, G. W., Sanders, D. H., and Tornatzky, L. G.,* Creating Change in Mental Health Organizations. *New York: Pergamon Press, 1974, p. 77.)*

TABLE 11.2
COMPARISON OF PASSIVE-ACTIVE MODES OF PRESENTATION

| | Mode of presentation | | |
Change score	Brochure	Workshop	Demonstration ward
	Number of hospitals		
1 No change	26	17	64
2 Permitted persuasion attempt	55	58	12
3 Persuaded to change	4	10	11
	$X^2 = 69.39^*$ (4 df)		

*$p < 0.001$
Source: Fairweather, G. W., Sanders, D. H., and Tornatzky, L. G., *Creating Change in Mental Health Organizations.* New York: Pergamon Press, 1974, p. 77.

experiment (Table 11-1). This study involved the random assignment of the twenty-five hospitals that agreed to adopt to two conditions in the activating phase. The sampling technique and design was described as follows:

It was decided that those hospitals that had been persuaded to establish the lodge would be divided into matched pairs on the basis of their previous experimental exposure, and then randomly assigned to either a written or action consultation approach to implementation. One group of hospitals would receive a written manual that clearly described each step in the movement from the hospital into the community, while a second group would receive periodic visits from an action consultant who would aim them in carrying out the move into the community. By comparing the progress made in movement toward adoption by those hospitals receiving the manual with those having active consultation one could clearly evaluate whether an action consultant was necessary and what the processes of these different forms of consultation happened to be. These two conditions (written and action consultation) constituted the major dimensions of the Activating Phase of the experiment (Fairweather, Sanders, & Tornatzky, 1974, p. 39).

The critical outcome in evaluating the effectiveness of the action consultant and written manual condition was the movement of each hospital toward complete adoption. In order to assess outcome differences, each hospital was measured on its task accomplishment on a number of adoption tasks whose completion was necessary to establish a lodge society. Before a lodge could be implemented, legal services for the members, and business and financial arrangements all had to be completed. Table 11-3 presents the nonparametric (Wilcoxan Matched Pairs Test) test of these effects. It shows that significantly higher adoption scores were obtained in the three central adoption tasks and in overall task completion by the action consultant (face-to-face) approach contrasted with a written manual of directions. Thus, interpersonal interaction facilitated activating the innovation.

TABLE 11.3
COMPARISONS OF SELECTED MEAN TASK ACCOMPLISHMENT SCORES
FOR ACTION CONSULTATION AND MANUAL CONDITIONS

Task	Action consultant	Manual	T value
Business	4.58	3.08	0*
Legal	4.79	3.13	0*
Finances	5.17	4.00	1†
Mean omnibus change score	33.71	25.96	3†

*p < 0.05
†p < 0.005
Source: Fairweather, G. W., Sanders, D. H., and Tornatzky, L. G., *Creating Change in Mental Health Organizations.* New York: Pergamon Press, 1974, p. 164.

Throughout dissemination of the lodge society, a number of very descriptive procedures and measures were employed. A few of these are included here to give the reader a sense of the actual experience of conducting dissemination projects (Fairweather et al., 1974). An example of the extensive letter exchanges is presented below.

> Dear. . . .
> Well, it looks like they had gotten over the last major hurdle prior to moving out into the community—it will be a major accomplishment in and of itself and one not to be underestimated. Let me say that the experience you have recently had was very reminiscent of my experience with the prototype lodge. I received a great deal of vicarious gratification from what you reported on the telephone yesterday. The major purpose for my writing at this time is to confirm our visit to the psychiatric institute for the move to the community during the week of July 6. As the time approaches, if you find this date to be inappropriate, please let me know. Please continue to keep me informed of the project as we are very, very excited about the impending move.
> Sincerely,

A reply received from the hospital contact in early June read:

> Dear. . . .
> This is to confirm our move into the lodge. We are definitely moving on July 6 and will look forward to seeing you then. I may be in Chicago for the weekend of July 4 and 5 and, if so, would like to ride back on the plane with you. If you could, I would appreciate it if you could let me know what flight you are taking. If I am down there, I'll meet you at the airport.
> Sincerely,

An example of narrative description is found in the notes of the research team reporting the following on an actual move into the community:

> Wednesday, July 8: The lodge was operating nicely by this third day. The carpenter had finished with the remodeling and painting. The lodge contracted with the carpenter to pay for materials and his time spent in painting. Some of the labor was

donated to the lodge. The place is pretty well cleaned up now except for some of the bedrooms.

Thursday, July 9: The lodge continued to do well and is more and more autonomous. There was a big drinking party the night before among five of the lodge members. Apparently they made of lot of ruckus and kept people awake so that the executive committee met and decided that there would be no drinking in the rooms and that one fellow who got in particularly bad shape would not be able to drink at the lodge at all for a period of time. They called this their restricted list. Some people at this point were talking about wanting to leave the lodge and look for work. The lodge members supported this and offered to let the persons stay and look for work and housing from the lodge. I clued them in: they should not be paid if they did not go to work, and that they ought to set up a sick leave and time off policy. The ideas stressed the fact that the lodge is a business and that members do not just get a work pass anytime they don't feel like going to work. A testimonial dinner was held for all connected with the lodge tonight. Members of the lodge were not there since they were pushing the "therapeutic community" concept, i.e., separate lives and autonomy for patients. It was lots of fun and a good experience for all.

Friday, July 10: The lodge continued to be in good shape. Their training was excellent and the program is running smoothly. No incidents or evidence of extreme anxiety. The hospital contact told me that he was somewhat surprised since they had really gotten frightened as the date to move neared.

After the activation phase was completed, the diffusing phase began. This was accomplished by a follow-up of all 255 hospitals in the study. The rate of spontaneous subsequent diffusion was assessed during a 2-year follow-up interval. Table 11-4 shows the relationship between the hospital's status in the original experiment and the amount of subsequent diffusion observed.

TABLE 11.4
AMOUNT OF DIFFUSION BY HOSPITALS SHOWING A DIFFERENTIAL RESPONSIVENESS TO ADOPTION DURING THE PRECEDING PHASES OF THE EXPERIMENT

Willingness to adopt lodge in *original* experiment	Gained knowledge of lodge (N)	(%)	Permitted persuasion attempts (N)	(%)	Decision and/or confirmation to adopt (N)	(%)
1 No willingness	36	84	14	14	2	2
2 Some willingness	79	68	32	27	6	5
3 Completely willing	5	20	5	20	15	60

$X^2 = 115.70^*$ (4 df)

*Significant at .001 level
Source: Fairweather, G. W., Sanders, D. H., and Tornatzky, L. G., *Creating Change in Mental Health Organizations.* New York: Pergamon Press, 1974, p. 164.

Table 11-4 also presents the chi square comparing the amount of diffusion that occurred in the three types of hospitals. The most striking result is the lack of diffusion. Only 23 hospitals of the 244 investigated actually proceeded beyond discussion of the lodge concept. Of these twenty-three, fifteen were adopting volunteers in the hospital study and had received help from the research team in the activation phase of the experiment. For the hospitals that originally permitted no entry, little diffusion occurred. For those that permitted a persuasion attempt but did not adopt, diffusion is somewhat greater and for those who volunteered to adopt, adoption continued and sometimes expanded to other hospitals. Thus, Table 11-4 shows that diffusion is directly related to the initial willingness of a hospital to become involved in the change process. Once involved, the process is likely to continue until one or more replicates have been established.

By presenting an example of an actual dissemination experiment, it is hoped that the reader has a better understanding of the possible options available for experimentation at each phase of the dissemination process. It should also be clear that only through the use of research methods which are equal to the task can our state of knowledge concerning planned social change be improved.

As the reader knows by now, dissemination research is an extremely trying experience. It should be obvious to the reader that there are many disappointments as well as happy events in the dissemination process itself. It is, therefore, necessary to develop a rather philosophical position about life and particularly about the possibility of changing cultural processes. To aid the dissemination experimenter in this process a few thoughts were set down in the dissemination experiment just described. It appears worthwhile listing them again so that some understanding of the problems involved and of the philosophical position that one needs to adopt becomes clear to the potential experimentalist. Fairweather, Sanders, and Tornatsky (1974) advised potential experimentalists to consider the following:

1 Don't worry about where the organization is. Cleveland is likely as good as San Francisco to the limited extent that location affects internal change.

2 Don't worry about how much money the institution has. If change is possible, money will be found; if change isn't coming, then money is irrelevant.

3 Don't expect anything to be too systematic, predictable, or organized.

4 Be very skeptical of verbal promises. Verbal change is *not* the same as institutional social role and status change.

5 If you, or someone like you, doesn't change the organization, it likely won't change by itself.

6 Limit your initial forays into the organization in intensity and scope, and then gradually expand the action and commitment required.

7 Don't worry excessively about seducing the powers-that-be in the organization. You may, or may not, need their support, but don't focus exclusively on them.

8 Try to get a number of people and power blocks involved in discussion and consideration of the innovation. Maximize participation and then gradually focus toward concrete action.

9 Work to develop an adopting group, or focus attention on a preexisting group that could become the adopting group. Concentrate on their viability as a group.

10 Your change activities will probably arouse the anxieties of some persons within the organization. Try to alleviate this condition.

11 While trying to ameliorate undue anxieties, do not yield to pressure to modify the major dimensions of the innovation so that the end product will be so watered-down it will not work well.

12 Develop a technique to quickly and effortlessly "pick yourself up off the floor" when knocked down. Perserverence may not pay off but change cannot occur without it.

13 Learn to lose gracefully.

14 Hope.

CHAPTER 12

ON BECOMING A COMMUNITY EXPERIMENTALIST

In other chapters throughout this book the authors have attempted to make clear to the reader that persons who become community experimentalists need to have a variety of different interests and skills. In some ways this role might be called the twenty-first century role for the "Renaissance person" since it represents the meeting point among scientific interests, humanitarian values, and an action orientation. Persons who enter this field must have an interest in all three of these areas and feel comfortable in all three areas. While this may appear to be a big order, and it is, this new role also has substantial rewards. One of the important rewards for the young community scientist is the positive feeling of being involved in something meaningful and important. It is difficult to conceive of a role where there is a greater potential to make a contribution to contemporary and future societies.

Such rewards are based upon the futuristic orientation that community experimentalists need to have. Since the end goal of community experimentation combined with humanitarian values is to provide future generations with a livable planet and a high quality of life, it becomes necessary for such persons to have a vision of the future in which the scientist's role is a central one in providing information upon which democratic decisions can properly be made. Such futuristic concerns make their present work rewarding for those who share the goals of a just world and a livable environment. Besides the central concerns for the future of society and the planet earth, there are a number of characteristics and procedures that will prepare persons who have an interest in these new roles. It is now important to look more carefully at the necessary role characteristics. Some of the new roles and their characteristics have been the concern of several behavioral scientists in recent years (Bevan, 1976; Kiesler, 1980; Fisher, 1982).

ROLE CHARACTERISTICS

Personal Style

It is undoubtedly true that persons entering this new professional role, even though it is an integration of bits and pieces from other more established professional roles, are beginning a risk-taking venture. While it may be true that nothing succeeds like success, it is equally true that success is often defined in terms of existing social and professional roles. Accordingly, a willingness on the part of an individual to take some risks while engaging in problem-solving activities is essential for this kind of work. Young scientists who wish to solve human problems will need to create innovative models which themselves will of necessity differ from those currently accepted in the society. Such activities will not always be completely and generously supported by persons who hold administrative roles in existing organizations. This is often true of those who have the responsibility and budgetary power for controlling programs in a particular area. For example, should one question the validity of a particular energy program, mental health treatment, environmental design, or the like, it is highly likely that such questioning may be viewed as insubordination by those whose job it is to preserve the status quo. It is, therefore, sometimes necessary for the community scientist to be able to take the risks and accept the criticisms that come from those who perceive themselves as the protectors of the status quo. This sometimes puts the community scientist at odds with professional societies and/or selected disciplines (Mayo, 1982). A certain amount of risk is necessary and accompanies the development of any innovation.

There are, however, other personal attributes necessary to be successful in this new field. A second attribute is that the person should feel as much at home in the library as he or she does in the community. From a personality perspective we are defining individuals who are able to be introverted upon occasion and engage in individual study and self-examination and who at the same time are able to engage in the extrovert behavior needed to communicate with a wide variety of people holding a number of different professional positions. This requires that a person be able to play a rather quiet, scientific role at one moment and at another be able to lead discussions in a community setting with numerous interest groups. While it is often thought that these two types of activities cannot be accomplished by one individual it is clear from the authors' experiences in training students to carry out these tasks over the last several years that these two sets of skills do often reside within the same individual.

The importance of the thoughtful aspect of the community scientist's role cannot be overemphasized. The use of a number of theoretical ideas in planning, design, implementation, operation, and evaluation reflects the need for creative thinking by the community scientist. Yet at the same time the community scientist must be able to participate in the research team and interact with community constituencies. This flexibility requires that a person have empathy for others and an ability to put himself or herself in the shoes of the other.

Since a great number of human problems involve individual participants who are often unable to escape their particular social position in the society, it usually is necessary for the interested community scientist to understand these persons' roles, which often reflect their lowly social position, and to be able to gain for them an audience with social administrators. It is, therefore, absolutely essential that the social experimentalist have an egalitarian view of society in which all persons are accepted in discussion and planning and none are eliminated by virtue of any characteristic they might possess.

It may be that this is a utopian value which cannot be realized completely. However, it is true that persons who strive to eliminate prejudice and create social justice should themselves question their own motives in an attempt to eliminate such biases from their own activities and perceptions. This also means that the community experimentalist must have a sensitivity to other persons as well as an awareness of the differences in cultures and subcultures that exist in this and other societies. While it is clearly impossible for any individual to have a complete and detailed knowledge of each and every culture and subculture, it is possible for the concerned community scientist to make a serious attempt to understand the values of persons who come from them.

What we are discussing here is an open-mindedness which should go along with the creativity inherent in the community scientist role. While it is essential to be open-minded, it is not enough in this role. It is also necessary for the individual to be able to create new programs or models that will theoretically reduce the injustices, environmental degradations, or any other negative force that can cause future difficulties for those involved. As mentioned in Chapter 3, innovation creativity is a very difficult aspect of human perception and behavior to describe. Despite this difficulty it is essential to human survival and, therefore, each community experimentalist must develop his or her own creative abilities as much as possible. To briefly review, some of the components of personal style necessary for a community experimentalist are: (1) willingness to take risks, (2) flexibility, (3) open-mindedness, and (4) innovation creativity.

Educational Background

The prospective community experimentalist should get as broad an educational background as possible with specific emphasis upon scientific methodology. Because a scientific background is so important, it has been reserved for separate discussion. In this section we will discuss the undergraduate background that would prepare an individual for a community experimentalist's role. First, it is important that he or she gain a background in the ethics of interpersonal relationships and the philosophy underlying different cultures. Thus, for example, an understanding of the development of western and eastern cultural ethics could serve as excellent background information.

It is also important that the person receive a multidisciplinary perspective. Such a background could be gained from an economic, political, religious, psychological, sociological, or anthropological approach. While it would undoubtedly be in the best interest of the prospective community experimentalist to be grounded in as many disciplines as possible, it is often quite impossible from a practical point of view. Since most students will have to major in a particular discipline such as psychology, sociology, and the like, one should attempt to augment those particular disciplines with a broad knowledge of subdisciplines within the discipline and some of the important concepts from related disciplines. For example, suppose the student is a psychologist. It would be important that he or she gain some background in experimental, personality, organizational, and social and clinical psychology. In addition, other areas of importance would be cultural anthropology, sociology, and history.

While, on the one hand, it is necessary to get an in-depth knowledge of a particular discipline, it is also necessary to see relationships between a particular discipline and other disciplines—psychology and sociology, for example. One need not be sacrificed for the other. Thus, when students have a background sufficient in one discipline to meet their undergraduate requirements—such as political science, for example—they should also take related courses in other disciplines to gain a well-rounded background.

Scientific Training

There has been an emphasis throughout this book on the need for a scientific approach to human problem solution. This emphasis is the subject of much recent discussion among social scientists, particularly psychologists (Good, Simon & Coursey, 1981; Stern & Gardner, 1981; Hobbs & Robinson, 1982; and Weiss, 1983). This section is, therefore, concerned with the young researcher's development of scientific interests and skills.

The broad multidisciplinary background and innovation creativity discussed earlier are, of course, part of the knowledge and background experience needed when a scientist approaches a problem. But such training alone is not sufficient for the prospective scientist. In addition, specific scientific training such as can be obtained by taking courses in logic, statistics, and the philosophy of science (which lend themselves to making inferences) should be assimilated during the early educational years. While it is undoubtedly true that education is a constant process and, therefore, no person is completely educated regardless of age and experience, it is also true that students should attempt to become as educated as possible for their specific career by gaining knowledge about general and specific areas of importance. Accordingly, in addition to courses in logic and statistics, it is also important that the neophyte scientist take courses that stress experimentation. Courses in the natural sciences can be helpful, as well as experimental courses in disciplines such as psychology and biology. A proper scientific background is gained by accumulated experience in understanding experimental methods and their logic through coursework and its application.

Turning now to application, students should obtain some actual scientific experience in order to accumulate knowledge and assess the congruence of their interests with the actual role. For example, courses in interviewing techniques can be of value, as can other courses stressing the design of questionnaires for surveys, such as questionnaires used to collect the census data. Performing actual ratings of peoples' behaviors is an important training experience. The gaining of knowledge through interviews, questionnaires, and ratings provides a background which can later be developed further to provide techniques for gaining information about problem definition, model creation, and evaluation.

In addition, it is exceedingly important that in these experiences the student at the undergraduate level have some experience as a subject in one or more experiments. One of the best ways to gain an understanding of the feelings and perceptions of those who might later participate in a social model experiment is for the prospective scientist to participate as a subject in an experiment. Such experiences help the prospective community experimenter understand the role of an experimental participant. In this vein, it is also helpful for the prospective community researcher to gain as much knowledge about interpersonal relations as possible. Being able to perceive a human problem from the perspective of others is important in planning solutions for those problems.

Finally, courses in particular problems are helpful. For example, specific courses or lectures organized around contemporary human problems such as acid rain, energy depletion, overpopulation, mental health, and health care can help students understand not only the subject matter but their relationship to the future of a society. In this regard, it would be important for the prospective community scientist to gain access, whenever possible, to visiting scholars who might discuss issues such as world health problems, world food supply, nuclear war, and so on. These scientists are often individuals who have faced or are now facing the problems with which contemporary societies are currently involved and they have often attempted to find solutions, at least from a philosophical and theoretical perspective.

Generally, in-depth knowledge in a particular discipline with an emphasis upon scientific methodology is paramount for the prospective community experimentalist. In addition, information relating philosophy and science, interpersonal relations, and scientific inquiry to the community experimentalist's role in the society should be of interest to any prospective community experimenter. While many of the conflicts inherent in such issues may be unresolved, the prospective community scientist will at least be knowledgeable about their existence and aware of the need for their resolution.

Administrative Knowledge

Community experimenters will usually have to manage a research team and a large number of individuals in the community who may have quite different skills and views of a problem. It is part of the role of the community experimentalist to bring together these diverse individuals—mentioned earlier as participants, social administrators, and scientists—to plan solutions to problems in which they all might have an interest. Such planning involves many group processes which, in most instances, will need to be approached from an administrative position. Accordingly, the development of administrative knowledge and skills, particularly those used in group decision making and conflict resolution, is of the utmost importance in this area. In addition, administrative experience should include the development of some background knowledge of finances and costs.

Courses in business and management may be taken or, at the very least, lectures attended and books read addressing these issues. This is particularly important when a social problem such as health care becomes the area of interest. Health care is one of the most expensive aspects of American society (Freeland & Schendler, 1983). Accordingly, it is essential that aspects of costs as they concern health care are to be addressed. Quite aside from the interpersonal skills and the business knowledge that need to be acquired, there is a growing field of organizational behavior concerned with how organizations function, which focuses on organizational decision making, organizational practice, management strategies, and labor relations. It is important for a community experimentalist to have an understanding of organizational structure and decision making as well as organizational linkages in community settings. Any courses, discussions, seminars, or speeches that would provide a background in understanding organizational processes and linkages would benefit the student.

Community Experience

All of the aforementioned should be augmented by actual experiences in the community. The actual form such experiences take (e.g., administrative internships, mental health aides, assistants for legislators, etc.) is less important than experiencing the community processes. It is important that these social activities involve experiences with persons of different socioeconomic positions, cultures, and races. Thus, for example, a student might take an aide's position with a senator and might also have some experience in working in a food stamp program, suicide prevention center, or some other problem situation where participants are actually experiencing the results of legislators' deliberations. In one role the student learns about defining and deciding what the social programs will be. In the other he or she learns what those funded programs actually do at the day-to-day level for participants in such programs. An understanding of each of these roles along with their liabilities and assets should soon occur. These experiences equip the prospective community experimentalist with a broad general view of the personal, organizational processes and actions involved in attempting to solve social problems.

These actual experiences can also be viewed as a training ground in interpersonal relationships. Community experimentalists will need to meet with a wide variety of people in different social positions in order to discuss with them contemporary problems and their solutions. Accordingly, the more skill in interpersonal relationships one acquires the better. The action experience also has the added value of giving the potential community experimentalist some idea of the human problem areas that might be of the most interest to her or him. This is important because in future experimental work the community scientist will need to spend a great deal of time with the problem population and the problem itself. To make the time and effort personally worthwhile, the human problem chosen should be an area of interest to the potential community experimentalist. Thus, community experience in an area of human problem interest is an important background ingredient in becoming a community experimentalist.

EMPLOYMENT FOR COMMUNITY EXPERIMENTALISTS

In this section we shall address different contemporary social roles and detail how the community scientist role might fit into each one of them. Even though there are now a limited number of such roles available, more and more community researchers will be necessary in the future. To create the needed positions the community experimentalist may need to accept a position where he or she can define the contemporary role behaviors, including the rights and obligations of a scientist. Let us now explore how this might occur.

Political Role

Persons with training in community experimentation who are also interested in a career in the political arena can find a role in the political spectrum that will help our society solve human problems. First, persons with such training who hold political office can take the lead in demanding scientific evidence about proposed programs or existing programs before decisions about activating statewide or national programs occur (Kiesler, 1980). Because of their scientific knowledge, they can also play a major role in writing legislation that requires scientific evaluation as part of the activation process for any new program. In this regard and through constant consultation with contemporary scientists working in the problem area of the politician's concern, the scientifically trained politician can help write legislation that reflects the best possible scientific evidence currently available. In many legislative bodies there are staff persons with a scientific background who act as advisors to legislators, legislative committees, and to the legislative body as a whole (Massad, Sales, &

Sabatier, 1983). These persons are often requested to evaluate or obtain an evaluation of the effectiveness of particular programs. A background in community experimentation is very helpful in these positions.

In addition to these activities, persons with a community experimental background can attempt to bring together the politicians, service workers, and scientists involved with a particular human problem by taking the lead in advocating the establishment of research projects when scientific information is essential to appropriate legislation. They can also propose and support funding legislation to disseminate productive innovative social models that have been found to be beneficial upon evaluation. At the same time they can become advocates for the establishment of research projects which legislators can use to secure scientific information about specific human problems before legislation is finally written. Thus, it is possible for persons with training in community experimentation to make an impact on the political scene by advocating in the legislative process the need for and use of problem-solving scientific knowledge.

Private Practitioner

Private practitioners have great access to freedom of inquiry and freedom from bureaucratic constraints. This gives them opportunities generally not available to politicians, administrators, and others who are, to some extent, kept in check by the bureaucracy. Accordingly, persons holding private practicing positions can take advantage of this situation by evaluating their own work and through this research process provide information about human service innovations. Historically, there has been little interest expressed by private practitioners in the daily use of research techniques, yet it is clear, especially to those who have scientific training, that their own future private practice directions should be improved by adequate evaluation.

Persons with a background in community experimentation can enter the field of private practice by obtaining a license or certification when required and establishing offices where they can carry out service and research work simultaneously. If not interested in service work itself, trained experimentalists can work jointly with service personnel by contract. This interaction can lead to important contributions because of the freedom permitted persons in private practice.

An example can be found in the work of Keith (1977, 1982). After completing graduate school, Keith entered private practice in a traditional psychotherapeutic role. In his early research in 1974, prior to private practice, Keith created a counseling program for emotionally and physically handicapped persons who could not find employment. His innovative program consisted of helping handicapped clients understand their vocational interests and opportunities in a supportive group context, and then using group support to aid them in job placement. Working mainly with continuously unemployed persons, he found in his first experiment that the particular program he created resulted in a significant increase in employment—42 percent employment contrasted with 10 and 12 percent in the traditional vocational rehabilitation programs currently available for this group of unemployed disabled persons.

At this point, Keith entered private practice where he found a large number of middle-class persons interested in career changes who came to him for advice and counseling. To accomodate these people, Keith modified his original program, extended it to several group sessions in which each person's career interests were discussed, developed a new set of counseling techniques, and provided each person with a network of individuals whom they could contact and work with about changing careers and the accompanying new employment. The program lasted for as long a period of time as the client needed to develop and implement new career plans. During this process, Keith became curious about finding out the effectiveness of combining some of the middle-class persons in the program with unemployed handicapped persons. He thought this integration might raise the level of employment of both groups and add to their satisfaction by helping others.

During the next 6 years Keith continued his private practice and his career counseling. He became convinced that the heterogeneity of the group—mixing persons who had employment but wanted career changes and those who were unemployed—aided in everyone's job placement and satisfaction. Accordingly, Keith (1984) proposed a randomized experiment in which some vocational rehabilitation patients would participate in the traditional state vocational employment program and its community employment network. The development of the concepts inherent in these long-term support groups and their employment networks was enhanced through Keith's scientific interest and by combining it with his private practice. The role flexibility interest in private practice permitted this integration.

The Private Consultant Role

The private consultant is in the unique position of being able to advise persons about their organization's services without having to take responsibility for the day-to-day operation of a particualar organization and the persons whom they serve. While this frees the consultant to think from a more comprehensive point of view about the organization's practices, at the same time it deprives him or her of the responsibility for organizational functioning. For this reason, it is important that consultants spend a good deal of time meeting with persons in an organization who wish to carry out research, helping them plan innovations, design experiments, select and create instruments, and complete data collection and analyses as well as helping them make inferences. A consultant can guide and direct others to carry out research programs with a maximum of efficiency. Many research organizations do consulting work, some worldwide. The consulting role is one in which community experimentalists can use all their background information and experience to help a group or organization evaluate their own products and processes as well as those of others with whom they are interrelated.

An example of a private community consultant's role can be found in the professional work of Harris (1984). He began consulting with a number of programs for the treatment of alcoholics country in his work as full-time research consultant. He aided professionals in establishing programs for alcoholics and helped them establish appropriate researchers to evaluate these programs. As new information was found he was able to pass it along to other persons and organizations with whom he was also consulting to help them improve their own programs for alcoholics. Eventually, his research consultation went beyond the area of alcoholism into other mental health and health areas. He also began advising organizations about how to conduct research in the dissemination of their new programs. His background knowledge in experimental field work and research procedures served as the basis for establishing his research consulting career.

Service Worker

The service worker's role is one of the most prolific in our society. It presents some assets and some liabilities as far as community experimentation is concerned. The positive aspect of the role is the direct human service planning for the worker engaged in delivering services to persons with problems. The liabilities of the service worker for community experimentation are the dangers of becoming more attuned to personal and professional needs than the needs of the target population, the lack of checks and balances on the effectiveness of the services provided, and, finally, the few avenues for innovation available in the service role.

Despite these shortcomings of the traditional service worker's role so far as research is concerned, it is still possible for aggressive, scientifically interested service workers to expand their activities to incorporate an experimental component. An example of this kind of expansion can be found in the early work of Fairweather (1960, 1964). To evaluate the validity of different types of psychotherapy for different patient groups, as mentioned in Chapter 4, Fairweather (1964) accepted a position as a ward psychologist. Cooperating and interested staff—a psychiatrist, social worker, nurse, and attendants—formed the rest of the research team. In addition to administering the different programs to be evaluated, the team planned and carried out an extensive and well-controlled randomized experiment. This research was conducted as part of their role as service persons treating persons on a mental hospital ward. By persuading the research committee of the hospital that a scientific comparison of the different treatment methods was important to the services the hospital offered, many difficulties were overcome. It is important to recognize here that within a traditional service role—that of ward psychologist—the interested scientist was able to develop a research program which permitted the evaluative setting necessary for scientific experimentation.

The same type of service–research situation existed for Tucker (1974), who was a high school counselor at the time he became interested in poor reading and its relationship to bilingual learning, as mentioned in Chapters 4 through

9. Tucker persuaded high school administrators and other teachers that an experiment could yield information that would otherwise be unavailable and that the results could aid in the development of a program that might improve poor readers' skills. Accordingly, he added a dimension to his role as student counselor by persuading those in the organization to help him carry out an experiment of the type just mentioned. Through these negotiations he was able to gain support for a randomized experiment that eventually demonstrated its value in improving reading skills.

There are numerous other scientists who have historically carried out quality research in service situations. The important point to remember here, for those interested in becoming community experimentalists, is that such a role expansion requires advocacy for the use of scientific innovation and evaluation that is pivotal to the community scientist's role as a service person.

Administrator

The administrator's role provides a number of role behaviors which can be helpful to the community scientist. These include directing programmatic operations, program change and innovation, and having access to decision-making groups who control policy and finance. Some negative attributes for research also exist here. Mainly they involve too little contact with the target population in the typical administrator role, which often results in isolation from the target population.

The administrator's role is probably the least understood by scientists and is, at the same time, one that provides an excellent power base for the possibility of community experimentation. The time demands of the job and adherence to organizational policy (both central to the administrator's role) are certainly drawbacks in developing innovative programs. However, this policy-making position also provides the administrator with an opportunity to work directly with research personnel who might carry out actual field experimental work in a human problem area.

Many examples of this type of role exist in both the state and federal government. Some scientists work for the National Institutes of Health and Mental Health as administrators responsible for funding selected research programs. Such positions are also found in state governments. Generally, these positions involve making or facilitating decisions about: (1) what research is the most important from a governmental perspective, (2) what research will be funded from the applications received, (3) reporting research needs and outcomes to members of the administration and Congress when appropriate, and so on. The administrative role is thus an important one in determining research directions. Community experimentation training provides an excellent background for such positions.

An example of the promotion of community research from an administrator's position can be found in the public health role of Taylor (1984). As head of the Division of Maternal and Child Health in the Michigan Department of Public Health, he is responsible for planning and funding research aimed at improving the quality of health care to this population. An example of a recent research sponsored by Taylor (1984) and its effect upon public health policy is presented below.

The research involved evaluating a new model of health care, maternity and infant care team clinics (Sprague & Taylor, 1983). The major outcome variable was the death rate in the perinatal time period (fetal gestation of 20 weeks or more through the first 28 days of life). In this research, health care delivered by physicians, nurses, nutritionists, social workers, and public health field nurses for low-income people for prenatal care was compared to medical care only. A reduction in fetal and neonatal death rate previously ranging from 99 to 128 deaths per 1000 live births to 28 deaths per 1000 live births occurred. This was a critically important finding because it demonstrated that infant mortality rates could be significantly decreased by using a different model of health care. Because of these findings, standards and guidelines have been written in Michigan which mandate team care and prescribe the types of services which must be provided.

University Professor

There are some similarities between the private consultant's role discussed earlier and the research role the university professor can play. But the private consultant's role also differs from the university professor's because the professor has teaching responsiblities that the private consultant does not have, and also incoming monies from research contracts are not absolutely essential to the professor's consulting role. Although this is not true in all organizations, as a general rule the income from research projects pays the salaries of the research consultant whether or not the person is a private consultant working alone or whether he or she is a consultant working for a nonprofit research corporation. In either case, the work effort of such individuals often involves obtaining research grants which fund consultations.

In a university setting, professors are mainly supported by the university— usually a state or private organization—and their primary role is as teachers and researchers. Community consultation is an additional role that some professors may choose to carry out because the university professor typically has a teaching role outside the realm of funded research.

Consulting by the professor involves many of the same advantages and pitfalls that occur in the private consultant's role mentioned earlier. The advantage of having a broad view of the problem from the perspective of a university chair gives the professor the opportunity to sometimes perceive aspects of research that those closer to it cannot see. On the other hand, university professors typically do not have access to service populations and must spend considerable time developing those contacts so that there is a liaison with community service persons and researchers. The development of such interpersonal relationships as a primary goal of consultant personnel has been given considerable emphasis in Chapter 11.

Even though it is sometimes difficult, there are opportunities for the university researcher to work directly in the community for extended periods of time, either on leave from the university or by making community research part of his or her university-sponsored role. Davidson (1984) has done this with juvenile delinquency. He has spent considerable time with judges and other personnel in the criminal justice system helping to establish the basis for the research and supervising field research in juvenile delinquency. Fairweather's (1964) lodge society research had university personnel serving in various research capacities. Some of the recent researches conducted by university professors in the fields of education, energy conservation, criminal justice, and health are presented in volumes 1 through 4 of the *Applied Social Psychology Annual* (Bickman, 1980, 1981, 1982, 1983).

If the research that the professor is interested in is not supported from within the university itself, which is often the case, monies must be obtained through contracting for research grants with the government or private organizations. Thus, the university professor often finds research by contracting with an outside agency and carrying out that research by hiring a research team to aid him or her in conducting it.

Full-Time Researcher

Full-time research roles exist which fit nicely into community experimentation training directly. While these are sometimes difficult to find, they do exist and are often the role most suitable for community experimentalists. The Veterans Administration, for example, has research positions in which the researcher is paid to devote his or her entire career to research alone. The same is true of other federal agencies such as the Institutes of Health. Usually, the researcher's salary is paid by the government and he or she also has the right to apply for outside monies. Thus, there are federal government research positions established for career researchers.

In addition, there are research associate positions in many universities, where the associate's entire workday is spent on a particular research project. For example, a university professor can receive a research grant in a particular area and, if appropriately funded, can hire other persons to help carry out the research in full-time research roles. Some foundations offer career research positions. Recently, for example (and very uncommon), the MacArthur Foundation has funded a number of individuals considered to be outstanding in their field. Frequently, medical schools and school districts establish research positions where the role is defined as a career research position. Other roles exist in private research organizations such as the Stanford Research Institute, the Research Triangle Institute, and the Battelle Research Institute. These and many other research organizations are concerned with national and international problems. They provide full-time research positions for their staff. The number of such research positions fluctuates with time, the funds available, and the political philosophy of the moment. Thus, in some historical periods funding for social research has been greater than in other periods. Nonetheless, such positions do currently exist and some will continue to be available for interested and qualified people.

Kushler's (Kushler & Jeppeson, 1981) role serves as an example of a full-time researcher's role. Kushler is a project manager in the evaluation division of the Michigan Energy Administration. In the course of his employment with that agency, he has had the opportunity to utilize fully his training in community experimentation by conducting numerous research and evaluation projects concerned with energy conservation and renewable energy programs.

In addition to the use of such techniques as needs assessments and quasi-experimental research, some of the more noteworthy evaluations he has conducted have been actual experiments, complete with random assignment and control groups. Perhaps the best example involved the youth energy education programs operated in conjunction with the Federal Energy Extension Service (EES) program. In the late 1970s, Michigan was selected as one of the ten states to operate a pilot program for EES. Michigan's program was unique among the ten states, however, in that its proposal included funding for providing energy conservation education to students.

Administratively speaking, the perfect opportunity for experimental research had been presented. A source of funds for a new program initiative was available. At the same time, there was little or no prior experience with the task at hand (i.e., providing energy conservation education), either in Michigan or elsewhere in the country. Given these factors, a strong case was made that the Energy Administration should utilize a variety of service approaches, together with a careful program evaluation, in order to learn from its initial experience and subsequently design improved methods of service.

What ensued was a 3-year period of experimental research in energy conservation education, with each year's programming built upon the evaluation results of the previous year. To begin, the broadest variety of educational approaches was tested (i.e., large assemblies, small theatrical presentations, student-to-student presentations, workshops for teachers). The results of this effort revealed that the most promising approach was to utilize teacher training. Therefore, the next year's progam experimentally tested different approaches in teacher training. At its zenith, the Michigan Youth Energy Education Project involved ninety different high schools throughout the state, randomly assigned to various treatment and control conditions (Kushler & Jeppesen, 1981).

In addition to the empirical fact that Michigan developed a very effective program of energy education, this research helped make Michigan one of the national leaders in energy education evaluation. The Youth Energy Survey attitude and behavioral evaluation instrument utilized in this research (Stevens & Kushler, 1979) was developed and extensively tested for reliability and validity under a special additional U.S. Department of Energy grant. As part of this project, the instrument was administered to over 40,000 students in 161 high schools in eight states, in order to develop regional and national norms.

Ultimately, through requests for assistance received by the Energy Administration, this instrument has been utilized in over thirty states.

The Private Business Sector

A commonly heard cliché in American society is that "the business of business is business." However, this expression obscures the importance of such factors as employee absenteeism, health, safety, training, and motivation to the success of the private sector enterprise. Until very recently, managers in industrial companies and private-sector service organizations such as retail stores, banks, restaurants, and insurance companies, generally considered the bottom line of profit margin to dwarf other organizational objectives. However, within the past 50 years, an accelerating trend has become evident within private sector organizations. This trend recognizes that all organizations are made up of imperfect and socially active human beings, rather than the perfectly knowledgeable "rational man" of classic economic theory.

Two important aspects of this organizational development are that: (1) understanding the company's dynamic environment (e.g., technological advances, government policies, and social attitudes) is recognized as critical to organizational effectiveness; and (2) improving the quality of work life is now valued by many managers as a means to organizational survival and success, and by some managers as a worthwhile goal in and of itself.

This change in organizational thinking has created opportunities for community experimentalists to find employment in private sector organizations. Four reasons argue in favor of considering this role:

1 Many individuals in our society spend at least 8 hours a day, 5 days a week, working in private sector organizations.

2 Individuals can be said to "define themselves" to a large extent in terms of their work.

3 Research has shown that satisfaction with one's work may be the strongest predictor of longevity and general well-being (House, 1975).

4 Our society pays for social programs with tax revenues. When the economy lags, so does economic support for education, health, and welfare programs. Therefore, if community experimentalists can improve the economic health of the society, these positions should be considered as potential career opportunities.

What are the kinds of jobs and projects which can be undertaken by community experimentalists in the private sector? The position a community experimentalist might hold would normally be located within a designated department of the organization—personnel, for example. If this were the case, in addition to his or her training as a community experimentalist, an individual would need a background in more traditional personnel areas such as employee selection, training, and development. Job titles might include such labels as internal consultant, organization development specialist, personnel manager, and the like. A large variety of potential projects might be undertaken by a community experimentalist in the private sector. For example, a recent article (Nicholas, 1982) reviewed the results of sixty-four organization development "intervention studies." To qualify for the review, studies had to be empirically based. Pre-post measures, comparison groups, and control procedures were all required. The types of interventions included:

1 Human process approaches
   a Structured laboratory training—group training experiences that focus on interpersonal behavior and group process issues.
   b Team building—a variation of laboratory training in which emphasis is on improving team problem-solving ability and effectiveness in natural work settings.
   c Survey feedback—the systematic feedback of survey data to groups with the intent of stimulating discussion of problem areas, generating potential solutions, and stimulating motivation for change.
2 Technostructural approaches
   a Job design and job enlargement—attempts to increase satisfaction and performance by consolidating work function from a "horizontal slice" of the work unit to provide greater variety and a sense of the whole task.
   b Job enrichment—work functions from a "vertical slice" of the unit are brought together into a single job to provide greater task identity and significance, employee autonomy, and feedback from the job.
   c Sociotechnical systems design—directed at the fit between the technological configuration and the social structure of work units. This approach results in the rearrangement of relationships among roles or tasks or a sequence of activities to produce self-maintaining, semiautonomous groups.
3 Multifaceted approaches
   a These are interventions that employ multiple techniques, such as survey feedback, team-building, and job enrichment.

A final issue concerns the role of the "internal consultant" (employed by the organization in which the intervention is carried out) contrasted with the role of the "external consultant." Managers frequently view "outsiders" as bringing a fresh perspective and a breadth of experience to the organization's problems. However, the requirement of a trusting relationship between employees and the scientist is especially important in the private sector, where concerns about competition and proprietary interests easily lead to suspicion. In such an environment university professors can be perceived as ivory tower types with no appreciation for the harsh demands of the real world, and external consultants are sometimes perceived as hit-and-run specialists who do not have to live with the results of their mistakes. Consequently, the community experimentalist who is actually employed within a private sector organization may find the attainment of research controls and administrative cooperation to be easier than the professor or external consultant seeking to intervene in such an organization.

In this chapter we have suggested some of the attributes of successful community experimenters. We have also presented some contemporary roles available in our society for these persons. Now, let us turn our attention to the future and try to understand, predict, and influence it by looking ahead.

13

THE FUTURE OF COMMUNITY EXPERIMENTATION

To return to the central theme of this book it is necessary to reiterate that in the process of human life, change is inevitable. If there is one central scientific law extant on this planet it is that biological, environmental, and social change occur as ongoing processes. The real issue for those of us living here is not whether change will occur—it will—the real issue is toward what end will this change occur and what legacy will we leave our children because of it. For this reason, it appears inevitable that extensive humane environmental planning of both social and natural environments will be necessary if human beings are to continue to occupy the planet and if a meaningful quality of life is to be maintained. Any long-range plan for the future of the environment requires continuous experimentation so that effective directions for the future of human beings on the planet can be ascertained. Not only is this necessary because the composition of our natural and social environments changes rapidly but there are even predictions that the earth itself is gradually changing. This book has been devoted to a discussion of the theory, methods, and practice of community experimentation. This chapter will explore the projected future need for such experimentation.

Whether or not the needed experimentation can be carried out in contemporary societies for the long term is a question that can only be answered through the experiences of the next several years. But what is certain now is that new approaches to training and research in social experimentation will need to emerge. There are many barriers that exist within society's organizations that may themselves require change before extensive social experimentation can occur. To understand what they are, let us briefly review the requirements for establishing new programs for social experimentation.

If there is to be community experimentation of a significant nature in the future, social scientists will have to make substantive contributions to the actual solution of human problems as they emerge. Organizations within which these scientists function will need to advocate the basic parameters described in Chapter 2 and examine the degree to which society's current organizations fulfill these parameters. This is important because the future of community experimentation depends upon the degree to which the parameters for an adequate decision process are available to those individuals who wish to become involved as both scientists and human problem solvers at one and the same time.

The need for planning and change *before* crises occur seems to be the only logical way in which the quality of life can be maintained or improved. It is obvious that what happens in one part of the earth, in this day of mass communication, air transport, and ecological sophistication can and will affect the other parts of this planet. If all people do not help preserve our oceans and waterways, for example, they will eventually become large cesspools that will contribute to our demise rather than to a brighter future. The air mass, as our daily television reports tell us, is worldwide and air flow in one area of the world affects the flow in another. In this same dynamic manner, ecological problems not solved in one area of the world infest other areas. The same appears to be true of social conflicts.

This can be seen rather clearly in the population overgrowth in particular areas of the world. Taking an example close to home, the annual population growth rate in Mexico is reported currently to be stabilized somewhere between 2.5 and 3.5 percent (Barney, 1980). If the growth rate continues in this range, within 30 to 50 years the population of Mexico will double. If Mexico is perceived as an isolated island affecting only itself it might be believed that the problem exists only in the country of Mexico and need not concern people in other nations. Such a myth simply denies the reality of living, for the rapid influx of migratory workers into the southwestern part of the United States who wish to improve their economic and living situation is ample evidence that the overflow from Mexico is even now occurring. Thus, the limited arbitrary boundaries established by governments do not solve international problems such as these. Inevitably, high population growth rates will affect the lives of all persons who live on this planet.

In other problem areas the need for international solutions is equally obvious. We need only repeat here the need for international control of nuclear weapons if the planet and its inhabitants are to survive.

Thus, in the final analysis certain problems demand an international solution and in this event problem-solving experimentation, or a modified version thereof, done in one culture could be tried in other cultures. At the very least, all cultures must participate in nuclear arms control, population regulation, and in matters of environmental cleanliness if the planet earth is to maintain its productive capacity and its ability to support people with a quality of life that makes living worthwhile. It is, of course, a matter of hope and advocacy at this time that governments can plan programs internationally but the spread of scientific methods across national boundaries has occurred in some of the sciences and it, therefore, seems possible that their use in solving social problems in different cultures can occur in the future.

While international solutions to some problems are essential, it seems clear that beneficial new programs within American society also need to be found. Such programs need to be countywide, statewide, and in most cases nation-wide to be effective. The piecemeal approach to solving contemporary human problems with the continuous "reinvention of the wheel" cannot be successful, considering the magnitude of the social problems with which we are faced today.

Whether research is international or national, to be of social value experimentation must be continuously carried out quickly so that society's needs can be met from one moment to the next. This requires monitoring of the society to detect problems at the earliest possible moment. Such monitoring permits problems to be identified and solutions found and implemented before crises arise. To accomplish this monitoring function, research must continuously be done to assess the needs of a society, not only the social needs of the society, but also the needs of the natural environment. The changing needs for maintenance of an adequate environment should be available to society's managers at all times. The readiness to act on this information depends on the validity of this continuous assessment information. For example, information about new toxins infiltrating our water and their effects on persons need to be known from a constant monitoring of toxicity levels so that the water quality necessary for human life can be maintained. Social needs assessment should be as rigorously and continuously carried out.

As time passes norms and values change. As this occurs, social programs that have been helpful in the past may no longer be useful. Continuous monitoring informs society's managers that changes need to be made at a particular time so that the quality of life in our society can be maintained or improved. *Thus, the primary use of research in our society is the constant assessment of the environment with the location of problem areas where change is required as such areas emerge and before they become crises.*

Such constant monitoring will result in need identification, and discovery of the need will usually require social innovation because the existence of the need itself usually shows that the problem is not being solved by contemporary programs. In such cases, new programs will have to be created on a small scale for trial and evaluation before they are implemented at a county, state, national, or international level. Examples of creating new programs in several different problem areas (poor readers, environmental degradation, juvenile delinquency) have been presented in this book.

A second use of research in our society is experimentation in social innovation. This is an area which will likely grow and expand in the future because of the increasing complexity of society. It seems axiomatic that as society increases in its complexity the number of problems and the solutions needed will also increase.

A third basic use of research is experimentation in dissemination of beneficial innovations. If the experience with the dissemination of complex social programs like that of the lodge society is a realistic example of the time lag that exists between the discovery of a new beneficial social program and its adoption, it seems very clear that constant dissemination needs to be understood and undertaken. Such activity is necessary so that the public can use the programs that have been found to be beneficial. As with problem identification and innovation experimentation, research on the processes and outcomes of dissemination needs to be continuously undertaken. This will provide the disseminators with feedback information that they can use to improve their capacity to spread new programs. Almost all the dissemination research literature points to the fact that few, if any, new programs will be used unless an active attempt is made to disseminate them. Further, the more complex the social program, the more difficult is its implementation. As programs become more and more complex it will be increasingly difficult to implement them on a nationwide basis. For this reason, dissemination research must be placed at the same level of importance as need assessment and social innovation research.

While such research can be carried out now to a limited extent through the roles mentioned in Chapter 12, future innovation and innovation dissemination research require an organizational structure in which social experimentation can be done. Perhaps the foremost obstacle to needs assessment, social innovation, and dissemination experimentation lies in the startling fact that there is no organization within society established with these research activities as primary goals. While it is important that as many scientists as possible become engaged in these three research areas (needs assessment, innovation, and dissemination experimentation), it is most important that we attempt to define and establish an organizational structure whose basic purpose would be to implement the scientific activities necessary for national and international problem solving. Let us now turn our attention to what the central characteristics of such an organization need to be and how it might be created in the future.

CHARACTERISTICS OF NEEDED SOCIAL STRUCTURES

For any program to aid the society in decision processes for social policy, it is necessary that such a program have a *democratic organization and operation.* There are many reasons for this necessity. Paramount among them is the relationship between the *means* of attaining desired goals and the *desired ends* those goals represent. This means–ends relationship has been a value issue throughout history. While there are those who maintain that the ends justify the means, that is not the position taken here. The position of the authors is that the means must be consistent with the ends, since the means can determine the ends and may, in fact, become the ends themselves. It is therefore essential that the processes operating in a social change mechanism be democratic so that the influence such an organization has upon the society at large improves the democratic processes of that society. It should be noted that some of those who claim that the ends justify the means are not interested in democratic societies. Often such persons believe that a minority of people should superimpose their will on the remainder of the society. This philosophical position frequently is held by individuals who believe that *they* know what a society must do and therefore *they* are justified in the destruction of the society to create what *they* believe is a just society. Such an approach, of course, results in a few people dictating to the majority. This often happens as an end product of revolutions. This is not to say that what happens in revolutions is "bad," or that they are not morally justified; it is simply the case that when one small group of individuals determines the future of any society it is an authoritarian approach incompatible with democratic processes.

One way of creating a democratic approach to problem solution is to represent all concerned societal groups in that problem solution. Since at any given moment in a society there are a number of individuals suffering from a particular problem—poverty, racism, mental health stigmatization, etc.—those individuals who daily suffer from such problems should be represented in the creation, dissemination, and evaluation of social programs designed to solve that particular problem. In addition, it is necessary that social administrators representing the elected officials and their organizations—typically governmental agencies—also be involved so that whatever programs are created can be utilized by the society if they are found to be helpful. Finally, it is necessary for scientists to become involved so that they can help establish, evaluate, and disseminate the new programs. Essentially, these three groups of individuals—the problem population, the social administrators, and the scientists—need to be adequately represented and involved in the planning, evaluation, and spread of new social programs designed to alleviate any human problem.

But such democratic processes cannot be aimed at problem solution unless these involved groups have *freedom of inquiry*. Often, in designing new social programs for particular problem populations within the society, those who plan the program are removed in time and distance from the program and the participants. Once the social decision makers have determined what a particular social program will be, they usually do not want to explore different alternatives. So the process of experimentation must occur before such decisions become final. Essentially, freedom of inquiry means that different alternative social policy decisions can be explored prior to widespread implementation. This is essential so that the outcomes of such programs can be assessed with as much certainty as possible prior to their implementation on a broader scale. Thus, individuals who represent the three groups mentioned above (participants, social administrators, and scientists) should not be tied to any special interest groups, either within or outside the government. To take one example, it is often stated that military research restricts scientists by requiring them to do only the particular research that the military will support. Consequently, ideas that might occur to outsiders as possible solutions to military problems are typically not funded for research by the military. Another classic example comes from the job corps program, where an entire program of training individuals in skills was underwritten by the federal government during the "great society" years. The assumption was that training individuals who were unskilled and often minority members would result in upgrading their job skills and hence result in subsequent employment. This program was initiated nationally with little concern for what its outcomes were concerning the population it was intended to benefit. Even today, its outcomes are unknown from a scientific perspective. Such issues as how many failures of job placement could have been the result of racial discrimination rather than lack of skills were not addressed.

Democratic process and freedom of inquiry, while essential, are not the only aspects of a social policy decision process that need to be established. In addition, it is necessary for social policy decision makers to be engaged in creating new social models so that these models can be compared to other models. Very often when old programs fail to work—such as is now obvious in areas like population growth, the elimination of poverty, and the like—it is because contemporary programs do not meet these needs. Accordingly, new programs need to be created and their problem-solving potential evaluated. Much of what is called social program evaluation today is simply the monitoring of programs that have been created by social administrators without any input or voice in the program itself from the problem population *or* from problem-solving concerned scientists. Frequently, the role that scientists play involves feeding back selected information to those who create programs rather than being involved in planning and creating the program itself. When this occurs, one of the greatest potential sources of new ideas is lost—the scientists themselves. Certainly, scientists contribute a great deal to the creation of new knowledge in biology, medicine, the natural sciences, space exploration, and the like. These programs, however, do not have a monopoly on scientific thinking and it is especially necessary now in our society that the creative problem-solving ability of scientists be exercised in human problem solution. It is for this reason that any social decision process which has meaning for the future will not only permit but encourage participants, social administrators, and scientists to create new social programs for evaluation. Creating small-scale models is a very different matter than evaluation. It is also a different matter than creating broad national programs which have typically been carried out by our political system without scientific or participant input. The advantage of such small model comparisons prior to implementation is clearly delineated in Chapter 5. Such comparisons help eliminate programs that could not result in valid social problem solution if implemented. It helps social decision makers determine *before* national implementation what the results of alternative social programs will probably be. With this information available, the decisions of a democratic society's representatives should be greatly enhanced.

An adequate social policy decision process must also have a *dissemination capability*. New programs created and found to be valid will not become available to the problem population throughout society as a whole unless such programs are actively disseminated. The trickle-down theory of science which has held that "if you build a better scientific discovery people will beat a path to your door"—a take-off on the old mousetrap axiom—just does not happen. Social innovations are at best difficult to spread and must have active promotion with advocates at various levels of the society "selling" others on the value of the particular social program so that the society as a whole can adopt new programs. Eventually, the desired social process would have the legislators deciding among alternatives whose value has already been established at a high probability level. Their dissemination could occur through the experimental dissemination processes described in Chapter 11. However, the history of democratic decision processes in American society shows that most often new social programs are only adopted at times of extreme crisis—such as the programs under Franklin Delano Roosevelt in the Depression of the 1930s—and without any attempt at establishing outcome validity. When scientists help create and evaluate new social programs in the future, they will probably be the only ones who know the relationship of all the social processes needed for success and they should, therefore, be actively involved in the dissemination process.

Thus, scientists can help create new programs and help others implement them throughout the society. After several problem-solving innovations have been established and support bases built within the adopting communities, the successful participants and their associates can bring new and important information to present to the decision makers. If the replicates produce the same results as the prototype model, the decision makers should be more inclined to support the further adoption of the new program. The success of replicates is very important to innovation dissemination and is another reason that scientists who develop and test the innovative model and thereby know its daily operation and validity must become involved in the innovation's early dissemination.

Of course, *evaluation* is central to the entire problem of combining science and social planning. While creating social programs and disseminating them are matters of equal concern to the scientist and social planners, without an evaluation of those two efforts, science cannot be adequately utilized in the process of social innovation and dissemination. As mentioned in past chapters, it is rare that actual scientific experiments have been carried out in community settings. However, it is undoubtedly true that unless actual experiments are created and carried out in field settings, our knowledge from a scientific perspective will continue to be vague and often not too helpful for human problem solving. It is therefore of the utmost urgency that techniques designed to gain information about human problems and their solutions be supplemented by actual field experiments in both the areas of program development and dissemination efforts so that in-depth knowledge of these processes can be gained.

Using all the contemporary comparative and associative processes, including actual field experiments, provides scientists with the broadest base of evaluation techniques available. Planning and supervising the field operation of the models along with the participants and social administrators makes the scientists' knowledge of any particular problem complete enough so that the interpretation of comparative and associative results is likely to be valid.

It is the acquisition of scientific knowledge about a problem which provides the logical basis upon which further social innovation and dissemination efforts can be built. Thus, the scientists must not only mutually create and scientifically compare different social models on different outcomes, but they must also double their efforts to advance experimentation into the field of dissemination. It is a matter of primary importance to discover answers to a number of pressing dissemination questions. What type of innovation (a small-scale educational model contrasted with a health model for example) can be more quickly adopted by what sort of organization—a small school contrasted with a large school or a small satellite hospital contrasted with a centralized hospital? What types of interventions are most successful with different individuals and organizations? Should we attempt to persuade the entire organization, administrators only, workers only, or workers and administrators together, and so on. Whatever these answers happen to be, the central issue here is that the most accurate scientific evaluation possible must be done so that we can better understand the processes of innovation dissemination.

Another essential aspect of the innovation dissemination process is that it must be done over a long period of time. This calls for a change in the approach of most of the government and privately funded research that exists today. If we take any contemporary problem—polluted air and water, primary education, and so on—the types of information required to understand these problems, not to mention finding their solutions, can only properly be gained over a period of time. In fact, it is highly likely that scientists only become experts in any given problem area after many years of research because so little is now known about these problems from a scientific perspective. It is for this reason that longitudinal studies and the longevity of experimental social organizations must be maintained if answers that have value in social policy considerations are to be discovered.

Again, we return to a familiar theme. It is that any adequate social problem-solving mechanism must be *multidisciplinary* in orientation (Chapter 2). It should be clear to all the readers of this book by now that any social problem—regardless of what its discipline is traditionally considered to be—is cross-disciplinary. Human problems often have components which are biological, psychological, sociological, legal, and medical. No single discipline can provide all the answers. It is therefore essential that scientists involved in these human problem research efforts, as well as social administrators and lay people, acquaint themselves with the thinking of people from the various involved disciplines and attempt to integrate their ideas into a conceptual whole. For example, people working in the area of pure air must recognize that without funding from political sources there can be no adequate research to clean up the air. In addition, the problem itself is chemical, biological, social, and personal—no adequate solution, even if found, can be implemented unless a wide variety of people and organizations participate in the solution. In this day and age, it is very clear that the psychology, economics, sociology, and politics of a problem are as important in its solution as are its physical and natural elements. It is for this reason that a multidisciplinary orientation is essential.

Finally, *training opportunities* for educating a new generation of socially conscious social scientists need to be incorporated into any program oriented toward human problem solution. Since very few of our scientists have had an opportunity to be trained in a problem-solving multidisciplinary framework and fewer still have had an opportunity to be trained in actual human problem settings, it is necessary that concerned scientists, social administrators, and problem participants join together to provide training opportunities for a new generation of socially conscious scientists. For this reason, training should begin with undergraduate school for those in colleges now. Eventually it should begin in grade school and continue in high school. If this could be done, individuals who later become politicians, administrators, and lawyers would have the academic background that would help them understand the value of integrating science into social problem solving. It is for these reasons that training needs to be accomplished.

How and where can such programs be carried out? Essentially, what we are talking about here is where can organizations be located that would be willing to engage in the types of endeavors just discussed. It is important, and indeed necessary, for a cooperative effort to take place among educational institutions, governments, the private sector of our economy, and other interested individuals and groups. It is quite clear though that at the beginning the young scientists interested in involving themselves in problem solutions will probably need to make a home wherever they can find it (Chapter 12). Some departments and centers in universities may provide the support for field research and multidisciplinary integrative thinking along with a background in humanitarian values. The same may be true of some governmental organizations that can combine science and social decision making as a primary obligation. Indeed, some research roles currently exist in the fields of mental health, health, and education departments in states and counties where administrators have established research organizations around the parameters mentioned in Chapter 12. Private research organizations can also lend a hand in this development. They can contract with governments, industries, and other segments of the private sector of the society to engage in research which will help answer pressing human problems. It is from all these organizations and groups that a concerted effort must come for the fusion of science and social problem solution if future generations are to benefit from the educational institutions and democratic processes currently available in America.

In the future, community experimentalists themselves should help to establish centers where politicians and private groups can meet and discuss issues of importance. Such collaborative efforts could result in researches that would provide all such individuals with information that would be invaluable to them and society. For example, if such centers existed, community experimentalists could directly contract with legislators who wished to gain scientific information about alternative solutions to a particular problem. Through the evaluation of the outcomes and processes of these models knowledge would be gained. In such a case, legislators would have a fairly clear idea of what the probabilities would be that a given alternative would succeed prior to making decisions. Accordingly, this could improve decision-making processes for the government and would, at the same time, expose special-interest legislation for what it actually was. For example, assume a number of legislators from a certain region of the country supported Program A and the evaluation revealed that Program A would not accomplish the desired goals but that Program B most likely would. If Program A was still supported after its evaluation despite the evidence that it would probably not be successful, it would soon be clear to everyone that the legislators had based their decisions on selecting Program A for some reason other than its potential success—personal friendship, perhaps. Whether or not such egocentric decisions could long endure in a democratic society where the alternatives were public information is highly questionable. Thus, community experimentation could improve decision processes in a democratic society.

Centers could also be used to train community experimentalists. If appropriately administered, the participants, social administrators, legislators, and scientists would meet together in goal-directed behavior oriented toward solving particular human problems. Currently, this is beginning to happen in the area of technological development, at least with universities and industries. Some universities are beginning to work closely with industries through the use of research centers in order to establish information that could be of value to the American public from a technological perspective. What is needed is that the same interest and consideration be given to the human problems of our era such as environmental degradation, social injustices, and the like. Centers, thus, could be central places for the meeting of concerned citizens from all groups in a society who were interested in human problem solution. Innovations could be planned and created and their outcomes evaluated prior to congressional adoption of a particular program. The implementation of such working research centers could sharpen the democratic processes and, in the final analysis, add a dimension to democratic decision making not yet attained in this or any other society.

BIBLIOGRAPHY

Alexander, J. F., & Parsons, B. V. (1973). Short-term behavioral interventions with delinquent families. *Journal of Abnormal Psychology, 81,* 219–225.

Altmann, J. (1980). *Baboon mothers and infants.* Cambridge, Mass.: Harvard University Press.

Altschuler, A. (1970). *Community control.* New York: Pegasus.

Anastasia, A. (1982). *Psychological testing* (5th ed.). New York: Macmillan.

Anderson, K. K., & Fine, J. (1978). Older workers and client placement services. *Aging and Working,* Winter, 52–57.

Andrejewski, N., Homer, C., & Schlesinger, R. (1972). Consumer participation in health planning. *Health Education Monographs, 32,* 23–26.

Asch, S. E. (1956). Studies of independence and conformity: A minority of one against a unanimous majority. *Psychological Monograph, 70*(9). (Whole No. 416).

Ashworth, W. (1982). *Not any drop to think.* New York: Summit Books.

Azrin, N. J., Philip, R. A., Barch, L., & Basalel-Azrin, V. (1978). *The job club as a method for obtaining employment for welfare-eligible clients: Job club procedures and their applicability to the WIN program.* (Report No. 51-17-76-04.) U.S. Department of Labor.

Bachrach, L. L. (1982). Assessment of the outcomes of community support systems. *Schizophrenia Bulletin, 2,* 39–61.

Bales, R. G. (1950). *Interaction process analysis: A method for the study of small groups.* Rollings Meadows, Il.: Addison-Wesley.

Bandura, A. (1969). *Behavior modification.* New York: Holt.

Banton, M. (1983). *Racial and ethnic completion.* New York: Cambridge University Press.

Bardach, E. (1977). *The implementation game: What happens after a bill becomes law.* Cambridge, Mass.: MIT Press.

Barnett, H. D. (1953). *Innovation: The basis of cultural change.* New York: McGraw-Hill.

Barnett, R. W. (1984). *Beyond war: Japan's concept of comprehensive national security.* Pergamon-Brassey's International Defense Publishers.

Barney, G. O. (1980). *The global 2000 report to the President of the U.S. entering the 21st century.* A report prepared by the Council of Environmental Quality and the Department of State, Pergamon Press.

————, Maiman, P. (Eds.). (1983). *Global Perspective Quarterly* (Vol. 1) Decatur: Ga.: Gerald O. Barney & Associates.

Beck, A. A. (1973). *The application of small group techniques to training in community participation: A field experiment.* Unpublished doctoral dissertation, Michigan State University, East Lansing, Mich.

Becker, H. C. (1963). *The outsiders.* New York: Basic Books.

Berger, B. M. (1976). Comments on Mel Kohn's paper. *Social Problems, 24,* 115–120.

Berman, P., & McLaughlin, M. W. (1978). *Federal programs supporting educational change* (Vol. VIII). Santa Monica, Calif.: Rand.

Bermant, G., Kelman, H. C., & Warwick, D. P. (1978). *The ethics of social intervention.* New York: Halstead Press.

Bernard, H. S., & Efran, J. S. (1972). Eliminating versus reducing using pocket timers. *Behavioral Research and Therapy, 10,* 399–401.

Bernstein, D. A. (1969). Modification of smoking behavior: An evaluative review. *Psychological Bulletin, 71,* 418–440.

————. (1976). Modification of smoking behavior: Progress and problems. *Addictive Behaviors, 1,* 89–102.

Best, J. A. (1975). Tailoring smoking withdrawal procedures to personality and motivational differences. *Journal of Consulting and Clinical Psychology, 43,* 1–8.

Bevan, W. (1976). The sound of the wind that is blowing. *American Psychologist, 31,* 481–491.

Bickman, L. (Ed.). (1980, 1981, 1982, 1983). *Applied Social Psychology Annual, 1, 2, 3, 4,* Beverly Hills, Sage.

————. (1981). Some distinctions between basic and applied approaches. *Applied Social Psychology Annual.* Beverly Hills: Sage.

————. (1980). Applied social psychology, SPSSI, and Kurt Lewin. *Applied Social Psychology Annual 1.* Beverly Hills: Sage, 7–18.

Bijou, S., Peterson, R., & Ault, W. (1968). A method to integrate descriptive and experimental field studies at the level of data and empirical concepts. *Journal of Applied Behavioral Analysis, 1,* 175–191.

Blakely, C., Emshoff, J., & Roitman, D. (1984). Innovation processes in organizations: An empirical test of the modified RD & D model for managing public sector innovation dissemination. In S. Oskamp (Ed.), *Applied social psychology annual* (Vol. 5). Beverly Hills: Sage.

Bleier, R. (1984). *Science and gender: A critique of biology and its theories on women.* New York: Pergamon.

Borgstrom, G. (1969). *Too many.* London: Macmillan.

Boruch, R. F., Anderson, P., Rinkskopf, D., Amidjaya, I., & Janson, D. (1979). Randomizing experiments for planning and evaluating local programs: A summary on appropriateness and feasibility. *Public Administrative Review, 39.*

Bray, R. M., & Kerr, N. L. (1982). Methodological considerations in the study of the psychology of the courtroom. In N. L. Kerr and R. M. Bray (Eds.), *The psychology of the courtroom.* New York: Academic Press, Inc., 287–323.

Breines, W., & Gordon, L. (1983). A review essay: The new scholarship of family victims. *Sign's Journal of Women in Culture and Society, 8,* 490–531.

Brown, L. R. (1976). *World population trends: Signs of hope, signs of stress.* Washington: Worldwatch Institute.

Burkhart, L. C. (1981). *Old values in a new town: The politics of race and class in Columbia, Maryland.* New York: Praeger.

Campbell, D. T. (1969). Reforms as experiments. *American Psychologist, 24,* 409–429.

———, & Fiske, D. W. (1959). Convergent and discriminant validation by the multi-trait multi-method matrix. *Psychological Bulletin, 56,* 81–105.

———, & Ross, L. N. (1965). The Connecticut crackdown on speeding: Time series data on quasi-experimental analysis. *Law Society Review, 3,* 33–53.

———, & Stanley, J. C. (1966). *Experimental and quasi-experimental designs for research.* Chicago: Rand McNally.

Chein, I., Gerard, D. L., Lee, R. S., & Rosenfeld, E. (1963). *The road to H.* New York: Basic Books.

Cialdini, R. B. (1980). Full cycle social psychology. *Applied Social Psychology Annual, 1,* 21–47.

Cloward, R. E. & Ohlin, L. E. (1960). *Delinquency and opportunity: A theory of delinquent gangs.* New York: Free Press.

Cobb, S., & Kasi, S. V. (1972). Some medical aspects of unemployment. *Industrial Gerontology, 12,* 8–15.

Cobb, J. A. (1972). The relationship of discrete classroom behaviors to fourth grade classroom academic achievement. *Journal of Educational Psychology, 63,* 74–80.

Coch, L., & French, J. J. (1948). Overcoming resistance to change. *Human Relations, 1,* 512–532.

Coelho, R. J. (1983). *An experimental investigation of two multi-component approaches on smoking cessation.* Unpublished doctoral dissertation, Michigan State University, East Lansing, Mich.

Coleman, J. S., Katz, E., & Menzel, H. (1966). *Medical innovation: A diffusion study.* New York: Bobbs-Merrill.

Collins, B., & Guetzkow, H. (1964). *A social psychology of group processes for decision-making.* New York: Wiley.

Committee on Resources and Man of the Division of Earth Sciences. (1969). *Resources and man: A study and recommendations.* National Academy of Sciences–National Research Council with the cooperation of the Division of Biology and Agriculture. San Francisco: W. H. Freeman and Company.

Commoner, B. (1963). *Science and survival.* New York: Viking.

Conover, W. J. (1980). *Practical nonparametric statistics.* New York: Wiley.

Cook, S. W. (1979). Social science and school desegregation: Did we mislead the Supreme Court? *Personality and Social Psychology Bulletin, 5,* 420–437.

Cook, T., & Campbell, D. (1979). *Quasi-experimentation: Design and analysis issues for field setting.* Chicago: Rand McNally.

Costle, D. M. (1979). The benefits of a cleaner environment. *EPA Journal,* 2–3.

Cottingham, C. (1982). *Race, poverty, and the urban underclass.* Lexington, Mass.: Heath.

Cowen, E. L., Gardner, G., & Zax, M. (1967). *Emergent approaches to community mental health.* New York: Appleton-Century-Crofts.

Cronbach, L., Glesser, G., Nanda, H., & Rajaratnam, N. (1972). *The dependability of behavioral measurements.* New York: Wiley.

Daft, R. L. (1982). Bureaucratic versus nonbureaucratic structure and the process of innovation and change. *Research in the Sociology of Organizations* (Vol. 1). Greenwich, Conn.: JAI Press, Inc.

Darwin, C. R. (1859). *On the origin of the species by means of natural seletion, or the preservation of savored races in the struggle for life,* London: John Murray.

Davidson, W., & Rapp, C. (1976). A multiple strategy model of child advocacy. *Social Work, 21,* 225–232.

———, Seidman, E., Rappaport, J., Berck, P., Rapp, N., Rhodes, W., & Herring, J. (1977). Diversion programs for juvenile offenders. *Social Work Research and Abstracts, 13,* 41–49.

———, Koch, J. R., Lewis, R. G., & Wresinski, M. D. (1981). *Evaluation strategies in criminal justice.* New York: Pergamon.

———, Redner, R., & Saul, J. (1983). Models of measuring social and community change. In E. Seidman (Ed.), *Handbook of community assessment.* Beverly Hills: Sage.

Delahunt, J., & Curran, J. P. (1976). Effectiveness of negative practice and self-control techniques in the reduction of smoking behavior. *Journal of Consulting and Clinical Psychology, 44,* 1002–1007.

Deluca, J. (Ed.). (1982). *Alcohol and health monographs No. 1: Alcohol consumption and related problems.* National Institute of Alcohol Abuse and Alcoholism. Washington, D.C.: U.S. Government Printing Office.

Dixon, W. J., & Brown, M. B. (1979). *BMDP biomedical computer programs P series, 1979.* Berkeley: University of California Press.

Downs, G., & Mohr, L. (1976). Conceptual issues in the study of innovation. *Administrative Science Quarterly, 21,* 700–715.

Dubey, S. N. (1970). Community action program and citizen participation: Issues and confusion. *Social Work, 15,* 76–84.

Dubos, R. (1970). *Reason awake: Science for man.* New York and London: Columbia University Press.

Duncan, O. D. (1966). Path analysis: Sociological examples. *American Journal of Sociology, 72,* 1–6.

Eckholm, E. (1982). *Down to earth.* New York: Norton.

Edgington, E. S. (1969). *Statistical inference: The distribution free approach.* New York: McGraw-Hill.

Edwards, A. L. (1984). *An introduction to linear regression and correlation* (2d ed.). New York: Freeman.

———. (1960). *Experimental design in psychological research* (rev.). New York: Holt.

Ehrlich, P. R. (1968). *The population bomb.* New York: Ballantine.

Eipper, A. W. (1970). Pollution problems, resource policy and the scientist. *Science, 181,* 11–15.

Empey, L. (1967). *Alternatives to institutionalization.* Washington, D.C.: U.S. Government Printing Office.

Environmental Protection Agency. (1979, March 29). *Health benefits from stationary air pollution control appear substantially more than costs.* EPA Press release.

Erickson, M. L. (1973). Group violations, socioeconomic status, and official delinquency. *Social Forces, 52,* 41–52.

Ethical principles of psychologists. (1981). *American Psychologist, 36,* 633–638.

Fairweather, G. W. (1967). *Methods for experimental social innovation.* New York: Wiley.

—— (Ed.). (1964). *Social psychology in treating mental illness: An experimental approach.* New York: Wiley.

——. (1972). *Social change: The challenge to survival.* Morristown, N.J.: General Learning Corp.

—— (Ed.). (1980). The Fairweather lodge society: A twenty-five year retrospective. *New directions for mental health services: A quarterly sourcebook.* San Francisco: Jossey-Bass, Inc.

——, Sanders, D. H., Maynard, H., & Cressler, D. L. (1969). *Community life for the mentally ill.* Chicago: Aldine.

——, Sanders, D. H., & Tornatzky, L. G. (1974). *Creating change in mental health organizations.* New York: Pergamon Press.

——, Simon, R., Gebhard, M. E., Weingarten, E., Holland, J. C., Sanders, R., Stone, G. B., & Reahl, G. E. (1960). Relative effectiveness of psychotherapeutical programs: A multi-criteria comparison of four programs for three different groups. *Psychology Monographs, 74.*

——, & Tornatzky, L. G. (1977). *Experimental methods for social policy research.* New York: Pergamon Press.

Fallid, F., & Brown, B. (1983). *Statistics for behavioral sciences.* Homewood, Ill.: The Dorsey Press.

Faust, F. L. (1973). Delinquency labelling: Its consequences and implications. *Crime and Delinquency, 19,* 41–48.

Feldman, R. A., Wodarski, J. S., Flax, N., & Goodman, M. (1972). Treating delinquents in traditional avenues. *Social Work, 17,* 71–78.

Ferguson, A. (1981). *Statistical analysis in psychology and education* (5th ed.). New York: McGraw-Hill.

Fiedler, F. E. (1967). *A theory of leadership effectivensss.* New York: McGraw-Hill.

Fishbein, M., & Ajzen, I. (1975). *Belief, attitudes, intention, and behavior: An introduction to theory and research.* Reading, Mass.: Addison-Wesley.

Fisher, R. J. (1982). The professional practice of applied social psychology: Identity, training, and certifications. *Applied Social Psychology Annual.* Beverly Hills: Sage.

Freeland, M. S., & Schendler, C. E. (1983). National health expenditure growth in the 1980's: An aging population, new technologies and increasing competition. *Journal of Health Care Financing Review, 4,*(3), 1–58.

Freeman, H. E., & Simmons, O. G. (1963). *The mental patient comes home.* New York: Wiley.

French, J., Jr., Ross, I. C., Kirby, S., Nelson, J. R., & Smyth, P. (1959). Employee participation in a program of industrial change. *Personnel Journal, 37,* 16–29.

Frieze, I. H., Parsons, J. E., Johnson, P. B., Ruble, D. N., & Zellman, G. L. (1978). *Women and sex roles: A social psychological perspective.* New York: Norton.

Fromm, E. (1968). *The revolution of hope.* New York: Harper & Row.

Fry, J. (1978). *Instructional skill training methodology.* Learning and Evaluation Services, Michigan State University, East Lansing, Mich.

Fuchter, B. (1954). *Introduction to factor analysis.* Princeton: Van Nostrand.

Galbraith, J. K. (1958). *The affluent society.* Boston: Houghton-Mifflin.

Gates-MacGinitie Test. (1969). *Survey F, Form 1 M.* New York: Teachers College, Teachers College Press, Columbia University.

Gerard, H. B. (1983). School desegregation: The social science role. *American Psychologist, 38,* 869–877.

Giedt, F. H., & Schlosser, J. R. (1955). *Movement of patients through a neuropsychiatric hospital.* Unpublished manuscript, Medical Library, Veterans Administration Hospital, Perry Point, Md.

Gilmer, B. (1966). *Industrial psychology.* New York: McGraw-Hill.

Glueck, S., & Glueck, E. (1950). *Unraveling juvenile delinquency.* Cambridge, Mass.: Harvard University Press.

Goffman, E. (1962). *Asylums.* New York, Doubleday.

Gold, M. (1974). A time for skepticism. *Crime and Delinquency, 20,* 20–24.

Goldberg, E. D. (1976). *The health of the oceans.* Paris: UNESCO.

Goldenberg, I. (1971). *Build me a mountain.* Cambridge, Mass.: MIT Press.

Goldfried, M., & Kent, R. (1972). Traditional versus behavioral personality assessment. *Psychological Bulletin, 77,* 409–420.

Goldstein, A., Carr, E., Davidson, W. S., & Wehr, P. (1981). *In response to aggression.* New York: Pergamon Press.

Good, P., Simon, G. C., & Coursey, R. D. (1981). Public interest activities of APA members. *American Psychologist, 36,* 963–971.

Goodman, P. S., Bazerman, M., & Conlon, E. (1978). Institutionalization of planned organizational change. In B. M. Staw & L. L. Cummings (Eds.), *Research in organizational behavior* (Vol. II). Greenwich, Conn.: JAI Press.

Gorsuch, R. L. (1974). *Factor analyses.* Philadelphia: Saunders.

Gouldner, A. W. (1962). Anti-minotaur: The myth of value free sociology. *Social Problems, 31,* 199–213.

Gray, D. O. (1980). *A job club for older workers and retirees: An experimental evaluation of outcome and process.* Unpublished doctoral dissertation, Michigan State University, East Lansing.

Grey, A., & Dermody, H. (1972). Reports of casework failure. *Social Casework, 53,* 534–543.

Grobecker, A. J., et al. (1975). *The effects of stratospheric pollution by aircraft.* Report on the Climatic Impact Assessment Program, Washington, D.C.: Department of Transportation.

Gunn, C. F. (1973, Fall-Winter). The amazing Ralph Heintz: Portrait of an inventor. *The Stanford Magazine.*

Guttmann, M., & Marston, A. (1967). Problems of S's motivation in a behavioral program for reduction of cigarette smoking. *Psychological Report, 20,* 1107–1114.

Hage, J., & Aiken, M. (1970). *Social change in complex organizations.* New York: Random House.

Hamilton, S. B., & Bornstein, P. H. (1979). Broad-spectrum behavioral approach to smoking cessation: Effects of social support and paraprofessional training on the maintenance of treatment effects. *Journal of Consulting and Clinical Psychology, 47,* 598–600.

Hammond, A. L. (1971). Mercury in the environment: Natural and human factors. *Science, 171*(3973), 789.

Hare, F. K. (1970). How should we treat environment? *American Association for the Advancement of Science, 167,* 352–355.

Harris, R. (1984). Personal communication.

Harris, L. S. (Ed.). (1983). Problems of drug dependence, 1982. Proceedings of the 44th Annual Scientific Meeting, The Committee on Problems of Drug Dependence, Inc., Department of Health and Human Services. *National Institute on Drug Abuse Research Monograph, 43.*

Havelock, R. G. (1979). *Planning for innovation through dissemination and utilizing of knowledge.* Ann Arbor, Mich.: The University of Michigan, CRUSK.

Hays, W. L. (1981). *Statistics* (3d ed.). New York: CBS College Publishing.

Helwig, J. T., & Council, K. A. (Eds.). (1979). SAS user's guide. Raleigh, N.C.: SAS Institute, Inc.

Hobbs, N., & Robinson, S. (1982). Adolescent development and public policy. *American Psychologist, 37,* 212–223.

Hollander, M. B., & Wolfe, D. A. (1973). *Nonparametric statistical methods.* New York: Wiley.

Hollingshead, A. B., & Redlich, F. C. (1958). *Social class and mental illness: A community study.* New York: Wiley.

House, E. R. (1975). *The politics of educational innovation.* Berkeley, Calif.: McCutchan.

Hunt, W. A., & Matarazzo, J. D. (1973). Three years later: Recent developments in the experimental modification of smoking behavior. *Journal of Abnormal Psychology, 81,* 107–114.

Irwin, J. (1974). The trouble with rehabilitation. *Criminal Justice and Behavior, 1,* 139–149.

Ives, W. R. (1974). *An evaluation of two drug abuse programs in Lansing, Michigan.* Unpublished doctoral dissertation, Michigan State University, East Lansing.

Jackson, J. M., & Saltzstein, H. G. (1956). Group membership and conformity processes. Ann Arbor, Mich.: University of Michigan, Research Center for Group Dynamics, Institute for Social Research.

Jeger, A. M., & Slotnick, R. W. (1982). Guiding values of behavioral-ecological interventions: The merging of ethics and practice. In *Community mental health and behavioral ecology.* New York: Plenum Press.

Jesness, C. F. (1975). Comparative effectiveness of behavior modification and transactional programs for delinquents. *Journal of Consulting and Clinical Psychology, 43,* 759–779.

Jones, M. (1953). *The therapeutic community: A new treatment method in psychiatry.* New York: Basic Books.

Jordan, V. E. (1974). The system propagates crime. *Crime and Delinquency, 20,* 233–240.

Judd, C. M., & Kenney, D. A. (1981). Process analysis. *Evaluation Review, 5,* 602–619.

Kaswan, J. (1981). Manifest and latent functions of psychological services. *American Psychologist, 36,* 290–299.

Katz, I., & Benjamin L. (1960). Effects of white authoritarianism in biracial work groups. *Journal of Abnormal Psychology, 61,* 448–456.

———, & Cohen, M. (1962). The effects of training negroes upon cooperative problem solving in biracial terms. *Journal of Abnormal Psychology, 64,* 319–325.

Keith, L. T. (1974). *An analysis of teacher interns' verbal and nonverbal classroom behaviors.* Unpublished masters thesis, Michigan State University, East Lansing.

Keith, R. D. (1982). *Unlimited career horizons.* East Lansing, Mich.: Rokeith, Inc.

———. (1984). *Improving the employment status and community adjustment of handicapped persons.* Unpublished manuscript, East Lansing, Mich.: Rokeith.

———, Engelkes, J. R., & Winborn, B. B. (1977). Employment seeking preparation and activity: An experimental job placement training model for rehabilitation clients. *Rehabilitation Counseling Bulletin, 21,* 159–165.

Kelly, J. G. (1971). The quest for valid preventive interventions. In G. Rosenblum (Ed.), *Issues in community psychology and preventive mental health.* New York: Behavioral Publications.

Keppel, Geoffrey. (1982). *Design and analysis: A researcher's handbook* (2d ed.). Englewood Cliffs, N.J.: Prentice-Hall.

Kerr, N., & Bray, R. (Eds.). (1982). *Psychology of the courtroom.* New York: Academic Press.

Keutzer, C. S., Lichtenstein, E., & Mees, H. L. (1968). Modification of smoking behavior: A review. *Psychological Bulletin, 70,* 520–533.

Kiesler, C. A. (1980). Psychology and public policy. *Applied Social Psychology Annual, 1,* 49–67.

———. (1980). Mental health policy as a field of inquiry of psychology. *American Psychologist, 25,* 1066–1080.

Klecka, W. R. (1980). *Discriminant analysis.* Beverly Hills: Sage.

Koenig, H. E. (1979). *Shaping our energy future: Foundations for community initiatives.* Unpublished manuscript, Michigan State University, Center for Environmental Quality, East Lansing, Mich.

Kohn, M. L. (1976). Looking back: A 25 year review and appraisal of social problems research. *Social Problems, 24,* 94–112.

Kushler, M. G., & Jeppesen, J. C. (1981). Teenage consumers and energy conservation. In *Consumer behavior and energy conservation: An International perspective.* New York: Praeger.

Lando, H. A. (1976). Self-pacing in eliminating chronic smoking. Serendipity revisited? *Behavior Therapy, 7,* 634–640.

———. (1977). Successful treatment of smokers with a broad spectrum behavioral approach. *Journal of Consulting and Clinical Psychology, 45,* 361–366.

LaPiere, R. T. (1965). *Social change.* New York: McGraw-Hill.

Lawson, D. M., & May, R. B. (1970). Three procedures for the extinction of smoking behavior. *Psychological Record, 20,* 151–157.

Leakey, R. E., & Lewin, R. L. (1977). *Origins.* New York: Dutton.

Leedom, N. J. (1980). *Energy conservation education: A task-oriented approach.* Unpublished master's thesis, Michigan State University, East Lansing, Mich.

Lemert, E. M. (1974). Beyond Mead: the societal reaction to deviance. *Social Problems, 21,* 457–461.

———. (1971). *Instead of court: Diversion in juvenile justice.* Washington, D.C.: U.S. Government Printing Office.

Lerman, P. (1975). *Community treatment and social control.* Chicago: University of Chicago Press.

Lerner, M. J., & Fairweather, G. W. (1963). The social behavior of chronic schizophrenics in supervised and unsupervised work groups. *Journal of Abnormal Psychology, 67,* 219–299.

Leventhal, H., & Cleary, P. D. (1980). The smoking problem: A review of the research and theory in behavioral risk modification. *Psychological Bulletin, 88,* 370–405.

Levine, A. G. (1982). *Love Canal: Science, politics, and people.* New York: Lexington Books, Heath.

Levitt, E. L. (1971). Research on psychotherapy with children. In A. Bergin and S. L. Garfield (Eds.), *Handbook of psychotherapy and behavior change.* New York: Wiley.

Lichtenstein, E., & Danaher, B. G. (1976). Modification of smoking behavior: A critical analysis of theory, research, and practice. In M. Hersen et al. (Eds.), *Progress in behavior modification,* Vol. III. New York: Academic Press.

Lilienthal, D. E. (1945). Research has a moral responsibility. *The Christian Century, 62,* 786–787.

Lincoln, S. B., Teilmann, K. S., Klein, M. W., & Labin, S. (1977). *Recidivism rates of diverted juvenile offenders.* Paper presented at the National Conference on Criminal Justice Evaluation, Washington, D.C.

Lindemann, J. E., Fairweather, G. W., Stone, G. B., & Smith, R. S. (1959). The use of demographic characteristics in predicting length of neuropsychiatric hospital stay. *Journal of Consulting Psychology, 23*(1), 85–89.

Linton, R. M. (1970). *Terracide.* Boston, Mass.: Little, Brown.

Logue, J. N., Melick, M. E., & Hansen, H. (1981). Research issues and directions in the epidemiology of health effects of disasters. *Epidemiological Reviews, 3,* 140–162.

Malthus, T. R. (1971). On population. New York: The modern library, 1960 (first published in 1789). In A.R. Omran (Ed.), *The health theme in family planning.* Chapel Hill, N.C.: Carolina Population Center.

Marris, P., & Rein, M. (1967). *Dilemmas of social reform.* New York: Atherton.

Martinson, R. (1974). What works. *The Public Interest, 35,* 22–54.

Massad, P. M., Sales, B. D., & Sabatier, P. (1983). Influencing state legislature decisions. *Applied Social Psychology Annual, 4,* 95–116.

Matza, D. (1964). *Delinquency and drift.* New York: Wiley.

Mayhew, D. (1974). *Congress, the electorial connection.* New Haven: Yale University Press.

Mayo, C. (1982). Training for positive marginality. *Applied Social Psychology Annual.* Beverly Hills: Sage.

Mead, M. (1971). *Coming of age in Samoa.* New York: Morrow.

Medler, J. F., Schneider, P., & Schneider, A. (1981). A statistical power analysis and experimental field research. *Evaluation Review, 5,* 834–850.

Mednick, S. A., & Christiansen, K. O. (1977). *Bisocial bases of criminal behavior.* New York: Gardner Press.

Meier, E., & Kerr, E. A. (1967). The capabilities of middle-aged and older workers: A survey of the literature. *Aging and Work,* 147–156.

Merton, R. K. (1957). *Social theory and social structure.* New York: Glencoe Press.

Messé, L. A., & Crano, W. D. (1981). The role of assessment in effective utility communication programs. In G. W. Selnow et al. (Eds.), *Energy essays.* East Lansing, Mich.: Michigan State University.

Messick, S. (1980). Test validity and the ethics of assessment. *American Psychologist, 35,* 1012–1027.

Michigan Department of Natural Resources. (1984). *Fish consumption advisory.* Lansing, Mich.

Miller, W. B. (1983). Choice, chance, and the future of reproduction. *American Psychologist, 38,* 1198–1205.

Mills, C. W. (1956). *The power elite.* New York: Oxford University Press.

Mischel, W. (1968). *Personality and assessment.* New York: Wiley.

Monahan, J. (1980). *Who is the client.* Washington, D.C.: American Psychological Association.

———. (1981). *Predicting violent behavior.* Beverly Hills: Sage.

Moncrief, L. W. (1970). The cultural basis for our environmental crisis. *Science, 170*(3957), 508–512.

Mook, D. G. (1983). In defense of external invalidity. *American Psychologist, 38*(4), 379–387.

Moos, R. H., & Insel, P. M. (Eds.). (1974). *Issues in social ecology.* Palo Alto, Calif.: National Press Books.

Morrell, J. A. (1979). *Program evaluation in social research.* New York: Pergamon Press.

Moses, L. E. (1952). Nonparametric statistics for psychological research. *Psychological Bulletin, 49,* 122–143.

Murray, T. (1982). Ethics, power, and applied social psychology. *Applied Social Psychology Annual.* Beverly Hills: Sage.

Myrdal, G. (1944). *An American dilemma.* New York: Harper & Row.

McClosky, H., & Brill, A. (1983). *Dimensions of tolerance: What Americans believe about civil liberties.* New York: Russell Sage.

McClure, L., Cannon, D., Belton, E., Sullivan, B., Allen, S., Connor, P., Stone, P., & McClure, A. (1980). Community psychology concepts and research base. *American Psychologist, 35,* 1000–1011.

McCord, J. (1978). A thirty year followup of treatment effects. *American Psychologist, 33,* 284–288.

McCord, W., & McCord, J. (1959). *Origins of crime.* New York: Columbia University Press.

McFall, R. M., & Hammen, C. L. (1971). Motivation, structure, and self-monitoring: Role of nonspecific factors in smoking reduction. *Journal of Consulting and Clinical Psychology, 37,* 80–86.

——— (1978). Smoking-cessation research. *Journal of Consulting and Clinical Psychology, 46,* 703–712.

McGlothin, W. H. (1975). Drug use and abuse. *Annual Review of Psychology, 26,* 45–64.

McReynolds, P. (1982). The future of psychological assessment. *International Review of Applied Psychology, 31,* 117–139.

Nagel, S. S. (1977). *Policy studies,* Vol. I. Beverly Hills: Sage.

Nagel, W. G. (1973). *The new red barn: A critical look at the modern American prison.* New York: Wackor.

National Academy of Sciences. (1976). *Halocarbons: Environmental effects of chlorofluoromethane release.* Washington, D.C.: National Academy of Sciences.

National Advisory Commission on Civil Disorders. (1968). *The Kerner report.* Washington, D.C.: U.S. Government Printing Office.

National Commission on Community Health Services. (1967). *Health is a community affair.* Cambridge, Mass.: Harvard University Press.

National Commission on Marijuana and Drug Abuse. (1973). *Drug use in America: Problem in perspective.* Washington, D.C.: U.S. Government Printing Office.

National Council on the Aging. (1975). *The myth and reality of aging in America.* A study conducted by Louis Harris and Associates, Inc., Washington, D.C.

National Science Foundation. (1983, May). *The process of technological innovation: Review of the literature.* Productivity Improvement Research Section, Division of Industrial Science and Technological Innovation.

Nicholas, J. M. (1982). The comparative impact of organizational development intervention on hard criteria measures. *The Academy of Management Review, 7*(4), 531–542.

Nie, N. A., Hull, C. H., Jenkins, J. J., Steinbrenner, K., & Bert, D. H. (1975). *SPSS: Statistical Package for the Social Sciences,* (2d ed.). New York: McGraw-Hill.

Olsen, M. E., & Goodnight, J. A. (1977). *Social aspects of energy conservation.* Unpublished manuscript, Battelle Human Affairs Research Center, Seattle, Wash.

Olshansky, S. (1960). The transitional sheltered workshop: A survey. *Journal of Sociological Issues, 16,* 33–39.

Olum, E. P. (1975). *Ecology: The link between the natural and the social sciences* (2d ed.). New York: Holt.

Oppenheimer, J. R. (1954). See U.S. Atomic Energy Commission, Personnel Security Board Hearing, Washington, D.C., p. 33.

Ortner, S., & Whitehead, H. (Eds.). (1981). *Sexual meanings: The cultural construction of gender and sexuality.* Cambridge: Cambridge University Press.

Oskamp, S. (1984) *Applied social psychology.* Englewood Cliffs, N.J.: Prentice-Hall, Inc.

Page, B. (1983). *Who gets what from the government.* Berkeley, Calif.: University of California.

Palmer, B., Sisson, R., Kyle, C., & Hibb, A. (1972). Community participation in the planning process. *Health Education Monographs, 32,* 67–78.

Paul, G. L. (1981). *Psychosocial treatment of chronic mental patients.* Cambridge, Mass.: Harvard University Press.

Paulus, P. B. (1980). *Psychology of group influence.* Hillside, N.J.: Lawrence Erlbaum Associates.

Pederson, L. L., Serimgeour, W. G., & Lefcoe, N. M. (1975). Comparison of hypnosis plus counseling, counseling alone, and hypnosis alone in a community service smoking withdrawal program. *Journal of Consulting and Clinical Psychology, 43,* 490.

Pedhazur, E. J. (1982). *Multiple regression in behavioral research* (2d ed.). New York: Holt.

Polier, J. W. (1973). Justice for juveniles. *Child Welfare, 52,* 5–13.

Polk, K., & Schafer, W. K. (Eds.). (1972). *Schools and delinquency.* Englewood Cliffs, N.J.: Prentice-Hall.

Powell, D. R., & McCann, B. S. (1981). The effects of a multiple treatment program and maintenance procedures on smoking cessation. *Preventive Medicine, 10,* 94–104.

Postal, S. (1980, July & August). Air pollution, acid rain, and the pollution of forests. *American Forests, 90*(7), 25–30 & *90*(8), 12–40.

President's Commission on Law Enforcement and the Administration of Justice. (1967). *Juvenile delinquency and youth crime.* Washington, D.C.: U.S. Government Printing Office.

President's Commission on Mental Health. (1978). *Commission on Mental Health Report,* Volumes I–IV. Washington, D.C.: U.S. Government Printing Office.

Pringle, L. (1982). *Water: The next great resource battle.* New York: Macmillan.

Proshansky, H. M. (1981). Uses and abuses of theory in applied research. *Applied Social Psychology Annual, 2,* 97–136.

Pumo, B., Sehl, R., & Cogna, F. (1966). Job readiness: Key to placement. *Journal of Rehabilitation, 23*(5), 18–19.

Pyke, S., Agnew, N. M., & Ropperad, J. (1966). Modification of an overlearned maladaptive response through relearning program: A pilot study of smoking. *Behavior Research and Therapy, 4,* 197–203.

Radnor, M., Feller, I., & Rogers, E. (Eds.). (1978, July). *The diffusion of innovations: An assessment.* Evanston, Ill.: Center for the Interdisciplinary Study of Science and Technology, Northwestern University. (NSF, Office of Policy Research and Analysis, Grant No. PRA76–80388).

Rappaport, J. (1977). *Community psychology: Values, research, and action.* New York: Holt.

Rappaport, M., & Labaw, P. (1975, April). *General public attitudes and behavior regarding energy saving* (Research report). Princeton, N.J.: Opinion Research Corporation. (NTIS No. PB-244-989).

Raskin, M. (1971). Volunteer probation counselors: A new dimension in sentencing youthful offenders. *Marquette Law Review, 54,* 41-49.

Ready, W. (1972). The counselor's role in the politics of health planning. *Health Education Monographs, 32,* 51-58.

Rice, R. E., & Rogers, E. M. (1980). Reinvention and innovation process. *Knowledge, 1,* 499-515.

Richardson, L. W. (1981). *The dynamics of sex and gender.* Boston: Houghton Mifflin.

Richette, L. A. (1969). *The throwaway children.* Philadelphia: Lippincott.

Richlefs, R. E. (1980). *Ecology, 1980: Sunbury-on-Thames* (2d ed.). England: Nelson Publishing Company.

Riley, M. W., & Foner, A. (Eds.). (1968). *Aging and society: An Inventory of research findings* (Vol. 1). New York: Russell Sage.

Rogers, C. (1957). The necessary and sufficient conditions of therapeutic personality change. *Journal of Consulting Psychology, 21,* 95-103.

Rogers, E. M. (1983). *Diffusion of innovations.* New York: The Free Press.

——, & Shoemaker, F. F. (1971). *Communication of innovations: A cross cultural approach.* New York: The Free Press.

Rose, A. M. (1967). *The power structure.* New York: Oxford University Press.

Rosenthal, R., & Rosnow, R. (1969). *Artifact in behavioral research.* New York: Academic Press.

——, & Rubin, R. (1978). Interpersonal expectancy effects: The first 345 studies. *Behavioral and Brain Sciences, 3,* 377-386.

Rossi, P. H., Freeman, H. E., & Wright, S. R. (1982). *Evaluation.* Beverly Hills: Sage.

——, Wright, J. D., & Anderson, A. B. (1983). *Handbook of survey research.* New York: Academic Press.

Rothman, D. J. (1971). *The discovery of the asylum.* Boston: Little, Brown.

Rubin, H. T. (1977). The juvenile court's search for identity and responsibility. *Crime and Delinquency, 23,* 1-13.

Rubin, J. (1982). *Alternatives in rehabilitating the handicapped: A policy analysis.* New York: Human Sciences Press.

Runkel, P., & McGrath, J. (1972). *Research on human behavior.* New York: Holt.

Rutherford, J., & McDermott, D. (1976). *Diversion in juvenile court.* Washington, D.C.: U.S. Government Printing Office.

Ryan, W. (1971). *Blaming the victim.* New York: Vantage.

Sachs, L. B., Bean, H., & Morrow, J. E. (1970). Comparison of smoking treatments. *Behavior Therapy, 1,* 465-472.

Sanders, D. H., MacDonald, W. S., & Maynard, H. (1964). The effect of group composition on task performance and role differentiation. In G. W. Fairweather (Ed.), *Social psychology in treating mental illness: An experimental approach.* New York: Wiley.

Sarri, R. C., & Vinter, R. D. (1976). Justice for whom? Varieties of juvenile correctional approaches. In M. W. Klein (Ed.), *The juvenile justice system.* Beverly Hills: Sage Publications.

Saul, J. (1982). *Systemic effects of diversion programs.* Unpublished master's thesis, Michigan State University, East Lansing, Mich.

Saxe, L., & Fine, M. (1980). Re-orienting social psychology toward application: A methodological analysis. *Applied Social Psychology Annual, 1,* 71–91.

Scarpitti, F. R., & Stephenson, R. M. (1971). Juvenile court dispositions: Factors in the decision-making process. *Crime and Delinquency, 17,* 142–151.

Scheff, T. J. (1966). *Being mentally ill: A sociological theory.* Chicago: Aldine.

———. (1963). The role of mentally ill and the dynamics of mental disorder: A research framework. *Sociometry, 26,* 436–453.

Scheirer, M. A., & Rezmovic, E. L. (1982, July). *Measuring the implementation of innovations.* Annandale, Va.: American Research Institute.

Schenck, H., Jr. (1963, September 14). Myth-image of the scientist. *The Nation,* 140–142.

Schram, S. F., & Osten, D. F. (1978, Summer). CETA and the aging. *Aging and Work,* 163–174.

Schur, E. M. (1973). *Radical non-intervention: Rethinking the delinquency problem.* Englewood Cliffs, N.J.: Prentice-Hall.

———. (1969). Reactions to deviance: A critical assessment. *American Journal of Sociology, 75,* 309–322.

Schwartz, J. L. (1979). Review and evaluation of methods of smoking cessation, 1969–1977. *Public Health Reports, 94,* 558–563.

———, & Ride, R. G. (1978). *Review and evaluation of smoking control methods: The U.S. and Canada, 1969–1977.* (DHEW Publication No. CDD–78-8369). Atlanta: U.S. Department of Health, Education, and Welfare.

Scott, W. G., & Mitchell, T. R. (1976). *Organizational theory: A structural and behavioral analysis.* Chicago: Irwin.

Sechrest, L., & Below, J. (1983). Nonreactive measures of social attitudes. *Applied Social Psychology Annual, 4,* 23–64.

Secretary of Health, Education, and Welfare. (1974, June). *Alcohol and health: New knowledge. Second report to the U.S. Congress.* (DHEW Publication No. ADM–75-212). Washington, D.C.: U.S. Department of Health, Education, and Welfare.

Seidman, E. (Ed.). (1983). *Handbook of social change.* Beverly Hills: Sage.

———, & Rapkin, B. (1983). Economics and psychosocial dysfunction. In R. D. Felner et al. (Eds.), *Preventive psychology.* New York: Pergamon Press.

Severy, L. J. (1979). Residential migration and stress. *Journal of Population: Behavioral, Social, and Environmental Issues, 2,* 358–369.

———, Houlden, P., & Wilmoth, G. H. (1982). Community acceptance of innovative programs. *Applied Social Psychology Annual, 1,* 45–71.

Shaw, C. R., & McKay, H. D. (1942). *Juvenile delinquency and urban areas.* Chicago: University of Chicago Press.

Shaw, M. E. (1981). *Group dynamics: The psychology of small group behavior* (3d ed.). New York: McGraw-Hill.

Sheppard, H. L., & Belitsky, A. H. (1966). *The job hunt.* Baltimore: Johns Hopkins Press.

Shurcliff, W. A. (1970). *S/S/T and sonic boom handbook.* New York: Ballantine Books.

Siegel, S. (1956). *Nonparametric statistics for the behavioral sciences.* New York: McGraw-Hill.

Sidman, M. (1960). *Tactics of scientific research.* New York: Basic Books.

Sinnott, E. W., Dunn, L. C., & Dobzhansky, T. H. (1950). *Principles of genetics.* New York: McGraw-Hill.

Snedecor, G. W., & Cochran, W. (1981). *Statistical methods* (5th ed.). Ames, Ia.: Iowa State University Press.

Sowby, F. D. (1984). *Principles for limiting exposure of the public to natural sources of radiation.* International Commission on Radiological Protection, Publication No. 39.

Sowell, T. (1983). *The economics and politics of race: An international perspective.* New York: Morrow.

Spergel, I. A. (1973). Community-based delinquency-prevention programs: An overview. *Social Service Review, 47,* 16–31.

Sprague, H. A., & Taylor, J. R. (1983, August). The impact of maternity and infant care programs on perinatal mortality. *Perinatology-Neonatology.* Barrington Publishers.

Stachnik, T. J., & Stoffelmayr, B. E. (1981). Is there a future for smoking cessation programs? *Journal of Community Health, 7,* 47–56.

Stanton, A. H., & Schwartz, M. S. (1954). *The mental hospital.* New York: Basic Books.

Starr, R. H., Jr. (Ed.). (1982). *Child abuse prediction: Policy implications.* Cambridge, Mass.: Bollinger.

Steinberg, S. (1981). *The ethnic myth: Race, ethnicity, and class in America.* New York: Atheneum.

Stephan, W. G., & Stephan, C. W. (1983). The role of ignorance in intergroup relations. In N. Miller & M. B. Brewer (Eds.), *Desegregation: Groups in contact.* New York: Academic Press.

Stern, P. C., & Gardner, G. T. (1981). Psychological research and energy policy. *American Psychologist, 36,* 329–342.

Stevens, W. S., & Kushler, M. G. (1979). *An energy conservation attitude questionnaire: Reliability, validity, and uses.* Paper presented at the Midewestern Psychological Association Convention, Chicago.

Strauss, M. (1972). An interview with consumer representatives. *Health Education Monographs, 32,* 41–48.

Streib, G. F. (1956). Morale of the retired. *Social Problems, 3,* 270–276.

Stuart, R. (1971). Behavioral contracting withing the families of delinquents. *Journal of Behavioral Therapy and Experimental Psychiatry, 2,* 1–11.

Sullivan, H. S. (1953). *The interpersonal theory of psychiatry.* New York: Norton.

Sullivan, M. L. (1983). Youth crime: New York's two varieties. In D. Metzer (Ed.), *New York affairs,* Vol. 8 (pp. 31–49). New York: New York University.

Tannenbaum, A. (1968). *Control in organizations.* New York: McGraw-Hill.

Taylor, J. (1984). Personal communication.

Thigpen, C. H., & Cleckley, H. M. (1974). *The three faces of Eve.* New York: Popular Library.

Tornatzky, L. G., Eveland, J. D., Boylan, M. G., Hetzner, W. A., Johnson, E. C., Roitman, D., & Schneider, J. (1983). *The process of technological innovation: Reviewing the literature.* Washington, D.C.: National Science Foundation.

———, Fergus, E., Avellar, J., & Fairweather, G. W. (1980). *Innovation and social process: A national experiment in implementing social technology.* New York: Pergamon Press.

———, Hetzner, W. A., Eveland, J. D., Dunne, M. J., Ettlie, J. E., Gerwin, D., Hartman, D. B., Leonard-Barton, D., Scheirer, M. A., & Taylor, J. C. (In press). Fostering the use of advanced manufacturing technology. *Technology Review.*

Truax, C., & Carkhuff, R. R. (1967). *Toward effective counseling and psychotherapy: Training and pr*

Tryon, R. C. (1967). Predicting group differences in cluster analysis: The social area problem. *Multivariate Behavioral Research, 2,*(4).

———, & Bailey, D. E. (1966). The BC TRY computer system of cluster and factor analysis. *Multivariate Behavioral Research, 1,* 95–111.

Tucker, C. (1970). Teachers Incompetence. *Chicago Tribune,* Section C.

———. (1974). *The role of reading, speaking, dialect and associative bridging in behavioral achievement and attitude change.* Unpublished doctoral dissertation, Michigan State University, East Lansing, Mich.

Tumin, M. M. (1967). *Social stratification: The forms and functions of inequality.* Englewood Cliffs, N.J.: Prentice-Hall, Inc.

Turk, J., & Turk, A. (1984). *Environmental science* (3d ed.). New York: CBS College Publishing.

Tyler, F. B., Pargament, K. I., & Gatz, M. (1983). The resource collaborator: A model for interactions involving psychologists. *American Psychologist, 38,* 388–398.

U.S. Department of Economic and Social Affairs. (1973). *The determinants and consequences of population trends,* Vol. 1. New York.

U.S. Department of Health, Education, and Welfare. (1976). *Adult use of tobacco, 1975.* Atlanta, GA: National Institutes of Health.

U.S. Department of Health and Human Services. (1981). *The changing cigarette: A report of the surgeon general.* (DHHS Publication No. PHS–81–50156). Washington, D.C.: U.S. Government Printing Office.

U.S. Public Health Service. (1964). *Smoking and health.* Report of the Advisory Committee to the Surgeon General of the Public Health Service (PHS–11037). Washington, D.C.: U.S. Government Printing Office.

U.S. Water Resources Council. (1978). *The nation's water resources: 1975–2000.* Washington, D.C.: U.S. Government Printing Office.

Waldo, G. P., & Dinitz, S. (1967). Personality attributes of the criminal: Analysis of research studies from 1950–1965. *Journal of Research in Crime and Delinquency, 4,* 185–202.

Warner, W. S. (1960). *Social class in America.* New York: Harper & Row.

Webb, E., Campbell, D., Schwartz, R., Sechrest, L., & Grove, J. (1981). *Nonreactive measures.* Boston: Houghton Mifflin.

Webb, E. J., Campbell. D. T., Schwartz, R. D., & Sechrest, L. (1966). *Unobtrusive measures: Nonreactive research in the social sciences.* Chicago: Rand-McNally.

Weber, M. (1958). *The protestant ethic and the spirit of capitalism* (T. Parsons, Trans.). New York: Scribner's.

Weick, K. E. (1984). Small wins: Redefining the scale of social problems. *American Psychologist, 39,* 40–49.

Weiss, B. (1983). Behavioral toxicology and environmental health science: Opportunity and challenge for psychology. *American Psychologist, 38,* 1174–1187.

Whitaker, J. M., & Severy, L. J. (1984). Service accountability and recidivism for diverted youth: A client and service comparison on analysis. *Criminal Justice and Behavior, 17,* 67–74.

Whitman, T. L. (1972). Aversive control of smoking behavior in a group context. *Behavior Research and Therapy, 10,* 97–104.

Whyte, W. F. (1955). *Street corner society: The social structure of an Italian slum* (2d ed.). Chicago: University of Chicago Press.

Wicker, A. J. (1969). Attitudes and action: The relationship of verbal and overt behavioral responses to attitude objects. *Journal of Social Issues, 25.*

Wieland, G. F., & Ullrich, R. A. (1976). *Organizations: Behavior, design, and change.* Chicago: Irwin.

Wiggens, J. (1973). *Personality assessment.* New York: Wiley.

Willems, E. P. (1977). Behavioral ecology. In D. Stokols (Ed.), *Perspectives on environment and behavior: Theory, research and application.* New York: Plenum Press.

Williams, J. R., & Gold, M. (1972). From delinquent behavior to official delinquency. *Social Problems, 20,* 209–229.

Wilson, D. P. (1951). *My six convicts.* London: H. Hamilton.

———, & Prentice-Denn, S. (1981). Rating scales in the assessment of child behavior. *Journal of Clinical Child Psychology, 10,* 121–126.

Winer, B. J. (1971). *Statistical principles in experimental design.* New York: McGraw-Hill.

Wood, G. (1981). *Fundamentals of psychological research* (3d ed.). Boston & Toronto: Little, Brown.

Wortman, C. B., Abbey, A., Holland, A. E., Silver, R. L., & Janoff-Bulman, R. (1980). Transitions from the laboratory to the field: Problems and progress. *Applied Social Psychology Annual, 1,* 197–233.

Worrall, J. D., & Vandergroot, D. (1982). Additional indicators of non-success: A follow-up report. *Rehabilitation Counseling Bulletin, 26*(3), 88–93.

Wright, P. (1966, November). Technology transfer and utilization: Active promotion or passive dissemination? *Research/Development.*

Wright, S. (1960). Path coefficients or path regressions: Alternative or complementary concepts? *Biometrics, 16,* 189–202.

Wright, W. E., & Dixon, M. C. (1977). Community prevention and treatment of juvenile delinquency: A review of evaluation studies. *Journal of Research in Crime and Delinquency, 14,* 35–67.

Yablonsky, L. (1964). *The tunnel back.* New York: Macmillan.

Yates, F. (1949). *Sampling methods for censuses and surveys.* London: Griffin.

Zimbardo, P., Haney, C., & Banks, W. C. (1975). A pirandellian prison. In E. Krapat (Ed.), *Psychology is social.* Glenville, Ill.: Scott, Foresman.

Zito, G. V. (1979). *Population and its problems.* New York: Human Sciences Press, Inc.

INDEX